THE GREEK
FATHERS

THE
GREEK FATHERS

BY

ADRIAN FORTESCUE

Isti in generationibus gentis suæ gloriam adepti sunt et in
diebus suis habentur in laudibus.—Ecli. cxliv, 7

LONDON
CATHOLIC TRUTH SOCIETY
69 SOUTHWARK BRIDGE ROAD
LONDON SE

—

B. HERDER, 17 SOUTH BROADWAY, ST LOUIS, MO.

1908

Nihil obstat
SYDNEY F. SMITH. S.J.
May 28, 1908

Imprimatur
GULIELMUS F. BROWN
Vicarius Generalis
die 29 Maii, 1908

ΝΙΚΟΛΑΩΙ ΤΩΙ ΟΡΘΟΔΟΞΩΙ
ΑΔΡΙΑΝΟΣ Ο ΚΑΘΟΛΙΚΟΣ
ΑΜΦΟΙΝ ΤΩΝ ΠΑΤΕΡΩΝ
ΤΟΥΣ ΒΙΟΥΣ

PREFACE

WHAT is a *Father?* The word is used in various senses. Bishops are our Fathers in God, and the Chief Bishop is called, as by a special title, the Holy Father. The name is also given correctly to priests who are members of religious orders and sometimes, incorrectly, to priests who are not. The members of a general Council are the "Fathers" of Nicæa, of Ephesus, of Trent. And then by common consent rather than by any formal rule we speak of certain famous Christian writers as the *Fathers of the Church.*

For anyone to be called a Father involves these four conditions. First, he must be an *Author,* whose works are still extant. The fathers are important because they are quoted as authorities in theology. Obviously, then, they are all people who wrote works that we can quote. St Antony the Hermit, St Lawrence, St Sebastian are not fathers because they have left no writings. Secondly, he must be a *Catholic,* who lived in the communion of the Church, whose writings are correct and orthodox. Otherwise the writer's authority is of no value as a witness of the Catholic faith. Apollinaris of Laodicea (†c. 390) and Tertullian (†240) were learned and prolific authors; but they are not fathers because they were heretics. Thirdly, a father is a person of eminent *sanctity* as well as learning. The title is an honourable one given only to saints, or rather it includes and involves the title of saint.[1]

[1]The legal process of canonization is a late development. Alexander III in 1170 made the first rule about it. The present law dates from Urban VIII in 1634. None of the fathers was

So Clement of Alexandria (†c. 217) and Origenes (†254) are not strictly fathers, because they are not saints. As a matter of fact, the root of the matter in this case, too, is the want of orthodoxy that prevents them from being either saints or fathers. The fourth criterion is *antiquity*. This is the most difficult one to determine exactly. Antiquity of some kind is always supposed. The fathers are the great authorities for ancient tradition, they are witnesses of the faith in earlier times. The age of the fathers begins at once after that of the apostles; it is not so easy to say when it ends. No one calls St Thomas Aquinas (†1274) or St Francis de Sales (†1622) a father, because of their late date. The fathers end when the middle ages begin; and there is no clear line of division here. Practically, there is a chain of great Catholic writers, whom we call the fathers, in east and west; then after a time of comparative stagnation begins another line—that of the Schoolmen. It is in the case of a few saints who come in the intermediate time that one may doubt whether they are to be called the last fathers or the first mediæval writers. In the east the connected line ends with St Cyril of Alexandria (†444), in the west with St Gregory I (†604). After a long break come St John Damascene (†c. 754) in the east and St Bernard of Clairvaux (†1153) in the west. These two are generally called the last of the fathers, though St Bernard, at any rate, certainly belongs to the middle ages. By taking the eighth century as the limit, and by allowing St Bernard as the one later exception (since by common use

ever formally canonized. The title *saint* (it is much less of a technical term in Latin or Greek) was given originally by general consent, vaguely controlled by the local bishops.

he is called a father), we shall fix our period as it is generally accepted. Any saint, therefore, who wrote in defence of the Catholic faith between the first and the eighth centuries and whose works are still extant is a Father of the Church.[1] The Fathers are then further divided into these five classes: (1) The *Apostolic Fathers*, first in order of time and first in importance in every way. They are the immediate disciples of the apostles, whose age ends at latest by the year 150. All wrote in Greek. (2) The *Apologists*, who lived during the persecutions and wrote apologies of the Christian faith against Jews and pagans, nearly all in Greek. Their age ends when Constantine became emperor (323). The *Great Fathers*,[2] who wrote against the heresies of the fourth and fifth centuries, and so on till the beginning of the middle ages, namely (3) the *Greek Fathers*, (4) the *Latin Fathers*, and (5) the *Eastern Fathers*, chiefly Syrian, with whom may be classed any who wrote in Coptic, Armenian or other eastern language.[3]

This little book contains outlines of the lives of the great Greek fathers,[4] from Athanasius to John

[1]At the beginning we must of course mark off those writers of the New Testament who belong to a still higher class. No one counts St Paul as one of the fathers. The title of *Doctor of the Church* (now given by an act of Papal authority) on the other hand involves no idea of antiquity. All the fathers whose lives follow have been declared doctors too; but the line of doctors goes on till modern times. The last Doctor of the Church is St. Alphonsus Liguori (†1787). The title is a general recognition of eminent service as a theologian.

[2]They are called great because their works are so much more voluminous. All the apostolic fathers together make up a smaller book than the New Testament, whereas St Augustine alone, for instance, fills sixteen volumes of Migne.

[3]It is proposed to make other little books like this one, as soon as possible, that shall in the same manner treat of each of these other groups of fathers.

[4]The spelling of the Greek names in this book is not consistent. It cannot be so unless one spells them all in Greek or

Damascene, with list of their chief works[1] and a few bibliographical notes. No one will expect to find anything new in what does not profess to be more than a series of popular sketches. The only object of the book is to give in a small space, and in English, a general account of what is commonly known about these fathers. I have described their lives and adventures rather than their systems of theology. It is true that most fathers owe their importance chiefly to their works and to the theology contained therein. But to understand discussions about their schools and principles requires at least some training in technical theology; and this

all in Latin. Neither course seems possible. I wish one could spell all in Greek. But Athanasios, Basileios, Kyrillos would look pedantic and absurd. Still less would I make all Greek names into very bad Latin. That some such forms have made their way into English is no good reason for increasing the evil by making more. So I have used such Latin forms as seem too well known to be avoided; and have left all the others in Greek. Once one accepts this rule it is a matter of detail how many names fall into either class. I have reduced the Latinized ones and spelt in Greek as far as I dared. No doubt some people would put many in sham-Latin that I have left Greek. Certainly by using mixed principles one lays oneself open to an obvious objection of inconsistency: If one writes *Athanasius*, why not *Eusebius*? We could go further and ask: If *Basil*, why not *Euseb*, if *Antony*, why not *Euseby*, if *Antioch*, why not *Heracl*? I think the answer is that we all treat names in this way in every language. When a form is well known we use it, as *Rome*, *Milan*, *Naples*, *Vienna*; but in the case of smaller and less known names we leave them in their own language—*Rocca di Papa*, *San Michele*, *Heilig-Kreuz*. In English we all say *Florence*; but we all say *Fiesole*. I have done just in the same way in the case of these Greek names, except perhaps that I have admitted as few as possible to the well-known and therefore mutilated class.

[1] I have quoted the works in Latin too, as they are very often referred to under Latin titles, and it may be easier to find them by the Latin names. I have also in each case given an exact reference to the volume and page where they will be found in Migne's *Patrologia Græca*. Migne is very far from being the ideal edition, but it is the one still commonly used and best known.

little book is meant for laymen. My object has been
less ambitious than a scientific investigation of the
growth of theology. All these fathers have another
side too. Apart from their writings they stand out
as great figures in the church history of their time.
They are mighty patriarchs or famous bishops, they
lead councils, resist Cæsar and suffer persecution.
It is in this light that I have tried to present them.
It is easier to understand and appreciate this side
of their lives than to follow the development of
Origenism. And it will be something gained if people
who are not prepared to study a treatise of technical
dogmatic have at least an idea of who these fathers
were and what they did. For one does not need to
be a Greek scholar nor a theologian to honour the
memory of the Greek fathers. They lived a long way
off, a long time ago and spoke a strange tongue. But
they are joined to us in a closer bond than any tie of
race or language, for they, like us, were citizens of
that great Kingdom of God on earth that stretches
over land and sea and knows no division of nations.
These Greek fathers were Catholics as we are. They
belonged to the great united and visible Church in
communion with the holy Roman See, where sat
the bishop whom they, too, obeyed as the successor of the Prince of the Apostles. What they
defended was the Catholic faith that we profess.
We, who are the heirs of so great a tradition,
ought to know at least something about the story
of the long chain that joins us back to the first
Whitsunday. And if we are to know anything at
all about Church history we must not forget the
Greeks. Athanasius, Basil, Chrysostom should be
something more than mere names to us. They were
great and mighty men who stand out very clearly
in the long and changing line that stretches now

over twenty centuries. It would be a gross ingratitude to forget that they are just as important, did just as much for our cause as our own Latin fathers.

Letchworth, May 2, 1908.

Athanasii episc. conf. et doct. *duplex*.

Ἡ ἀνακομιδὴ τοῦ λειψάνου Ἀθανασίου τοῦ μεγάλου. κατάλυσις οἴνου καὶ ἐλαίου.

CONTENTS

PAGE

Chapter I. *St Athanasius* (293–373) 1–45

1. The beginning of Arianism 2
2. St Athanasius' early life 8
3. The first general Council (Nicæa 1, 325) 11
4. Athanasius patriarch (328) 16
5. The Arians and semi-Arians 19
6. The first attacks against Athanasius (335–339) 22
7. Appeal to Rome. The second exile (340–345) 26
8. Third exile, in the desert (356–362) 31
9. The fourth and fifth exiles (362–363, 365–366) 34
10. Athanasius' last years and death 35
11. Table of dates 38
12. Works 40
13. Literature 44

Chapter II. *St Basil* (330–379) 46–86

1. His family, birth and early years (330 –c. 345 ?) 46
2. Studies (345–357) 49
3. Baptism and journey to the monks (357–358) 55
4. Life as a monk (358–364) 58
5. His priesthood (364–370) 61
6. Basil metropolitan of Cæsarea (370– 379) 65
7. The affairs of the province. Basil's friends 68
8. St Gregory of Nyssa (c. 331–c. 395) 73
9. St Basil's death (Jan. 1, 379) 75
10. Table of dates 78
11. St Basil's works 79
12. St Gregory Nyssene's works 83
13. Literature 86

PAGE

Chapter III. *St Gregory of Nazianzos*
    (330–390)   87–108
  1. Early years (330–c. 345)   88
  2. Education at Cæsarea and Athens
     345 ?–357)   90
  3. Gregory's baptism, ordination and
     flight (357–c. 372)   93
  4. Bishop of Sasima. His hermitage at
     Seleucia (372–379)   96
  5. Gregory at Constantinople (379–381)   99
  6. The second general Council (381)   100
  7. Last years and death (381–390)   103
  8. Table of dates   104
  9. Works   105
 10. Literature   107

Chapter IV. *St John Chrysostom*
    (344–407)   109–149
  1. Early years (344–369)   110
  2. Baptism. Life as a monk (369–380)   115
  3. Ordination. Preacher at Antioch (381
     –397)   117
  4. The affair of the statues (387)   119
  5. Chrysostom's theology   123
  6. Patriarch of Constantinople (398)   129
  7. Eutropios's disgrace (399)   131
  8. The Synod at the oak tree and first
     exile (403)   133
  9. The second exile (404–407)   137
 10. Appeal to the Pope (404)   139
 11. Death and final triumph (407–438)   141
 12. Table of dates   143
 13. Works   144
 14. Literature   148

Chapter V. *St Cyril of Jerusalem*
    (c. 315–386)   150–168
  1. First years (c. 315–345)   150
  2. Priest and Catechist (345–350)   151

Contents

PAGE

3. Was Cyril ever a semi-Arian?   155
4. Cyril's theology   157
5. Bishop of Jerusalem, to Julian's accession (350–361)   158
6. The attempt to build the temple (c. 362)   161
7. From Jovian's accession to Cyril's death (363–386)   164
8. Table of dates   166
9. Works   166
10. Literature   168

Chapter VI. *St Cyril of Alexandria* (†444)   169–201

1. St Cyril before he was patriarch (—412)   170
2. Patriarch (before Nestorianism, 412–428)   171
3. Nestorius and his heresy   174
4. Before the Council of Ephesus (428–431)   180
5. The Council of Ephesus (June–July, 431)   186
6. After the Council (431–439)   191
7. The end of St Cyril (431–444)   194
8. Table of dates   197
9. Works   197
10. Literature   201

Chapter VII. *St John of Damascus* (†754)   202–248

1. The city of Syria   203
2. Before Iconoclasm (c. 680–726)   208
3. The Iconoclasts (726–842)   212
4. Revenue-officer and theologian (726–730)   220
5. Monk at Mar Saba (c. 730–c. 734)   223
6. St John ordained priest (c. 734)   227
7. St John's philosophy and theology   229

Contents

		PAGE
8.	St John's poetry	234
9.	St John's death (c. 754)	239
10.	Table of dates	241
11.	Works	242
12.	Literature	247

Index   249

THE GREEK FATHERS

CHAPTER I

ST ATHANASIUS (293–373)

ATHANASIUS, some time Patriarch of Alexandria, is the first and, without question, the greatest of the Greek Fathers. The apostolic fathers and apologists had written in Greek, but they form classes of their own. When we speak of the Greek fathers we mean the great saints who in the eastern part of the Empire wrote defences of the faith in various forms after the age of persecution was over, during the time of the great heresies, that is in the fourth and fifth centuries. Of these Greek fathers St Athanasius is the first in order of time. Against each of the heresies the Church had some one great champion, one leader who stood for the Catholic side against the heretics as the chief defender of the faith, who was the acknowledged guide of the others. The first heresy after the persecution was Arianism; it was also the most disastrous and far-reaching in its effects. And St Athanasius was the defender of the faith against the Arians. There were others too, St. Hilary in the West, St Basil and the Gregories. Every father of this time has something to say against the Arians, but they all acknowledged Athanasius as their leader. From the beginning he had been the chief opponent of Arius, so much so that "Athanasian" was often used as the name of the Catholic party, as opposed to "Arian." To tell the story of his life is practically to tell that of the Arian troubles. He lived through the whole movement. As a young deacon he saw it begin, and for nearly fifty years he fought it from his throne by the Nile. His name was always the watchword for either side. Every Arian synod declared its policy to be "away with Athanasius," every Catholic synod took up his defence. Under five emperors and five Popes he was the one tower of strength and rallying point to all Catholics in that hopeless confusion of synods and anti-synods, banishments and usurpations. Five times he himself was driven into exile for the faith, and when at last he died in his own home, the most famous bishop of his time, he had won his fight; Arianism was practically dead too. And he left a name whose glory no length of time can ever make us forget.

1. The beginning of Arianism.

WHEN Constantine (306–337) proclaimed the Edict of Milan (313), the Christians thought that the end of their troubles had come. The persecution was all over at last; no one would be banished nor burnt nor thrown to the beasts for the name of Christ any longer. What could they foresee but that the Church should now settle down in peace, spread her boundaries on every side and reign united and triumphant till her Lord came again in power and glory, to found his thousand years of earthly paradise? Naturally they thought so; and yet never were people more mistaken. The great heresies were coming as successors to the great persecutions, and the Church was to be more troubled and to suffer greater evils from her own children than she had from the sword of the

Roman magistrates. The first heresy was already
brewing while the happy bishops were reading the
new edict and thanking God for having sent his
servant Constantine. During the very lifetime of
the heroes who could show the glorious wounds
they had received under Diocletian, the Christian
Church was tossed by a raging storm that nearly
wrecked her. Bishops fell on every side, intruders
and counter-intruders filled every see, anathemas
and counter-anathemas thundered across the
empire from Tyre to Milan, so that the wretched
layman who wanted to serve God in peace may
well have wondered whether the old cry of *Christianos ad leones* were not on the whole pleasanter
than the shouts of *Homoüsios* and *Homoiüsios*, of
which he understood nothing except that, whichever he said, some one was sure to excommunicate
him.

In the beginning of the fourth century Bishop
Alexander reigned at Alexandria. He too, no
doubt counted on peace for his old age since Diocletian was gone, and he certainly did not foresee
how great a storm would grow out of a little cloud
that rose in his own city. For among his priests
was one Arius, a Libyan from the South. Few men
have left so unsavoury a memory as this Arius
("Αρειος)[1] He had been a well-meaning and
zealous person once, and had narrowly escaped
in the Diocletian persecution. If the Roman
governor of Egypt had been a little more zealous we
should, perhaps, now honour St Arius as a holy
martyr, instead of shuddering when we hear his ill-
omened name. He had then joined sides with

---

[1]If we call him by the Latin form of his name, we must
accentuate the *i* (Arîus) according to the Latin accent-rule,
because the i is long. In Greek "Αρειος is pro-paroxytone.

Meletios of Lykopolis. This Meletios (quite a different person from Meletios of Antioch, who made a more famous schism sixty years later) had got into trouble with his patriarch,[1] apparently for ordaining people outside his diocese, and had made a small schism in 306. But Arius soon left his Meletian friends, and was ordained priest by Achillas of Alexandria, Alexander's predecessor, in 311. Under Alexander we find him a parish priest with a Church in the city called the Baukalis (ἡ Βαύκαλις). Epiphanios says that he was a tall, thin ascetic-looking man, well-educated, popular with his parishioners, especially with pious women.[2] He explained the Scriptures[3] and in this explanation the poison appears, for what he taught was Subordinationism.

It will be well to explain at once what all the trouble was about, by drawing up the points in which Arius and his followers were heretics. In the first place Arianism did not spring full-grown and fully-armed at one moment from the mind of one man. We know now that no heresy ever really began like that. It is never the case that one man out of sheer wickedness suddenly invents a false doctrine. We can always trace germs and tendencies, that afterwards develop into the heresy, back to many years before the father of the sect was born. A movement begins, often very rightly, by insisting on one aspect of the faith, very often at first it is a vigorous and extreme opposition to some patently false teaching. Then this way of looking at things crystallizes and hardens; it is taken up enthusiastically by some school, it becomes a point of honour with a certain party

---

[1] Lykopolis is in Egypt.   [2] *Hær*. lxix, 3 and 9.
[3] Theodoret, H.E. i, 2.

to insist upon it, it is the national teaching of some
country. At last some one gets hold of the theory,
oversteps every limit in his defence of it, and is
eagerly supported by the rest of the party. And
then he finds himself condemned by the Church
and his name goes down to history as that of a
heresiarch. It was just so with Arius. Centuries
before he was born learned and most pious persons
naturally had been concerned as to how we are to
conceive the relation between the Persons of the
holy Trinity. It was especially the relation between
God the Father and God the Son that was in
question—one hears less about the procession of
the Holy Ghost at this time. Christians declared
their belief in one God. But they were everlastingly accused by Jews and pagans of having
at least two. Did they adore the God of Israel?
Certainly. Then if Jesus is a God as well, there are
two Gods, or is he the God of Israel, and if so who
is the Father to whom they pray through him?
A certain Sabellius, who had lived in Rome under
Pope Zephyrinos (202–218) had tried to solve this
difficulty by explaining that God the Father and
God the Son were merely two names for exactly the
same Person. There is only one God. To the Jews
he had revealed himself as the Father, and then
He had been pleased to become man and be called
the Son and the Word of God. Whenever he in
the Gospels seems to distinguish between himself
and the Father it is only a manner of speaking.
Father and Son are only two modes of existence of
the same Person. That is the *Sabellian* heresy: we
hear of it also as *Modalism* and *Patripassianism*
("Pater passus," the Father suffered, meaning that
God the Father became man and was crucified).
Against this the right teaching insisted on the

real difference between God the Father and
God the Son. Some people in opposing Sabellius
went too far. The great Origenes (†254) was one.
If the Sabellians quoted the text: "I and the Father
are one" (John x, 30), he and his school answered
with the other text "The Father is greater than
I" (John xiv, 28). These extreme anti-Sabellians
maintained that not only is God the Son really a
different person from the Father, he is even less
than the Father. They knew him to be the Son of
God, but is not a son necessarily in some way less
than his father? So there arose the school of
those who, while still calling our Lord God,
thought that in some vague way he is not quite so
much God as God the Father. These people are
the *Subordinationists*—they subordinate the Son
to the Father. And Arianism is nothing but an
extreme form of Subordinationism.

There were many Subordinationists before Arius.
Paul of Samosata (Patriarch of Antioch, 260–269)
taught something of the kind, further complicated
by a distinction of person between the Logos and the
man Jesus Christ,[1] and Lucian (†311), a priest of
Antioch, and martyr at Nicomedia under Diocletian, taught Subordinationism at the Antiochene school. It is very significant that Arius had
been his pupil. From this master, then, the heretic
had learned what he taught at the Baukalis
church at Alexandria. He further developed the
theory and at last it took this form. The root of the
heresy is that God the Son is not equal to God the
Father. In its perfect form Arianism may be
summed up in these six points: (1) The Son did
not exist from eternity. If he is the Son he must

[1]So this Paul had the unique distinction of being the remote
ancestor of two famous heresies—Arianism and Nestorianism.

have been born at some moment; so before his birth he did not exist. "There was a time when he was not"[1] was the favourite Arian formula. (2) He is not begotten of the essence of the Father —God's essence cannot be divided—but he was created by the Father out of nothing. (3) He is therefore a creature (ποίημα, κτίσμα). (4) He is the first and most exalted creature, through whom God created all the others. This is the Neoplatonic idea that God would be defiled by touching matter, so he creates and rules the world through an intermediary, a Demiurg (Δημιουργος). (5) He may be called God, but only in an extended and analogical sense; the Father made him a sort of God by his grace. (6) His will is created and fallible. He could commit sin. That is the teaching of which Arius at Alexandria maintained at any rate the germ.

In 318 the Patriarch Alexander heard of the trouble; he was told that Arius had fallen foul of other priests because of his Subordinationism. So he sent for him and reprimanded him. But Arius was obstinate and went on forming a party that included even many nuns. So in 321 Alexander summoned a synod to examine the matter. It should be noted as a sign of the great power and extent of the Patriarchate of St Mark that no less than 100 suffragan bishops of Alexandria attended this synod. They condemned and excommunicated Arius with all his followers, who included already two Egyptian bishops, Secundus of Ptolemais and Theonas of Marmarica. And while Alexander presided, by his side as his counsellor and secretary sat a young deacon, Athanasius.

---

[1] Ἦν ποτε ὅτε οὐκ ἦν.

2. St Athanasius' early life

The saint who from this point becomes the chief
opponent of Arius was then just twenty-eight
years old. Various statements made by people who
lived at the time make it practically certain that
he was born in the year 293.[1] His parents were
probably Christians; they were certainly Greeks of
Alexandria, members of the great Greek colony
that filled that city to the exclusion of native
Egyptians (Kopts) since the Ptolemies had reigned
there (B.C. 323–B.C. 30). Apart from the fact that
Athanasius never spoke nor wrote any language
but Greek and Latin, his name[2] shows that he
was one of that great multitude of people,
either born Greeks or completely Hellenized, who
filled the towns of the Levant since Alexander
(336–323 B.C.). One must remember that at this
time all the cities in eastern Europe, Syria and
Egypt were Greek. Peasants went on speaking the
old languages of their countries, but every one who
had any claim to culture, all townsmen, philosophers, governors and bishops used what was the
common tongue of the East, the late form of
Greek that we call Hellenic. Latin in the west and
Greek in the east were the two languages of the
civilized world.

Of St Athanasius' early years we know little
but what we can conclude from his later writings; and there is one legend that we should
not take seriously. He certainly had what we
should call a liberal education. His city, Alex-

[1] The chief witness is a Coptic panegyric (edited by O. v.
Lemm in the *Mémoires de l'académie imp. des sciences de St.
Pétersbourg*, Série vii, vol. 36, n. 11, Petersburg, 1888) which
says that when he became patriarch in 326 he was 33 years old.

[2] Athanasios ('Αθανάσιος) is Greek for *Immortal*.

andria, was at that time the chief centre of
learning in the empire, and its schools were the
most famous in the world. That he attended these
schools and there read the Greek classics whose
study formed scholarship in his days is plain from
the allusions he makes to them throughout his life.
Homer was the fountain of culture to Greeks always, and Athanasius knew Homer very well
(*cfr.* e. gr., *Orat. iv. ctra Arianos*, iv, 29). He knew
Plato, too, and could discuss Platonic and Neoplatonic theories (*Or. ctra Gentes*, 40). His language
is always that of a late Greek philosopher; he
writes naturally of archetypes and universals and
categories and immanent ideas. Sulpicius Severus
(ii, 36) says he had studied Roman law. When he
was accused at the Council of Tyre (335) he was
able to expose flaws in the technical legality of the
case against him.[1] And, lastly, he most certainly
had studied the Bible. Few of the fathers refer to
it so constantly as he does; he quotes from every
book, and has a special ease in quoting every kind
of text that suits his purpose. In reading his writings
one has the impression that he almost knows the
Bible by heart—so ready is he always with a
passage, often with one that seems quite out of the
way, to prove his point. So St Gregory of Nazianzos only confirms what we should in any case
have found out from his works by telling us that
he was very learned in both the Christian faith
and profane letters.[2] For the rest he is not eloquent
nor brilliant. He never rises to the splendid style of
St Basil, nor does he scatter flowers of rhetoric over
his work like St John Chrysostom. He is dignified,
very determined, short and categorical in his
assertions, clear and uncompromising rather than

[1]Sokrates, H.E. i, 31.   [2]*Oratio pan.*, xxi, 6.

persuasive. In his manner he has something of the Latin.

The legend about his childhood is one of the famous stories that are told of great saints. One day when Alexander the Patriarch was looking out of the window of his house he saw some children playing at church. Among them was Athanasius, who was taking the leading part as bishop. He was baptizing the other boys. Alexander was so impressed by what he saw that he foretold great things of this boy's future, and from that moment took him under his special care. He further asked very exactly how Athanasius had performed the rite of baptism in his play and, finding that everything had been done quite rightly, he recognized the baptisms as valid and would not allow these other boys to be baptized again. The story is told by Rufinus (H.E. i, 14) and repeated by Sokrates (H.E. i, 15). The dates make it very unlikely. Alexander began to reign in 313, so Athanasius was then already seventeen years old. And boys of seventeen do not play at church— Greek boys in the fourth century still less than western boys now. Moreover it is less edifying than it at first seems. That Athanasius did all the rites correctly is very well—but what about his intention? Rufinus and Sokrates did not think of that. But boys playing at baptizing have not anything like the intention that is required for sacraments. So any theologian would say at once that these baptism-games were invalid from want of intention, as well as exceedingly naughty.

To come back to what are real facts. Athanasius was ordained Reader (ἀναγνώστης, *lector*) either by Alexander or by his predecessor Achillas; and he

served as reader six years[1] Then he was made
deacon and became a kind of secretary to Alexander, who was a very old man. During this first
period, before the Arian troubles began, he had
already written two theological works—*A treatise
against the Heathen* and *On the Incarnation* (p. 40).
It was also during this time that he made
friends with the first monks, the hermits who had
fled from the world to the great desert south of
Egypt. His admiration for and friendship with
these holy men lasted through his life. He knew
St Antony (whose life he afterwards wrote, p. 42)
and Pachomios well. He had stayed with them in
their huts and had waited on them as a young man.
So close were his relations and so often had he
shared their life, that after he had become patriarch his bishops describe him as having been "one
of the monks."[2] It was as an already well-known
man and as the confidential friend of the patriarch
that he attended the first synod against Arius.
And when Alexander, four years later, went to
expose his case against this new heretic to the
great council at Nicæa, he naturally took Athanasius with him as his theologian.

3. The first general Council (Nicæa i, 325)

Arius then was condemned and excommunicated
by his patriarch, and by the whole Church of
Egypt. But it did not occur to him to submit and
retract his views. We have seen that he had large
ideas about the independence of clergy from their
superiors, and that he had shown them in the
affair of Meletios of Lykopolis. Now he finds that he

[1]Coptic panegyric (*op. cit.*), p. 30.
[2]Athan.: *Apol. c. Arianos*, 6.

cannot do much in Egypt—Alexander was too strong for him; so he fortifies his party, arranges an alliance with his old friends the schismatical Meletians (they all eventually became Arians), tells his followers to be true to the Subordinationist faith and await his return, and sets off across the sea to Syria.

Arrived here he persuades a number of bishops to join him and wanders about Syria and Asia Minor making converts. He explained his ideas speciously enough, declared that of course he taught the divinity of Christ—in a wider sense, that he had not had a fair hearing, and so on; his opponents, who called him a Subordinationist, were themselves Sabellians. So in a short time he had an even greater following in Syria than in Egypt. His chief convert was Eusebeios, Bishop of Nicomedia, an important person and distant relation of Constantine himself, who became a leader of the extreme wing of strict Arians, and eventually lived to baptize the emperor. From Syria Arius wrote a meekly complaining letter to Alexander, and here he also composed a curious work containing discussions of theological questions, half in prose and half in verse, which he called the Thaleia (θάλεια, festival).[1] He also wrote songs for sailors, travellers, millers, etc.[2] His ideas by this time were known to every one, and even the heathen began to make jokes on the stage about these disputes among Christians. Alexander had written encyclicals to other bishops warning them against Arius and showing that his teaching was simply a revival of that of Paul of Samosata and Lucian of Antioch. Then Arius in

[1] The Thaleia has disappeared, but fragments of it are quoted in St. Athanasius' works.
[2] Philostorgios: H.E. ii, 1.

about 323 comes back to Alexandria, and defies
the patriarch in his own city. Some bishops,
notably Eusebeios of Cæsarea (the future father of
Church history, †340), tried to arrange a compromise and to suggest explanations that both Catholics and Arians could accept. These compromisers
are the beginning of the great semi-Arian party.
But then, as always, the Catholic Church would
have no compromise and no shuffling formulas.
Arius was utterly and completely wrong, and his
teaching must be utterly condemned. You must be
either a Catholic or an Arian.

Constantine came to Nicomedia in 323, after he
had defeated Licinius, and there the Bishop Eusebeios tells him all about this new quarrel. The
emperor was immeasurably annoyed. He neither
understood nor cared anything at all about the
nature of God the Son. He was not a Christian,
though it suited him to protect Christians. But
above all he wanted union and concord. He had at
last succeeded in joining the whole empire together under himself, and he wanted no more disturbance. He was braving the anger of the
immortal gods by being friendly to these Christians
and now he found that the Christians had two
parties and, whichever he defended, he would
have the other for an enemy. So he thought that
he could patch it all up before the trouble went
any further. He sends Hosius, Bishop of Cordova,
with letters to both Alexander and Arius at
Alexandria. He tells both that the whole question
does not matter in the very least—what is the good
of quarrelling over words? Arius ought not to have
begun, and Alexander ought not to have stopped
him when he did begin. Now they must both be
quiet and say whatever they like, only not annoy

each other. Constantine was a person with a modern mind. Obviously his letters did no good. Arius had the courage of his convictions as much as the Catholics, and of course, quite rightly, neither side would consent to tolerate the other. So then Constantine proposed his second plan: Let all the bishops come to discuss the matter at Nicæa in Bithynia. He provided carriages and horses, and offered them hospitality while the council lasted.

From every part of the Levant the bishops came, venerable fathers who had seen the days of persecution, many of whom still bore the marks of torture suffered for Christ, some famous as workers of miracles, others renowned for their learning. From Egypt they hurried across Syria, Potamon of Herakleia, Paphnutios of the Thebais, from far Nisibis came James, Nicholas from Myra, Leontios from Cæsarea in Cappadocia, Spiridion across the sea from Cyprus, Eustathios from the great and God-beloved city of Antioch, Makarios from the Holy Place where the tomb of Christ still lay hidden. From Africa came Cæcilian of Carthage, Mark of Calabria from Italy, Nicasius from distant Gaul, and Hosius from the Gates of the West by the Pillars of Hercules. And old Alexander, the great Lord of Christian Egypt, came with his deacon. 318 fathers met at the city to whose name they were to give undying honour, so that even now the Christian traveller in Asia Minor braves the difficult journey to an unsavoury Turkish village, that at *Isnik* he may stand by the shattered palace wall and dream of the meeting of the fathers at the first and most famous of all Œcumenical synods.[1] It is not

[1] The first Council of Nicæa (325) is so much the most famous of all, that when we say simply the "Council of Nicæa"

necessary to tell again the story of that great synod. Arius appeared, was heard and condemned. He and his followers were solemnly excommunicated; and the emperor added a sentence of banishment. The council settled other questions too, the Meletian trouble in Egypt, the keeping of Easter and the validity of doubtful baptisms. It sat through the summer, and when all was finished Constantine entertained the fathers at a great banquet, and sent them home again. He had sat in the place of honour and had opened the proceedings with a speech. But Hosius of Cordova signed the acts first, "In the name of the Church of Rome, the Churches of Italy, Spain and all the West"; and with him sign two Roman priests, Vitus and Vincent.[1] So although the first of the patriarchs was not present, he was represented by his legates. And still Sunday after Sunday we sing at Mass the creed drawn up by this council. It is not a general profession containing the whole Catholic faith, but a definite opposition to Arius' heresy. So the memory of this first great heresy and of the venerable assembly at Nicæa hovers round our altars as we, too, declare our faith in the absolute equality of God the Son and God the Father; it is the voice of the 318 "holy and divinely inspired Fathers" that sounds through our churches still after seventeen centuries, as we declare against the Arians that we believe in one Lord Jesus Christ "ex Patre natum ante omnia

or "Nicene Synod," this one is always meant. There was, however, a second Council of Nicæa (the seventh general Council, in 787) against the Iconoclasts. All the eastern Churches still keep a feast in memory of "the 318 holy and God-inspired Nicene Fathers" (the Orthodox and Melkites on the Sunday in the Octave of the Ascension).

[1] Mansi, ii, 692, etc.; 882, 927.

sæcula. Deum de Deo, lumen de lumine, Deum
verum de Deo vero. Genitum non factum, con-
substantialem Patri, per quem omnia facta sunt."[1]
And throughout the council already the chief
defender of the Catholics—their chief spokesman
against Arius, Eusebeios of Nicomedia and the other
heretics—was Alexander's deacon, Athanasius.

4. Athanasius patriarch (328)

Three years after Alexander had come home
from Nicæa he died (April 17, 328). It is said that
he had already strongly recommended his clergy
to elect Athanasius as his successor (Sozomenos
ii, 17). But in any case that was a foregone con-
clusion. Very grave and troublesome times had
already begun in Egypt, and no Catholic could
have doubted for a moment that there was only
one man fit to take up the burden left by the dead
bishop. By an overwhelming majority Athanasius
was elected Patriarch of Alexandria (*Apol. c.
Arianos*, vi). He was consecrated by his suffragans;
and from now till his death, for forty-five years
(328–373) he filled the succession of St Mark in the
second see of Christendom, of which his name has
become the chief glory.

The title "Patriarch" in the fourth century
was still used loosely for any specially venerable
bishop; it did not become the technical name of a

[1] The council drew up twenty canons about points of discipline, anathemas against the Arians, and especially the Nicene
creed, which, however, ends with the words: "and in the Holy
Ghost." The rest of the creed we now say was added later,
probably by the next general Council (Constantinople I, 381;
but *see* Duchesne, *Églises séparées*, Paris, 1905, p. 79). The
original Nicene creed is in *Denzinger*, No. 17, 18. There were
about 20 bishops present who favoured Arius, but most of
them retracted. The history of the council is given by Hefele:
Conciliengeschichte 2 ed., i, 252, *seq*.

definite rank in the hierarchy till gradually in the fifth and sixth centuries. But in the time of Athanasius there was no doubt as to the fact that high above all other bishops, metropolitans and primates stood three great Princes of the Church at Rome, Alexandria and Antioch. He did not live to see the slowly climbing ambition of Constantinople, and though the Nicene Synod had given special honour to Jerusalem it had refused it any place even among the metropolitan sees (can. 7). That synod had recognized the "ancient custom" that gave the first places to the three old sees only (can. 6); so during St Athanasius' life no one disputed that Alexandria was the first throne in the east, the second (after Rome) in the whole Christian world. He ruled all Egypt and the lands to the South, Ethiopia[1] and part of Nubia that were converted from Egypt. And whether he sat on his throne by the great harbour in the richest and most famous centre of the Hellenic world, or wandered in exile in the west, or the desert, every Catholic looked up to Athanasius as the Lord of the East, who brought to their cause not only his learning and virtues, but the honour of so great a see. And yet, great as was the place he filled, there was little cause to envy him. When the bishops left Nicæa they must have thought that the trouble was all over. The Church had spoken. For the first time since the Apostles had settled the question of the old law at Jerusalem (Acts xv, 6–29), she had solemnly declared her faith by a general assembly of her rulers. Here was a plain case to which to apply the text: "Who hears you

---

[1] In the second year of his reign (329) Athanasius ordained St Frumentius Bishop of Axuma, and sent him to convert the Ethiopians.

hears me, and who despises you despises me
(Luke x, 16)." And Cæsar had spoken too, so that
whoever was not moved by excommunication
would be by banishment. And yet the Arian
troubles had really only just begun. The council
that should have ended the whole question only
closed the first and shortest period of its history.
From now till the end of the century the storm
becomes steadily worse and worse. The beginning
of the reaction against the council was when Constantine, who had hitherto been the stern enemy
of the Arians, suddenly veered round and began to
be their friend. His sister Constantia, widow of
Licinius, was an Arian. She died in 328, and on
her death-bed she implored the Emperor to have
pity on Arius and his banished friends. We have
seen that Constantine had never really understood
the question at issue. He had no convictions of
his own, and so he was easily moved to change his
policy. From now till his death he becomes a
favourer and protector of the heretics, and under
his sons, too, they have the court on their side as
long as the movement lasts. First the banished
Arian bishops are recalled; then they do all they
can to force Athanasius to restore Arius at
Alexandria. When they see how utterly hopeless
are all such attempts, and that in any case they
will never be able to make Athanasius even
temporize, they begin the long career of calumny
against him, and of persecution, that lasts nearly
till his death. At this point there also begins that
endless series of Arian and semi-Arian synods
that fill up the history of this heresy. Before we
come to them we may here give an outline of the
different parties into which the Arian body broke
up after the Council of Nicæa.

5. The Arians and semi-Arians

The Nicene Synod had declared that our Lord is *Consubstantial* with God the Father. That is a Latin word meaning "of the same nature." The Father and Son have the same identical divine nature; they are different persons in the same nature or substance. So obviously they are absolutely equal. Comparisons are made according to the natures of the things compared, and they have, not equal natures, but the very same nature. That is the Catholic faith that we have all learned in our catechisms. "Consubstantial" is Latin. We have it from the Latin translation of the Nicene Creed. The original Greek word is *Homoüsios*[1] (ὁμοούσιος). This word became the test-word of the Catholics. Whoever said our Lord is "Homoüsios" to the Father was a Catholic and no Arian. Homoüsians were Athanasians, Athanasians were Nicenes and Nicenes were Catholics. So we have a plain test for one side. The other side was, as heretics usually are, divided against itself. They all agreed in denying Homoüsios—the negative agreement one always finds; whatever they may think, they do not think what the Church has defined. Out of very complicated ramifications we can distinguish three chief parties of anti-Nicenes, though the boundaries between them were vague and changeable. First there were the strict and uncompromising Arians. Their words were *Anomoios* (ἀνόμοιος, "unlike") or *Heteromusios* (ἑτερομούσιος, "of another nature"). They said that our Lord is simply unlike, of a quite different nature from

[1] Whoever wishes to pronounce Greek properly must never sound the letter H in it. *Consubstantialis Patri* (in the Creed) in Greek is ὁμοούσιος τῷ πατρί.

God the Father. Of these was Arius himself as long as he lived, Eunomios of Kyzikos[1] and Aetios, a deacon of Antioch. They are called *strict Arians*, *Anomoians* and *Eunomians*. Then there were the people who hoped for a compromise between Athanasius and Arius, the people who thought both went too far and that a *via media* could be arranged by taking what is good from both. We know them in all controversies, the people who tell us that no doubt there is a great deal to be said on both sides. In this controversy that attitude was represented by the *semi-Arians*, and, as usual, they satisfied no one. Their word was *Homoiüsios* (ὁμοιούσιος, "of a similar nature"). They thought our Lord was neither of quite the same nor of a quite different nature. His nature was similar, very like, almost the same as that of the Father. The semi-Arians formed for a time a very large party of their own. Their leaders were Basil of Ankyra,[2] George of Laodicea, Theodor of Herakleia and, in the west, Auxentius of Milan.[3] Then, lastly, between the utter Arians and the compromisers there were the compromisers of a compromise, people between the Arians and the semi-Arians, three-quarter Arians. Their word was *Homoios* (ὅμοιος, "similar"). They thought Christ to be like the Father, but not of a like nature, and preferred not to talk about his nature at all. Their leaders were Akakios of Cæsarea (in Palestine), Eudoxios

[1] He was a Cappadocian († 395) and a pupil of Aetios. As Bishop of Kyzikos on the Hellespont he became so great a leader of this party that they are generally called *Eunomians* after him.

[2] Ankyra in Galatia, now Turkish Engkür, Angora, where the Angora cats come from. The branch of the Baghdad railway from Eskijehr ends here, and you must go on six days' ride to Cæsarea in Cappadocia.

[3] St Ambrose's predecessor.

of Antioch,[1] Uranios of Tyre. They are called *Homoians*. Eventually the situation was simplified; the semi-Arians ended by falling in with the Catholics and the Homoians fell back to the strict Arians.

Since Gibbon[2] these discussions about one letter have been a favourite object of humour. What, it is asked, can the difference between Homoüsios and Homoiüsios matter? Was it worth while to rend the whole Church for the sake of an iota? Undoubtedly to a person who cares nothing for any dogmatic belief, to whom the Christian faith means either nothing at all or a vague humanitarianism, the discussion will seem absurd; so will any theological controversy. But to people who take historic Christianity seriously one may point out that the question at issue was the vital one of all. It was that of the Divinity of Christ. Are we to believe him to be God, or only some 'sort of superior creature having rather more likeness to God than we have? That is what is involved in the issue between Homoüsios and Homoiüsios. And that the two words look so much alike is due to an accident of Greek grammar and to the fact that the semi-Arians chose their word deliberately, because it looked like ours. These pass-words were technical forms that stood for very real differences.[3]

[1] He succeeded Eusebeios at Antioch and was then Bishop of Byzantion from 360–369.

[2] *Decline and Fall*, chap. xxi (ed. Bury, vol. II, 1897, pp. 351–353).

[3] The Russian arms look very like those of Austria, and are, as a matter of fact, a rather bad copy of them. But in the case of a war between these countries an Austrian soldier would not waver in his allegiance because of that. It is very obvious that the change of one letter in a word may completely alter its meaning. Cardinal Newman somewhere quotes the example of *Personage* and *Parsonage*. Scores of instances in any language will occur at once to anyone.

6. The first attacks against Athanasius (335-339)

As soon as the Arians feel their own position safe through Constantine's change of policy they move heaven and earth to have their great opponent degraded and banished. In 330 they had succeeded in deposing Eustathios, the Catholic Patriarch of Antioch, in a synod held in that city. Now they fly at higher game. In 335 they call together a synod at Tyre to try Athanasius. He came to it with forty-eight Catholic bishops of his patriarchate; against him were sixty Arian bishops. He was accused of these crimes: (1) He had sent a certain Makarios to persecute a pious priest named Ischyras. Makarios, acting under Athanasius' orders, had forced his way to Ischyras' altar, had broken the chalice and burnt the holy books. (2) Athanasius had murdered a bishop, Arsenios of Hypsele, had cut off the dead man's hand and used it for working magic.[1] The Arians even produced the hand. (3) He had committed sin with a certain woman. The dramatic and triumphant defence of Athanasius has been the joy of every Catholic ever since. He proved that Ischyras was not a priest at all; Arsenios came and showed himself, very much alive with two hands, and the lady did not even know him by sight when she saw him. But the Arians were not prepared to accept even that defence. They could not help Arsenios and the lady; but they promptly ordained Ischyras bishop, to make up for his not having been a priest before; they declared Athanasius contumacious,

[1] The bloody hand of a murdered man as a weapon of magic is a very old superstition. We know it in the "Hand of glory" in the Ingoldsby Legends.

deposed him, and forbade him to go back to Alexandria. Then they all went to Jerusalem, consecrated the new Anastasis church with great pomp,
and began their arrangements for deposing another
Catholic bishop, Markellos of Ankyra. Meanwhile
Athanasius went to Constantinople to ask Constantine to see fair play. So far Constantine, in
spite of his Arian leanings, had had a great respect
for the saint and had refused to countenance the
attempts of his enemies. Now he sends for the
leaders of the Arians at Tyre and asks them to
explain themselves. Eusebeios of Nicomedia and
others come, and they entirely change the ground
of their complaint. The former accusations,
although certainly striking in themselves, suffered from a deplorable want of evidence. Arsenios
was still going about with both his hands, and they
were not sure that the lady would recognize the
Patriarch even this time. Also the date of Ischyras'
ordination promised to be a difficulty. Moreover,
Constantine would not trouble much about a
broken chalice, and his own career had shown that
he had no very strong feeling against either
murder or rape. So on the way to Constantinople
they thought of a far better case. They said
nothing more about these misdemeanours; Athanasius had done something much worse—he had
stopped the corn from Egypt! Egypt paid her
taxes in corn, and the whole empire depended
on the yearly export from Alexandria. This corn
was by far the most valuable asset of all the taxes
to the government. So Constantine had no hesi-
tation when he heard that. Athanasius had stopped
the corn—Very well, he shall be banished to as distant a land as possible, where there is no corn.
The emperor would hear no defence, and Atha-

nasius was sent to Trier on the Mosel. This is the
first exile; it lasted till after Constantine's death
(335–338). In the same year (335) the Arians
carried out their plan of deposing Markellos of
Ankyra in a synod at Constantinople, and Pope
Sylvester I died (314–335). The next year, 336,
saw what Catholics have always remembered as
one of the most striking judgements of God in
history. The Arians had triumphed on every side
now. Only one thing was still wanting, the restitution of their founder, Arius, himself. In the
capital of the empire he was to be solemnly
received and restored. The emperor ordered the
Bishop of Constantinople, Alexander, to receive
him back into communion. Arius hurried to the
city from Alexandria; an enormous crowd of his
friends came with him. The Catholics of Constantinople shut themselves up in despair. The Nicene
synod had been held to no avail and the Nicene
faith was to be openly denied in the very heart of
the empire. And the Arians made the most of
their victory. The court was to receive the heretic
with every possible honour; they arranged a gor-
geous procession to pass through the city, to flaunt
the triumph of their side before the whole world.
The procession began, they sang out their hymns,
and there was the famous Arius himself marching
in the place of honour. Suddenly he felt unwell
and retired to a private place. The procession
waited, the hymns died out, and then gradually
the news was whispered among the crowd. Arius
was dead. In the midst of his triumph he had died
like Judas. In a shameful place his body had
burst open and his entrails were scattered over the
floor. *Crepuit medio,* and as his friends stole away
silently to lay aside their finery the amazed

Catholics learned that sometimes in this world too the strong arm of God is stretched out and that his awful vengeance had fallen at the very moment when he was being defied.[1] And then in the next year Constantine died, too. On his death-bed at last he made up his mind to be a Christian, and he was baptized by his Arian cousin, Eusebeios of Nicomedia. He died at Nicomedia on Whitsunday, May 22, 337. His body was robed in the Imperial purple, placed in a coffin of gold and brought to the city he had founded. There he lay in the church of the holy Apostles, first of the long line of Roman emperors who were buried around him, till in 1463 the Turk cleared away the burial-place of the Cæsars to make room for the mosque of Mohammed the Conqueror. The Orthodox Church has canonized him, as well as his mother, and on May 21 they keep the feast of "the holy, glorious, mighty, God-crowned, equal-to-the-Apostles sovereigns, Constantine and Helen." The Catholic Church, more difficult in her standards of sanctity, honours Helen only as a saint.[2] Nevertheless, a certain halo will always surround the figure of that mighty prince who joined together the whole empire under his rule, founded New Rome, summoned the Nicene fathers, and is remembered as the first Christian emperor. And Athanasius, among the Germans in distant Trier, heard the news of the awful death of his old enemy, Arius, and then of the tardy baptism and

[1] For Arius' death see Athanasius: *De morte Arii*, c. 2. *Ep. ad Ep. Aegypti*, c. 19. Sokrates, H.E. i, 37. Sozomenos, H.E. ii, 29. Theodoretos, H.E. i, 24.

[2] Constantine was, in any case, only a catechumen till his death-bed, and then an Arian. He persecuted the Catholic bishops and had a weakness for murdering his near relations. None of these things can be held up as examples of heroic sanctity.

death of his old friend the emperor. The exiled
patriarch had been received at Trier with great
honour by the bishop Maximinus. He had with
him some of his Egyptian clergy and he could
write letters to his flock at home. It was during
this time that he wrote his first Paschal letter
(p. 42). And Constantine, although he had banished
the lawful patriarch, had not allowed any intruder
to be set up at Alexandria.

7. Appeal to Rome. The second exile
(340-345)

After Constantine's death his three sons divided
the Empire between them. *Constantius* had the East
(Præfectura Orientis), *Constantine II* Gaul, and
Constans Illyricum and Italy. But this arrangement
only led to fighting between them. In 340 Constans
defeated and slew Constantine II at Aquileia. Ten
years later, in 350, a usurper named Magnentius
defeated and slew Constans, and after three more
years, in 353, Constantius defeated and slew Magnentius. So Constantius is again the only lord of
the Roman world (353-361). He reigned, of course,
at Constantinople, began to persecute the pagans
and was himself, without any sort of compromise,
a declared Arian. So the government and the
court are now even more enemies of the Nicene
faith than in Constantine's later years. However,
as soon as Constantine was dead, St Athanasius
was able to go back to his own city. The three sons
began their reigns by proclaiming a general
amnesty and restoring all exiled bishops. In 338,
Athanasius entered Alexandria again, to the great
joy of all faithful Catholics. But his enemies did
not mean to leave him long in peace. The next
year they set up an Arian anti-bishop, a certain

Pistos, at Alexandria and sent a long complaint against Athanasius to the three emperors and to the Pope, to persuade them to recognize Pistos. Athanasius then did what every Catholic bishop would do. He, too, formally appealed to the Pope. He "sought refuge in Rome as in a most safe harbour of his communion."[1] But in 340 Constantius, having refused to allow Athanasius to defend himself, let the Arians in a synod at Antioch again declare him deposed. Then he banished him and set up, instead of Pistos, one Gregory, a Cappadocian, as rival bishop. Gregory, of course an Arian, seized the churches at Alexandria with the help of the Imperial prefect of Egypt and began a fierce persecution of the Catholics. And St Athanasius set out on his *second exile*. The Pope, to whom he had appealed, had not forgotten him. Julius I (337–352) had succeeded Sylvester I. As soon as the complaint of the Arians and Athanasius' appeal reached him, he summoned both sides to Rome. Athanasius went at once, even before Gregory the usurper had arrived at Alexandria. But the Arians, denying the Pope's jurisdiction, like all heretics, did not appear.[2]

[1] St Jerome, *Ep.* 127, n. 5.

[2] Their language sounds curiously like what we hear in this country. They said they could not allow the Pope to discuss the matter, because it had been settled by councils. So it had, by a dozen councils; and every council had settled it in a different way. To appeal to councils is a splendid argument, when you are quite sure which councils are the right ones to appeal to. At that time there was a council of some kind every year somewhere, and some councils were Homoüsian, some Homoiüsian, some Homoian, and they all deposed somebody and set up somebody else, and they all anathematized everything done by all the others.

These Arians also told the Pope that he had no more authority than any other bishop; no doubt his see was a very important and venerable one, but he had no jurisdiction over them. Protestantism is an older movement than people suppose. For this impudent Arian letter to the Pope *see* Athanasius, *Hist.*

Pope Julius then, in 341, held a synod at Rome,
attended by fifty bishops, in which he declared
Athanasius to be innocent of all crimes of which
his enemies had accused him, and to be the only
lawful bishop of Alexandria. The story of St
Athanasius' appeal to the Pope and of the Pope's
judgement is one of the many famous cases of
appeals to Rome in the early Church. Here, again,
we see the greatest bishop in the east, the mighty
patriarch who held the second see of Christendom,
the leader of the Catholics against Arians, and
the greatest of eastern fathers solemnly appeal-
ing to the Bishop of Rome as his over-lord to
judge his case. It was no question of Roman
patriarchal jurisdiction. Egypt had nothing to do
with the Roman patriarchate. The only claim the
Pope could have to interfere in a quarrel at Alexandria was his claim to universal jurisdiction over
the whole Church of Christ. And St Athanasius
showed plainly enough what he thought of that
claim. He had always steadfastly refused to admit
the emperor's right to judge in ecclesiastical
affairs,[1] but when he was in really great trouble
he appealed to the Pope. This is Theodoret's
account of the matter: "The Eusebians, having
got together calumnies against Athanasius, had
denounced him to Bishop Julius, who then ruled
the Roman church. And Julius, following the rule
of the Church, ordered them to come to Rome,

Arian, c. 11, *Ep. Jul. ad Ant.* (quoted in Athan.: *Apol. ctra
Arianos,* c. 21–35); Sokrates, H.E. ii, 15, 17; Sozomenos, H.E.
iii, 7, 8, 10.

[1]For instance, he says triumphantly of this very Roman
synod in 341: "No Imperial governor was there, no soldiers
stood before the doors, the affairs of the synod were determined
by no laws of the government." (*Hist. Arian.* c. 11). Indeed,
throughout his life he never ceased protesting against the
interference of the state in these theological questions.

and he also summoned Athanasius to explain his
case. Athanasius, obeying the summons, started
at once on the journey. But they who had made
up the fable would not come to Rome, because
they knew that their lie would be found out."[1]
And Julius wrote a stern letter to these Eusebians,
saying: "Do you not know that this is the custom,
that you should first write to us and that what is
right should be settled here."[2] So St Athanasius
passed his second exile at Rome under the protection of the Pope. Meanwhile the bewildering succession of synods and anti-synods was going on
all over the empire. In the same year as the
Roman one (341) there was a great Arian synod
at Antioch, when the bishops met to dedicate
Constantine's Golden church.[3] In 343 the Catholics
met at Sardica (now Sophia in Bulgaria), defended
Athanasius and confirmed the right of appeal to
the Pope that every accused bishop has,[4] and at
the same time the Arians met at Philippopolis
and again declared Athanasius deposed. But Constans while he lived was Athanasius' friend, and
he at last persuaded his brother, Constantius,
to allow the patriarch's return. In February, 345,
Gregory, the Arian usurper at Alexandria, who
had ruthlessly persecuted the faithful subjects of
Athanasius, went too far and they rose up and
murdered him. Then Constantius invited the
lawful bishop back. He wrote him a very friendly
letter and offered him the use of the government's

[1]Theodoreti H.E. ii, 3 (M. P. G. lxxxii, 996).

[2]Ep. 3 Julii ad Eus. 22 (in Athan.: *Apol. c. Arianos*, 21–36).

[3]This is the Synod *in encœniis* (ἐν ἐγκαινίοις, "at the dedi-
cation").

[4]Canons 3, 4 and 5 of Sardica are the most famous instance
of an Eastern synod solemnly recognizing this right of appeal
to Rome.

conveyances. So in 345 Athanasius makes a second triumphal entry into his city. This return was the most famous of all. He had passed through Adrianople, Antioch and Laodicea (where another council met and declared him innocent), and when he came to Alexandria, "like another Nile,"[1] the people streamed out to meet him. They spread their carpets in the streets for him to walk upon and cut down palm-branches to carry before him. "Who," he says himself, "that beheld such peace in our church did not wonder at the sight? Who did not praise God for the joy of the people."[2] And Pope Julius wrote a letter full of praise of the saint and of joy at his return. "If precious metals are tried by fire, what shall we say of so great a man who has overcome so many trials? . . . Receive, therefore, my dear brethren, your bishop Athanasius, with joy and with thanks to God."[3] To this day the eastern churches keep a feast in memory of the end of Gregory's tyranny and Athanasius' happy return.[4] For ten years he now reigned in peace at Alexandria, restoring order in his patriarchate and writing one treatise after another against the Arian heresy.[5] Meanwhile the synods went on. In 344 the Arians at Antioch drew up another formula that was rejected by the Catholics at Milan in 345. In 351 an Arian Synod of Sirmium[6] proposed yet another form, carefully avoiding the word Homoüsios; in 353, at Arles, they

---

[1]Greg. Naz.: *Orat.* xxi, 27.   [2]*Hist. Arian.* 27.
[3]Athan.: *Apologia*, 52.
[4]In the Byzantine Church on Jan. 18.
[5]Throughout his life he was always occupied in writing defences of the faith. We shall come to these in the list of his works (pp. 40-43).
[6]*Sirmium* was in Lower Pannonia near the river Save. Now it is in Slavonia, north-west of Belgrad.

deposed and banished St Paulinus of Trier. And
in 355 they met again at Milan.

8. Third exile, in the desert (356-362)

This Arian Synod of Milan professed to depose
Pope Liberius (352–366), who had succeeded
Julius. He and Lucifer of Calaris in Sicily then had
to go into exile. It also deposed Athanasius for the
third time. Constantius had again changed his
mind. He was always an Arian, and he quite
rightly looked upon the great patriarch as the
most powerful and uncompromising enemy of his
belief. This time he tried to have him murdered.
On Febr. 9, 356, while Athanasius was keeping the
night hours in the church of Theonas at Alexandria it was surrounded by the emperor's soldiers, who shot their arrows into the church. At
last the Catholics succeed in breaking through
with their patriarch, and he flees for refuge to the
fathers of the Libyan desert.[1] This is the *third
exile* among the monks (356–362). St Athanasius
had always had a very great admiration for the
monks who lived away from the world in the great
Egyptian desert. We have seen that even before he
was patriarch he had known and served them
(p. 11). It is said that he was one of the founders
of western monasticism while he was at Rome,
and he had made many journeys to their settlements in his patriarchate. So it was natural that,
now that he was fleeing for his life, he should go to
these monks, where he could hide from the
emperor's soldiers in the desert and where he would

[1]Before he could get away he lay hidden in Alexandria while
the soldiers hunted for him in his friends' houses. Eudaimonis,
a nun, was tortured to make her say where he was; but she
kept the secret. Another lady hid him in her house for days
while the pursuit was hottest.

have the comfort of their company. For six years
he wandered about the different settlements of
these fathers south of the Thebais where the great
tawny lions crouch behind the burning rocks.
Meanwhile, in Alexandria, his Catholics were
fiercely persecuted. The soldiers hunted for the
patriarch throughout Egypt. As they could not
find him, they broke open and burnt down houses,
scourged his clergy (Eutychios, a subdeacon, died
under their rods), violated nuns and took away
all the churches to give them to the Arians.
Indeed, all over the empire there was now a furious
persecution of the "Athanasians." For a second
time the government set up an intruder in St
Athanasius' see, this time George, another Cappadocian. This George was a quite horrible person,
an Arian, of course. Sozomenos says that he was a
notorious drunkard and a man of evil life, stupid,
coarse and brutal (H. E., III, 7). He meant to make
money out of his place, so he secured monopolies
for salt, paper and nitre, and did a thriving trade in
coffins on his own account by refusing Christian
burial to anyone who was not brought in one made
at his own factory. Catholic bishops were deposed
and imprisoned, Catholic monasteries burnt down
and every meeting of Catholics interrupted by
soldiers, who scourged all the people they found,
sometimes even to death. But Athanasius, from his
hiding-place, still cared for his desolate church, and
wrote constantly to encourage his faithful subjects.
"Our churches," he says, "are taken from us and
given to the Arians; they have our places, but we
have the faith. They cannot rob us of that." Many
strange and romantic stories are told of the saint's
adventures while hiding in the desert. The loyal
hermits watched for the coming of soldiers and

sent him on from place to place, bearing themselves the brunt of the soldiers' rage when they
missed him. One story is famous. The soldiers
actually met him once face to face, but they did
not know him by sight. "Where is Athanasius?"
they asked. And he answered: "He is not far off."
So they hurried on, and he escaped. This story is
often told as an example of a mental restriction. It
was one of a very innocent kind. During this third
exile he wrote many of his most famous works,
including the *Apology for his Flight* (p. 41). While
he was there St Antony, the father of monks, died
and left his cloak of palm-leaves as a legacy to the
exiled patriarch.[1] Throughout the Church the hopeless confusion of synods went on. In 357 the
Arians met again at Sirmium and drew up an even
more uncompromisingly Anomoian formula than
that of the first Synod of Sirmium (in 351); the
semi-Arians held a synod at Ankyra in the same
year. In 358 came the famous third Synod of
Sirmium, with its semi-Arian formula that Pope
Liberius is said to have signed, in 359 the fourth
Synod of Sirmium, and the great Synod of Ariminium[2] that Constantius forced to accept the
fourth Sirmian formula. The trouble and confusion
were now at their height. There were at least
twelve different creeds[3] that claimed the allegiance
of the pious Christian layman; every shade of
Arianism and semi-Arianism clamoured for his
acceptance; only the faith of Nicæa and Athanasius was forbidden and persecuted. It is of this
time, just before Constantius died in 362, that St

[1] Athan.: *Vita Antonii*, 91.
[2] Rimini in Romagna on the coast between Ravenna and
Ancona.
[3] Five of Antioch, four of Sirmium, one of Constantinople,
one of Akakios of Kyzikos and the Nicene creed.

Jerome wrote: "The whole world groaned and wondered to find itself Arian."[1] But the simple people kept the faith through all this clash of quarrelling bishops,[2] and they looked out towards the hot Libyan desert where the column of the faith lay hidden till God should bring him back. St Athanasius' return after his third exile was brought about in just the same way as his former one. Julian (361–363) declared himself emperor, and Constantius died on his way to fight him (362). Julian began his reign by recalling all banished bishops, and George the intruder at Alexandria, who had made himself even more hated than his predecessor, Gregory, of unhappy memory, was murdered by the people. Only this time it was the pagans who murdered him, thereby earning the gentlest of reproofs from Julian, who thought that this time the zeal of his fellow-Hellenes had exceeded the bounds of moderation. So St Athanasius came back again to his city (362).

9. The fourth and fifth exiles (362-363, 365-366)

From this time the tide of Arianism turns back and the whole movement gradually disappears. But Athanasius has to go into exile twice again before he dies. He was by now without comparison the most famous man in the Christian Church and the acknowledged leader of the Catholics. At Alexandria he converts so many pagans that their priests complain to Julian that if he stays there there will soon be no more gods at all in Egypt. So

[1]Ingemuit totus orbis et arianum se esse miratus est (Hieron.: c. Luciferianos, 19).
[2]St Hilary († 366) says that the ears of the people were holier than the lips of the preachers (Ad Constantium, 4).

Julian again banishes the saint as being "an enemy
of the immortal gods," and he again goes to the
monks in the Thebais. This is the *fourth exile* (362–
363). It did not last long. Poor Julian was killed
fighting the Persians in 363, and his successor,
Jovian (363-364)), as usual, began his reign by
proclaiming an amnesty and the return of all
exiles. So Athanasius entered his city again. But
Jovian died after eight months, and Valentinian I
(364–375) appointed his brother, Valens, to be
regent of the east. Valens was a declared Arian,
and he immediately ordered that all Homoüsian
bishops who had been banished by Constantius
and restored by Julian should again leave their
sees (May 5, 365). Athanasius had to go, too, and
fled to his father's tomb by the Nile.[1] But there
was so great a tumult among his people at this
continued persecution of their patriarch that the
emperor had to give in and recall him after four
months. So this *fifth and last exile* (365–366) was a
short one. Once more, and for the last time, the
old patriarch entered his city in triumph, and from
now till his death he lives there in peace.

10. Athanasius' last years and death

The saint's last seven years were spent in finish-
ing the work of his life, the destruction of Arianism. And now, after all his troubles, he was able to
see the storm calmed before he died. Arianism
was disappearing as fast as it had arisen. In spite
of Valens, the Arian Cæsar, everywhere the
Nicene faith was being restored. Catholic bishops
were coming out of their hiding-places and a new
and younger band of defenders of the faith was

[1]Sokrates, H.E. iv, 13; Sozomenos, H.E. vi, 12.

routing the heresy in east and west. St Basil
(† 379), St Gregory of Nyssa († c. 395) and St
Gregory of Nazianzos († 390) on the one side,
St Ambrose († 397), St Jerome († 420) and St
Damasus the Pope († 384) on the other finally
destroyed the evil that had threatened to swallow
up the whole Church. And at last—but this was
after Athanasius' death—the great Catholic
emperor, Theodosius I (379–395), ruled over a
united Catholic empire, and Arianism became only
an episode of history and a memory of the most
fearful storm that has ever raged in the Church of
Christ.[1] And all these younger fathers looked up
with unbounded reverence to the old patriarch
who had borne the burden of the fight before they
were born, whom they recognized while he lived
as their leader and champion, whom they remembered after his death as the great standard-bearer
of the Nicene faith. He tasted this peace after so
great a storm during those last seven years. From
every side came news of the reconciliation of Arian
churches and the conversion of Arian bishops
In his own city he ordered everything peaceably
for the firm establishment of the Catholic faith,
and he saw the last poor remnants of paganism
and heresy gradually die out dishonoured and
unnoticed. Naturally from every side people
appealed to him in their difficulties. St Basil wrote
to him from Cæsarea asking for sympathy and help
in his own difficulties, and when a new heresy
began—that of Apollinaris—once more people
turned to Alexandria and begged the old patriarch
to refute this, as he had so often refuted the
Arians. His treatise *against Apollinaris* was almost

---

[1] Arianism went on outside the Empire for a long time still as
the religion of the Teutonic peoples. The Goths were Arians.

his last work. And then, after all his troubles, after
he had been hunted down, had fled for his life so
many times, after he had spent those long years of
exile hiding among the rocks of the desert, or wan-
dering in the distant western lands, after all he
died at home in the city that had been his since
his birth, that had become more famous because
of him than it had been in the old days of Alexander and the Ptolemies. On May 2, 373, the old
patriarch, who had fought his good fight, finished
his course and kept the faith, went to receive the
crown of righteousness that the Lord gave him at
that day. We are not surprised that the whole
Catholic world from end to end united to honour
his glorious memory. He was buried at Alexandria
with great honour by the people who had been
faithful to him through all the persecution. The
whole city formed a great pomp to follow his
relics to their rest. Gregory of Nazianzos preached
a glowing panegyric[1] of him. "To praise Athanasius is to praise all virtues. To name him is to
name a gathering of all that is admirable in one
man." He was the "Pillar of the Church, rich in
doctrine, edification and comfort, a triumph of
truth and right." Every one of these later fathers,
Greek or Latin, has something to say of the great
hero. To St John Damascene († c. 754) in far
Damascus he is the "Foundation-stone of the
Church of God," and to Vincent of Lerins in still
further Gaul he is the "most faithful of confessors,
most enlightened of teachers." Naturally, he is,
first of all, the great national saint of Egypt. Ask
any Egyptian Christian who is the greatest saint
of his country, and he will answer at once "Athanasius the Great." The four patriarchs who now

[1] *Oratio* 21 (M. P. G. xxxv, 1082–1128), probably in 380.

dispute the succession of St Mark[1] all claim him as their most glorious predecessor. And, beyond the boundaries of Egypt, east and west keep the memory of the champion of the faith against the greatest and worst of heresies. Orthodox and Catholics remember him every year on May 2, the day of his death. The Orthodox pray to him: "Speaker for God, Athanasius, who overcame endless dangers and trials, now you have become worthy of the delights of paradise. You followed God's commands, conqueror of justice, now you are crowned with the crown of the heavenly kingdom, glorious in your eternal triumph." And the Roman Church that he honoured and obeyed[2] honours him, and throughout the world her priests read on May 2 of the great saint who "for six and forty years during the greatest changes of times with very great holiness ruled the Church of Alexandria"; and we pray that God may hear the prayers that we say on the feast of blessed Athanasius, Confessor and Pontiff, and that he may forgive us all our sins through the merits of the saint who served him so worthily.[3]

11. Table of dates

293. *Birth of Athanasius.*

306–337. Constantine the Great, only emperor from 323.

311. Arius ordained priest.

313–328. Alexander of Alexandria patriarch.

314–335. St Sylvester I Pope.

[1]There are four Patriarchs of Alexandria, an Orthodox, a Monophysite Kopt, a Uniate Kopt and a Melkite. The Latin titular patriarch at Rome has no pretence of succession from the old line and need not be counted.

[2]Above, pp. 26-29.

[3]*Brev. Rom.* 2 Maii, Lect. vi and Collect.

c. 319. Athanasius ordained deacon.

321. Synod of Alexandria against Arius.

325. FIRST GENERAL COUNCIL AT NICÆA IN BITHYNIA.

328. *Athanasius Patriarch.*

335. Arian synod at Tyre.

335–337. *First exile at Trier.*

335. St Sylvester I †.

336. Arius †.

337. Constantine †.

337–362. Constantius emperor; he reigns alone from 340.

337–352. St Julius I Pope.

338. Athanasius restored at Alexandria.

340. Arian synod at Antioch against Athanasius.

340–345. *Second exile at Rome.* Gregory of Cappadocia intruded at Alexandria.

341. Synod at Rome defends Athanasius.

341. Arian synod "in encæniis" at Antioch.

343. Catholic synod at Sardica. Right of appeal to Rome.

344. Arian synod at Antioch.

345. Gregory of Cappadocia murdered. Athanasius restored. Feast of his restoration.

345. Catholic synod at Milan.

351. First Arian synod at Sirmium.

353. Arian synod at Arles. St Paulinus of Trier banished.

355. Arian synod at Milan. Pope Liberius (352–366) and Athanasius banished.

356–362. *Third exile in the desert.* George of Cappadocia intruded at Alexandria.

357. Second Arian synod at Sirmium.

357. Semi-Arian synod at Ankyra.

358. Third semi-Arian synod at Sirmium. Liberius signs its formula.

359. Fourth Arian synod at Sirmium.

359. Synod of Arminium.

361–363. Julian emperor, alone from 362.

362. George of Cappadocia murdered; Athanasius restored.

362–363. *Fourth exile in the Thebais.*

363–364. Jovian emperor.

364–375. Valentian I emperor; Valens Cæsar in the east.

365–366. *Fifth exile by his father's tomb.*

373 (May 2). *Athanasius †.*

12. Works

Throughout his whole life St Athanasius was engaged in writing, chiefly against the Arians, but we have treatises of exegesis and history, letters, sermons and apologies by him as well. His works were first collected and printed in Greek in 1600 at Heidelberg; the Benedictines of St Maur published what is still the best edition of them at Paris in 1698,[1] and they fill four volumes of Migne.[2] This is a list of the chief works only.

APOLOGETIC WRITINGS. While he was still only a deacon, before Arius had begun his heresy, he wrote a *Treatise against the Heathen* (λόγος καθ᾽ ἑλλήνων, Oratio contra gentes,[3] xxv, 3–96) and a *Treatise on the Incarnation of the Word* (λόγος περὶ τῆς ἐνανθρωπήσεως τοῦ λόγου, Oratio de humana natura a Verbo assumpta, xxv, 95–198).

DOGMA AND POLEMICS AGAINST THE ARIANS. His chief polemical work is the *Four treatises against the Arians* (κατ ἀρειανῶν λόγοι δ΄, Orationes IV

[1] 3 vols, edited by J. Lopin and B. de Montfaucon.
[2] M. P. G. xxv–xxviii, Paris, 1857.
[3] The Latin titles are useful for reference to Migne. For the same reason I give the volumes and pages in M. P. G.

contra arianos, XXVI, 11–526). Also *Of the appearance in the flesh of the Word of God and against the
Arians* (περὶ τῆς ἐν σάρκου ἐπιφανείας τοῦ θεοῦ λόγου
καὶ κατ᾽ ἀρειανῶν, De apparitione Verbi Dei in carne
et contra arianos, XXVI, 983–1028), *Exposition of
the Faith* (ἔκθεσις πίστεως, Expositio fidei, XXV,
199-208). *Two Books against Apollinaris* (κατ᾽
Ἀπολλιναρίου λόγοι β΄. Contra Apollinarium libri
II, M. P. G., XXVI, 1093–1166) were written at the
end of his life.

HISTORICAL WORKS. Three Apologies are specially valuable as telling the history of his own time,
the *Apology against the Arians* (ἀπολογητικὸς κατ᾽
ἀρειανῶν, Apologia contra Arianos, XXV, 247–
410), written in 350, the *Apology to the Emperor Constantius* (πρὸς τὸν βασιλέα Κωνστάντιον ἀπολογία,
Apologia ad imperatorem Constantium, XXV, 595–
642) in 356, and the *Apology of his flight* (ἀπολογία περὶ τῆς φυγῆς αὐτοῦ, Apologia de fuga, XXV,
643–680)[1] in 357. He wrote a *History of the Arians
addressed to the monks* (ἱστορία τῶν ἀρειανῶν πρὸς
τοὺς μονάχους, Historia arianorum ad monachos,
XXV, 691–796), between 335 and 337.

EXEGESIS. Of Athanasius' many interpretations
of holy Scripture only fragments remain that have
been preserved in Catenas.[2] Of these the largest
fragment is that of his *Commentary on the Psalms*
(XXVII, 55–590). There are also parts of his expo-
sitions of *Job* (XXVII, 1343–1347), the *Song of
Songs* (XXVII, 1348–1350), *St Matthew* (XXVII, 1363–

[1] The lessons of the third nocturn on his feast in the Roman
breviary are taken from this work.
[2] A *Catena* is a collection of interpretations from the fathers
arranged together under each text of Scripture in a "chain."
It was a favourite and very convenient way of making commentaries on each book in the middle ages, the commentary
consisting of a mosaic of quotations. St Thomas Aquinas'
(† 1274) *Catena aurea* is a well-known example.

1390), *St Luke* (XXVII, 1391–1404) and 1 *Cor.* (XXVII, 1404).

ASCETIC WORKS. His *Life of St Antony* (βίος καὶ πολιτεία τοῦ ὁσίου πατρὸς ἡμῶν ᾿Αντωνίου, Vita S. P. N. Antonii, XXVI, 835–976) is one of the great standard books on the spiritual life. It was done into Latin almost at once, and this version was one of the chief causes of St Augustine's conversion. He had heard a certain Pontitianus speak of St Antony's life and describe how he had found this book with his friends in a monastery while they were out for a walk; "and one of them began to read it and to wonder and be greatly moved, and while reading it to think about leading such a life himself and leaving the army to serve God" (Aug. *Confess.*VIII, 6). A number of St Athanasius' letters addressed to monks belong to this class too.

LETTERS. It is, perhaps, from these letters that one knows the saint best. He wrote a great number to all sorts of people, and in them he discusses every kind of subject; sometimes he tells the story of some synod or other event, often he again exposes the Nicene faith and argues against Arianism, or he writes exhortations and counsel for the devout life. The most important are the *Paschal Letters* (ἐπιστολαὶ ἑορταστικαί,[1] Litteræ festivales, XXVI, 1431–1444). It was the custom for the Patriarch of Alexandria soon after the Epiphany to write an encyclical to his suffragans announcing on what day Easter would fall in that year, and he used the opportunity to discuss any other important question of the time.[2] Besides the fragments of

---

[1] ἡ ἑορτή in Greek always means Easter.
[2] These Paschal letters then were like the Lenten pastorals that our bishops now write.

Athanasius' paschal letters extant in the original
Greek, a Syriac version of fifteen of them has been
discovered.[1] These were written between 329 and
348, many while he was in exile, and they contain
most important passages about his own life and his
theology. His letters to various monks, to Abbot
Drakontios (xxv, 523–534), two to Abbot *Orsisios*
(xxvi, 977–980), one to a monk *Amunis* (xxvi,
1169–1176), one addressed to the Egyptian monks
in general (xxvi, 1185–1188) are about the rules of
monastic life and asceticism. His letters to *Epiktetos*,
Bishop of Corinth[2] (xxvi, 1049–1070), to Bishop
Adelphios (xxvi, 1071–1084) and to a philosopher
named *Maximos* (xxvi, 1085–1090) explain the
Catholic faith against the Arians. They were
written at the end of his life, about 371. Two
Encyclical Letters, one to all bishops (ἐπιστολὴ
ἐγκύκλιος, Ep. encyclica, xxv, 221–240) in 341, and
one to the *Bishops of Egypt and Libya* (xxv, 537–
594) in 356, tell the history of the Arian attacks
against him. An encyclical about the *Decrees of
Nicæa* and one about the *Teaching of Denis of
Alexandria* (xxv, 479–522) were written between
350 and 354. He wrote two Latin letters to
Lucifer, Bishop of Calaris[3] (xxvi, 1181–1186) in
360, one to Bishop *Serapion* (xxv, 685–690) at
about the same time, one to the *Antiochene bishops*
(xxvi, 795–810), and one to *Rufinianus* (xxvi,
1179–1182) in about 362. There are also a number
of other letters which will be found in Migne's

[1] In 1847 in a monastery in the desert. Cureton edited them
in 1848 and a Latin version of them is given in M. P. G. xxvi,
1351–1444.
[2] This letter is specially famous; Epiphanios quotes it at full
length in his work *against Heresies* (Hær. 77).
[3] Cagliari in Sicily. This is the Lucifer who afterwards made
the Luciferan schism in Italy.

Greek series among his works. Lastly, it is hardly necessary to say that St Athanasius had nothing to do with the so-called *Athanasian Creed*. The clauses in this against the Nestorians and Monophysites alone are enough to show that it was written after those heresies (after the fifth century). As a matter of fact, we now know that it was composed in Latin in the west (in southern Gaul or Spain) and that it was not introduced into the Divine office (at Prime) till the ninth century.[1]

As a specimen of the great veneration with which the fathers received St Athanasius' works we may quote what Abbot Cosmas in the eighth century says: "If you find a book by Athanasius and have no paper on which to copy it, write it on your clothes."

13. Literature

For the Benedictine edition and Migne, *see* p. 40. Hurter has published a Latin version of the *Treatises against the Heathen* and *On the Incarnation* in his little series (*SS. Patrum opuscula selecta,* Innsbruck, Wagner, vol. XLIV), and an English translation of the chief works forms vol. IV of the second series of the Oxford *Select Library of Nicene and Postnicene Fathers* (J. H. Newman and A. Robertson). J. Dräscke (who is obsessed by Apollinaris and spends his life in trying to prove that he wrote every doubtful and many not-doubtful treatises of the fourth century) has attempted to show that his hero wrote "against the heathen" and "on the Incarnation"[2]. The standard life is still J. A. Möhler: *Athanasius der Grosse und die Kirche seiner Zeit* (2 vols, Mainz,

[1]Dom. G. Morin: *Les origines du symbole Quicunque* (La Science Catholique, 1891, pp. 673, *seq.*)
[2]*Athanasiana, Theol. Stud. u. Kritiken,* lxvi (1893).

2 ed., 1844). J. P. Silbert: *Das Leben des h. Athana-sius* (2 vols, Vienna, 1842). P. Barbier: *Vie de S. Athanase* (Tours, 1888). H. Voigt: *Die Lehre des Athanasius von Alexandrien* (Bremen, 1861). Ch. Vernet: *Essai sur la doctrine christologique d' Athanase le Grand* (Geneva, 1879). L. Atzberger: *Die Logoslehre des hl. Athanasius* (Munich, 1880). H. Sträter: *Die Erlösungslehre des hl. Athanasius* (Freiburg, i/Br. 1894). F. Cavallera: *Saint Athanase* (*La Pensée chrétienne*, Paris, Bloud, 1908). For Arianism see Gwatkin: *Studies of Arianism* (Cambridge, 2 ed. 1900); Schwane, *Dogmengesch. der patrist. Zeit* (Freiburg, i/Br., 2 ed. 1895); Harnack: *Lehrbuch der Dogmengeschichte*, vol. II (Freiburg, i/Br., 3 ed. 1894).

CHAPTER II
ST BASIL (330–379)

ST BASIL, Metropolitan of Cæsarea in Cappadocia, is the chief of the three Cappadocians[1] who defended the faith of Nicæa in the next generation after St Athanasius. Like all the fathers of that time he wrote against the Arians; and he wrote a famous work about the Holy Ghost. But he is not known chiefly because of his polemical works. He is remembered rather as a great Catholic bishop in a troubled time, as a man of very ascetic life and as the father of organized eastern monasticism. The Byzantine Church ascribes the older of her two liturgies to him; we know him, through his letters especially, as a very charming and sympathetic person, as, perhaps, personally the most attractive of the Greek fathers.

1. His family, birth and early years (330-*c.*345?)

Basil[2] came of a distinguished family of Pontus in Asia Minor. His forbears had filled important places in the government. At that time there was no sort of hereditary nobility in the empire, but certain families succeeded in getting high places for their children and relations as each generation grew up and so they gradually gathered together much wealth and large properties. St Basil's

---

[1] The other two are his brother St Gregory of Nyssa, and St Gregory of Nazianzos.

[2] Βασίλειος (Basilîus) means *Royal*. The Greek form is pro-paroxytone, the Latin pro-perispomenon.

family was of this kind. For a long time his relations had been persons of consideration because of
the offices they held; they had lands in Pontus and
Cappadocia; and they all had the natural instincts of
people of a certain social position. They show a
sense of distinction in style when they write; they
nearly all become orators, and they are very keen
hunters. St Basil's grandfather had been a great
man, whose table groaned under the weight of the
game he offered to his guests. He was also a Christian; he had fled to the mountains of Pontus with
his wife Makrine during Diocletian's persecution.
Here he lay hidden for a time, but comforted himself by shooting birds with his bow.[1] The saint's
father, also named Basil, was an orator at Cæsarea,
the capital of Cappadocia; although he was a fer-
vent Christian, he did not despise the old Greek
classics. Later his successors in the school that
thought it quite possible to join the Christian
faith with humanism note this as a point in his
favour.[2] The elder Basil married a certain Emmelia,
the mother of our St Basil, a lady who seems to
have brought to her husband every grace and
every good quality that a bride could have. She
was very rich and very beautiful, but every one
especially praises her wisdom, sense and piety. St
Basil owed his training to these ladies, Makrine, his
grandmother, and his mother Emmelia; he, his
brothers and all his friends constantly speak with
unbounded admiration of both. Of this marriage of
Basil the orator and Emmelia ten children were
born, five boys and five girls. The eldest of all was
a girl, called Makrine after her grandmother. This
Makrine became a nun and a saint, as we shall

[1] St Gregory Naz.: *Oratio*, xliii, 5–8.
[2] *Ib.* 11.

see (pp. 54, 58, 77). Then came our saint, Basil, the eldest son. He was born at Cæsarea in 330.[1] His younger brothers were Nausikrates, who became a monk and died young in 357, then Gregory (St Gregory of Nyssa, a bishop and one of the Greek fathers like his eldest brother), Peter, who became bishop of Sebaste in Armenia, and another who died quite young. The names of the other daughters are not known. It was then an eminently religious family; Basil, the father, gave to the Church three bishops, a monk and a nun, and three of his children are canonized saints.[2] The father was known as a pious Christian, but it was especially the two ladies, old Makrine and Emmelia, who brought up the children in the fear of God. St Basil is never tired of repeating that he owes everything to his mother and grandmother. "I shall never forget," he says, "the deep impressions made on me as a boy by the words and example of these venerable women." He was delicate from the first; all through his life he refers to his ill-health. The first years were spent at Cæsarea and then chiefly in Pontus, where the family had an estate near Neocæsarea. Here the father taught the boys the elements of secular knowledge and the mother and grandmother told them stories about the old days of persecution and the sufferings of martyrs and confessors in the bad times that had just passed. Old Makrine had known St Gregory Thaumaturgos († 270), the apostle of Pontus and bishop of Neocæsarea; and from her they learned to honour the memory of the great Christian bishop in whose footsteps three of them were to walk.[3] The boys

[1] There is some doubt about the date. It is sometimes given as 329 or 331.
[2] St Basil, St Gregory and St Peter.
[3] St Gregory Nyss. afterwards wrote his life (p. 85). There is

then spent these first years on their land in Pontus
in a great house full of slaves, where they had
every comfort that a rich establishment in the
fourth century could offer. We picture them hunting, fishing, riding through the forests along the
slopes of the mountains that stretch down towards
the Black Sea, then learning the first mysteries of
Greek grammar, logic and rhetoric with their
father or sitting round old Makrine and listening
to her stories of the dreadful days when to confess
the name of Christ meant torture and death.
After this we shall lose sight of the others to follow
our two saints, Basil and Gregory.

2. Studies (345-357)

Basil the father did not mean to keep his sons at
home all their lives. He naturally foresaw for them
a distinguished career as government officials or
orators, and the first condition of such a career
was to have studied at one of the great centres of
Greek learning under some famous professor. There
were then several cities that had great schools,
places that corresponded to our Universities.
There was Cæsarea, where he himself had practised
as an orator, the capital of Cappadocia and chief
town of all central Asia Minor; there was the
capital of the whole empire, Constantinople, still
glowing with the first whiteness of new marble,[1]
where Cæsar reigned with his court and all the

a pretty story about this St Gregory the Wonder-worker. As
he lay dying at Neocæsarea (a large and important town) he
asked how many pagans were left in it. They told him seventeen. "Thank God," he said, "when I came here there were
just seventeen Christians." This Gregory was said to have
literally carried out our Lord's words and by faith to have
moved a mountain. His name (θαυματουργός, wonder-worker)
shows that he had a special reputation for working miracles.

[1]Constantine the Great dedicated his new city in 330.

world came to stand before him. And there was
Athens, dangerous, perhaps, as one of the last
strongholds of the old gods, but most attractive
of all, since here the pure Greek culture still reigned
and the old city, mother of all Hellenism, still
gathered under her Akropolis the first teachers
and philosophers of the world. So to these three
cities Basil sent his sons. It was the custom then
for students to go from one centre to another,
learning what they could from each and then
going on to hear some other famous teacher else-
where. In the fourth century the love of Greek
letters was so little dead that it was still the chief
moving force to hundreds of thousands of eager
scholars. They had never forgotten the glories of
the old Greek classics. The one thing that gave a
man a position and a title to be honoured was a
knowledge of Homer, the tragedians, the history-
writers and especially the philosophers. Homer and
Plato were the greatest of all names to civilized
people in the east, who still spoke their language and
gloried in being the successors and descendants of
the citizens of the old Greek states. So great a power
were the Greek classics that the love of them
among all civilized people was the one thing on
which the emperor Julian (361–363) could count
in his war against Christianity. His argument was
always that this new religion would mean the
death of Hellenism; Christians were the enemies of
the Greek gods, therefore they were the enemies
of Greek culture; they were barbarians, worshipping a Jew, using barbarous Jewish Scriptures in a bad Greek version instead of the pure
glory of Homer and Plato. And his most subtle
form of persecution was to forbid Christian
teachers to explain the classics. Let them explain

their Septuagint, and let all who loved Hellas and beauty leave them to grovel in their debased superstition and come back to the worship of the immortal gods and the use of the optative mood. Christians, of course, indignantly denied that there was any necessary opposition between their faith and the love of what was beautiful in the old classics; Christian students flocked to the great teachers of Greek letters just as much as their pagan fellow-citizens. These students travelled enormous journeys and suffered great hardships, dangers[1] and discomfort for the sake of the austere joy of scholarship; and they continued their studies for a much longer time than the modern University student. Some of them at the age of thirty were still sitting round a professor and learning from him.[2] Basil and Gregory then went first to Cæsarea in Cappadocia. Here there was no danger for their faith; the city was almost entirely Christian,[3] but the schools were not the best that could be found. At that time Cappadocians had a reputation for being rustic, rather stupid and coarse.[4] It was here that the brothers first met a fellow-countryman, also named Gregory, who remained, but for one rather bitter quarrel, their very intimate friend and comrade through life. This is St Gregory of Nazianzos.[5] The two brothers and the friend form the company of

[1] St Gregory of Nazianzos was shipwrecked and nearly drowned once while travelling to Athens to hear Himerios lecture (*Poem. de se ipso*, xi, 130, *seq.*)

[2] So Greg. Naz. (*ib.* xi, 239).

[3] The town council had already ordered the two great temples of Zeus and Apollo to be broken up (Sozomenos: H.E. v, 4).

[4] Even in Latin "Cappadox" was almost a term of abuse, meaning "boor," "oaf."

[5] He was the son of the bishop of Nazianzos (Diocæsarea) in Cappadocia.

three great Cappadocians who by their learning
and eloquence, as much as by their virtues, have
redeemed the character of their fatherland, so
that we now remember that province with honour
as their birthplace. Gregory of Nazianzos says that
already at Cæsarea Basil was the most distinguished student in the city, even then surpassing
his professors.[1] From Cæsarea the brothers go on
to Constantinople, the other Gregory to Palestine
and Alexandria. Then they all meet again at
Athens. The city of Pallas Athene, crowned with
violets, was still ancient Athens. That wonderful
vision of gleaming marble and stately orders of
columns, the glowing colours of the Parthenon,
the shining golden helmet of the virgin goddess,
the cool arcades, crowded theatre and the glorious
Propyleia—all the splendours that we now try
to recall among the piteous ruins of the Akropolis—
were then real things. Where we look up from the
bay of Salamis and see only broken columns and
the split gable of the great temple—even now
incomparable in its ruin—there the sailor of the
fourth century saw the Parthenon radiant with
colour and the mighty statue of Athene lifting
her gleaming spear over the wine-dark sea. Athens
was still the heart of that rich and subtle com-
bination of philosophy, letters and perfect æsthetic
taste that make up *Hellenism*. Here were the temples and statues that formed the standard of
beauty for the rest of the world, in the Dionysiac
theatre under the Akropolis the chorus still sang
Aeschylus' strophes, the olive-groves at Kolonos
still sheltered the discussions of philosophers.
And Athens was still the heart of the old pagan
faith. The dying gods found a last refuge in the

[1] *Oratio xliii*, 13.

city where they had grown; so every Christian
knew that, beautiful and fascinating as Athens
was, priceless as was the erudition, the pure
Greek, the perfect style that could be learned only
there, still there was grave danger to the faith of
young students in the plausible discourse of the
Athenian philosophers. Basil took this risk, but
took also every precaution while he was exposed
to it.[1] He and Gregory of Nazianzos, now the closest
of friends, divided their time between their studies
and prayers. Gregory says that they only knew two
roads, that road to the lecture-room and the one
to the church. They kept away from the company
of pagan students and succeeded in the centre of
pagan philosophy in leading an almost monastic
life. "We were advanced in the fear of God by the
learning of the heathen, since we knew how to
ascend from the imperfect to the perfect, and to
find a support for our faith in the weakness of their
reason." They gloried in one thing only, "in that
great name of Christian."[2] We know the names of
the two most famous professors whom they heard;
the religions of these teachers are a sign of that
time of transition. For Himerios was a pagan and
Prohairesios a Christian. A hundred years before
no Christian would have been allowed to teach, a
hundred years later there were practically no
pagans left. Basil and Gregory studied grammar,[3]
rhetoric, logic, philosophy, astronomy, geometry
and mathematics, also a little medicine. Among
their fellow-students was the emperor's nephew,

[1] It is uncertain whether his brother Gregory of Nyssa went
to Athens with him or not. We know little about this Gregory
till he became a monk (p. 74).

[2] Greg. Naz. *Oratio xliii*, 21.

[3] Grammar then included many things, such as the art of
poetry, and even history.

Julian.[1] This meeting between the future champions of the Christian faith and its future enemy is historical. Julian had not yet declared himself, so he passed for a Christian too at that time. But Gregory says afterwards that even then they foresaw what Julian would become. He describes him as a young man "uncertain in manner, shifty in look and inconsistent in speech," and adds that he said at the time, "See what a scourge the empire here prepares for itself."[2] Then in 355, while Gregory stayed to continue his studies at Athens, Basil went back home to the family estate by Neo-cæsarea in Pontus.

When he arrived home he found his grandmother and father dead. Four of his sisters were married; the eldest, Makrine, had been engaged to a young man who died before the wedding. She kept his memory sacred, gave up all thought of ever marrying anyone else and lived at home helping to bring up her youngest brother Peter. Gregory (of Nyssa) was then an orator, and by no means specially pious,[3] Naukratios after a brilliant career as an orator at Neocæsarea had retired to the mountains as a kind of hermit and had there founded an almshouse for old men. He died soon after. Peter, the youngest, the future bishop of Sebaste, was being taught by Makrine, who was "not only his sister, but father, mother, guardian and tutor all in one."[4] Basil, after a short visit at home, set up as a teacher of rhetoric at Cæsarea. He was already a famous man. The news of his brilliant career as a student at Athens had reached

---

[1] Afterwards emperor, 361–363.

[2] *Oratio v*, 23, 24.

[3] He could not stand the long family prayers (Greg. Nyss. *Oratio ii in xl martyres*).

[4] Greg. Nyss. *De vita S. Macrinæ.*

his own country, so that the people of Neocæsarea tried in vain to persuade him to come and teach in their town. He preferred to stay at Cæsarea and here for two years he was the chief and most popular master in Cappadocia.

3. Baptism and journey to the monks (357-358)

The great turning-point in Basil's life was his baptism in 357. He had never been wicked in any way, so that one cannot properly call it a conversion. It was rather the natural piety he had inherited from his parents that made him at last determine to leave the world and live only for God. And his sister, Makrine, used her influence over him to persuade him to do so. She had always had great faith in him and had always hoped that he would become something better than a professor of rhetoric. So after two years of public life he is persuaded to give it all up and become a monk. The first step was that he should be baptized. According to the custom of that time, although he was so pious, although he had always gloried in the name of Christian, he was not really one yet at all. Like most people, he had put off his baptism to a mature age. Afterwards he and both the Gregories wrote strongly against this dangerous custom.[1] In 357, at the age of twenty-seven years, he was baptized by the bishop of Cæsarea, Dianeios. He then at once began to make ready to lead the life of a monk. There were at that time no organized monasteries with fixed rules anywhere; it is our saint who is looked upon as the founder of organized monasticism in the east as much as

[1]Basil: *Hom. xiii*, Greg. Nyss.: *Adv. eos qui differunt baptismum*, Greg. Naz.: *oratio xl*, 16, 17.

St Benedict (†543) in the west. But there were many monks. Great numbers of men left their families and the cares of the world to go out into some lonely place, build themselves a hut, live by tilling the ground and spend all the time they were not digging in praying, meditating and singing psalms. These were the *Ascetes* (ἀσκητής), a wrestler, warrior), *Hermits* (ἐρημίτης, dweller in the desert) or *Monks* (μοναχός, solitary man).[1] Some sort of organization had begun before St Basil's time. Naturally the hermits tended to form colonies, they would then look up to the oldest and most venerable among them as their leader, and young men when they first arrived would put themselves under the guidance of the older ones. So we have already the germ of a community with abbot, monks and novices. Then they would read not only the Scriptures but the lives of specially famous fathers of the desert, and they would form their lives on these models; what St Antony, for instance, did was a right and safe thing for any monk to do;[2] then the advice and example of old and wise hermits became accepted as a kind of law. So we have the beginning of a monastic rule. But there was as yet no legal establishment, no legal admittance to a religious order. Monasticism was still simply a manner of life, not a disciplined body. To be a monk a man had to flee the world and go away to some quiet place to serve God. He was then quite as much a monk as anyone else. It

[1]As far as its original meaning goes the word *Monk* is therefore more applicable to these first solitary hermits than to members of the organized communities that we know. Μόνος means alone, *single*; and so the root idea of all the words *monk, monastic, monastery* is solitude. Their secondary meaning is, of course, quite a correct one now.

[2]St Athanasius' Life of St Antony was a recognized model for monks to follow.

should be specially noted that monks were never
priests. The hierarchy of the Church consisted of
bishops, priests, and deacons; these persons
administered sacraments, said Mass and had the
care of souls. One did not say "secular priests"
because there were no others. For with all this the
monks had nothing at all to do. If a monk wanted
to receive a sacrament (it was not a very common
occurrence), he came out of his solitude and went
to the nearest priest. Occasionally a monk is made
a priest or bishop; but then the situation was quite
simple—by that very fact he ceased being a monk
and went back to the world. The greatest and most
famous colonies of monks were in Palestine, Syria,
Mesopotamia and especially in the great Libyan
desert south of Egypt. So when St Basil made up
his mind to be a monk himself he first undertook
a long journey to visit these places and to learn
from the holy men there how to follow in their
footsteps. He spent the two years after his baptism (357–358) in travelling "to Alexandria,
throughout Egypt, in Palestine, Hollow Syria, and
in Mesopotamia."[1] Here he lived with the Ascetes,
and, sharing their life, was filled with admiration
for "their fasting, their courage in their work,
exactness in long vigils of night-prayer, the high
and noble spirit that made them scorn hunger,
thirst and cold, as if they were free from the body
and already citizens of heaven."[2] Then he came
back to Pontus to copy this life at home.

[1]Ep. 223.   [2]*Ib.*

4. Life as a monk (358-364)

He found quite a large community waiting to
lead the monastic life under his guidance. His
young brother, Peter, was now grown up; there
were no more duties to be done in the house at
Neocæsarea. So his mother, Emmelia, his sister,
Makrine, Peter himself, nearly all their servants
and some friends had agreed to go out from the
world and spend the rest of their lives in the service of God. Basil chose a place called *Annesos*
not far from Neocæsarea, in the diocese of Ibora.
He had a strong sense of natural beauty,[1] and here,
on the border of the little river Iris, he found a
retreat among such beautiful surroundings as
would make up for the splendour of the city he
had left.

There is a high mountain, not easy to reach,
covered with woods; its green slopes lead down to
the clear river; banks of wild flowers cluster
around the roots of the trees; birds sing all day in
their branches and the river is full of fish. "No
place," he wrote afterwards, "ever gave me such
peace. No sound from the city ever reached us;
we were far away from the high road, and only
rarely some hunters came to disturb our life."[2]
Emmelia, Makrine and the women lived on one
side of the river, Basil, Peter and the men on the
other. As soon as he had settled here he tried to
persuade Gregory of Nazianzos to leave his mud,
bears and wolves and to come and join him by the

[1] In an amusing letter to Gregory of Nazianzos he criticizes
the scenery of Gregory's town, says it is full of mud, bears and
wolves, and that he cannot bear ugly country (Ep. 14).
Throughout his letters we notice this sense of beauty or
ugliness in scenery.
[2] Ep. 14.

Iris. Gregory would not come at first, because, he
said, his old father wanted him. However he came
eventually and lived some time as a monk under
Basil's guidance. Other people came, too, drawn
by the fame of these men, so there was soon a
large colony of monks. Every one acknowledged
Basil as their chief. He was the *Hegumenos* of the
Laura. They worked hard to till the ground,
carried wood, dug, planted, watered. Gregory was
very proud of a fine birch tree he had planted himself.[1] But sometimes the rocks nearly fell on their
heads, and the river was occasionally inclined to
be foggy.[2] They had a hard life; often Emmelia
from the other side had to send across bread
because they had none themselves. St Basil in a
long letter (written to Gregory of Nazianzos after
he had left the community) describes their life very
exactly.[3] They got up at sunrise and praised God
with psalms and hymns. Then they went out to
work and while they dug and planted they still
sang psalms. During the day hours are set apart for
reading the Bible; they read with it Origenes'
(† 254) commentaries. Then there are meetings for
prayer and the singing of psalms; once a day they
eat bread and green-meat, they drink only water.
They go to bed at sunset and get up again at midnight to sing. They dress in one tunic and a cloak,
and sleep on the bare ground. It will be seen that this
way of living only needs to be codified to make it
a monastic rule. The singing of psalms is the
divine office, abstinence from flesh-meat is always a
fundamental rule for eastern monks, the hand-work
in the fields was for centuries the normal occupa-
tion of all monks, and the tunic and cloak are the
"angelic dress." During these years at Annesos St

[1]Greg. Naz. Ep. 6.   [2]Ep. 4.   [3]Basil, Ep. 2.

Basil did codify it. He drew up a list of a monk's duties, arranged the division of the day and so organized the ascetic life in a system. This is the first monastic rule. It is the one still followed by very nearly all eastern monks, and because of it St Basil is looked upon as the founder of organized monasticism in the east, as St Benedict in the west.[1] He prefers greatly that monks should no longer live entirely separated from one another, but should group themselves into communities under a leader (*ἡγούμενος, leader,* is still the Greek title corresponding to our word *abbot*), living in huts arranged as a kind of village and coming together for public prayers.[2] And the new members are to be subject to strict discipline and tried before they are admitted as regular members. The public prayer is to take place at midnight, at dawn, and then four times during the day, at the third, sixth, ninth hours and at sunset. This is the divine office of the Byzantine Church. The psalms to be sung are fixed, and every monk must leave his work to attend. Celibacy is, of course, a strict law. There are long hours of silence; when speech is allowed it must be grave and edifying. St Basil led this life and ruled his monastery for five years, from 358 to 364. Then he had to leave his quiet retreat and go out into the world to defend the faith against the Arians.

[1] The eastern monks resent being called after any founder; as they have no distinction of various religious orders it is not necessary to use any special name for them. A monk is a monk, a "good old man (*καλόγερος*)" and that is enough. But Latins, who are used to speak of Benedictines, Cistercians, and so on, generally call eastern monks *Basilians*, and Melkite monks accept the name. If they are to have a special name, this is certainly the right one. There is a second edition of St Basil's rule, made by him later (*cfr.* p. 81).

[2] St Benedict begins his rule by expressing the same preference for " coenobitarum genus, hoc est monasteriale militans sub regula vel abbate." *Reg. Ben.* Cap I.

5. His priesthood (364-370)

During those years that Basil spent at Annesos the Church was passing through very terrible times. The Arian troubles were at their height. The emperor Constantius was fiercely persecuting Catholics; many otherwise excellent bishops had not the strength to resist, but gave in for a time and signed one of the endless Arian or semi-Arian formulas that the government sent round, with the alternative of banishment. Dianeios of Cæsarea, who had baptized Basil, was such a one. Basil had always loved and reverenced him; then he heard that his old friend had signed the Arian formula of Ariminium.[1] So at once he refused to have any communion with him. But poor Dianeios had only given way in a moment of weakness. On his death-bed he sent for Basil and solemnly assured him that he had never really meant to deny the faith of Nicæa. "God is my witness," he said, "that I signed in the simplicity of my heart. I never meant to renounce the faith taught by the fathers at Nicæa. Now I ask for only one thing, not to be separated from the 318 holy bishops."[2] So the saint came back into communion with the dying bishop. In 362, after Dianeios' death, Eusebeios was chosen to succeed him as metropolitan of Cæsarea by a stormy and irregular election. The same year saw the last attempt to enliven the dying embers of paganism by the emperor Julian (361–363). He was specially angry with Cæsarea because it was a very Christian town and because its citizens had destroyed two great temples (p. 51, n. 3). So he seized on the pretext of this irregular election to

[1] The Council of Ariminium (359) was Catholic, but Constantius forced the bishops who held it to accept an Arian formula.
[2] He means the 318 Fathers of Nicæa I (Basil, Ep. 51).

impose a heavy fine, confiscate all Church property, take away all privileges, even the right to be a city, and make all the clergy policemen. He did not try to hide his scorn and hatred of its citizens. "I cannot find a single Hellene," he writes (meaning a worshipper of the gods[1]), "among those Cappadocians."[2] Between the Arians and the pagan emperor the Catholics were in great straits. Julian further proceeded to punish every one connected with the destruction of the temples (which had taken place quite legally under a former government) with death or exile. And the bishop, Eusebeios, though a Catholic, was weak and uncertain. Under these circumstances, urged by Gregory of Nazianzos, Basil left his monastery, came to the city and was ordained deacon and priest by Eusebeios, in 364. He was by far the most important person in the church of Cæsarea; he was known as an unswerving defender of the Nicene faith, all the monks in the diocese were on his side, he had much more influence than Eusebeios himself. Eusebeios was jealous of his popularity and did not like to see himself eclipsed by one of his own priests. So there was friction, and there would have been grave trouble had not Basil avoided it by going back to Annesos. But he did not stay there long. Gregory of Nazianzos wrote to him again, imploring him not to forsake the church of Cæsarea at a time when it was in so great danger from its enemies, the Arians. Eusebeios meant well, but no bishop ever had greater need of support; nowhere was the presence of an uncompromising Homoüsian more necessary than at Cæsarea. "Go back since there is so much need of you. The

[1] *Hellene* always means pagan at this time and for many centuries afterwards. [2] Julian, Ep. 4.

heretics are all at work, some already troubling the
faithful with their arguments; we hear that others
will arrive soon. Truth is in danger."[1] St Basil
could not resist this appeal, so he went back to
Cæsarea, made friends with Eusebeios again and
stayed with him for five years, till the bishop's
death in 370. During these years he, with Eusebeios' consent, managed most of the affairs of the
diocese. His place corresponded to that of our
Vicars-General. And he used his power very zea-
lously to strengthen the position of the Catholics,
to improve whatever was lacking in the services of
the Church and to help the poor. Valens, the
brother of the emperor Valentinian I (364–375)
and Regent of the east under him, was a strict
Arian and a bitter enemy of Catholics. He came
to Cæsarea in 365 with a train of Arian bishops.
Gregory of Nazianzos says that Basil then was the
soul of the resistance against him. It was Basil who
encouraged waverers, restrained the excessive
eagerness of others and strengthened all to withstand Valens' persecution.[2] At this time he re-
formed the church services at Cæsarea. He shortened the prayers of the Liturgy and Office that were
too long, borrowed from Antioch the custom that
alternate choirs should sing the verses of psalms
alternately—as we and the Orthodox still do—
and arranged the various duties of each order of
clerks. This reform of St Basil was gradually
adopted by all churches that used Greek as their
liturgical language. His influence on the Byzantine
rite was as great as that of St Gregory the Great
(590–604) on ours. The older liturgy of the Orthodox Church[3] bears his name, though really he

[1]Greg. Naz.: Ep. 19.   [2]*Oratio, xliii, 32 seq*
[3]And of the Melkites, of course, too.

arranged and modified it rather than actually composed it all.[1] In 367 and 368 a dreadful famine spread over Cappadocia. Bad weather ruined two successions of crops, and people were dying of hunger. In this trouble, while the governor and magistrates did nothing, Basil alone came to the rescue. He sold all that was left of his property to buy corn for the starving people and persuaded merchants, who wanted to sell what they had kept in their barns at an enormous price, to sacrifice such iniquitous profit. He opened subscriptions, organized distribution, founded public kitchens, to which we are told that Jews were admitted as much as Christians,[2] and encouraged the people by his sermons.[3] So we are not surprised that every one at Cæsarea looked on him not only as the foremost churchman of the city, but as the saviour of the people, nor that when Eusebeios died in 370, every one, the people, clergy of the town and suffragan bishops of Cappadocia, with one voice elected Basil as his successor.

[1] The *Liturgy of St Basil* is used on the Sundays in Lent (except Palm Sunday), Maundy Thursday, Holy Saturday, the eves of Christmas, and the Epiphany, and on his own feast (January 1). On other days they use the *Liturgy of St John Chrysostom*, a shortened form of St Basil's. And St Basil's Liturgy itself is a modified form of the old Antiochene rite. His relation to the service that bears his name is much the same as that of St Gregory I to the "Gregorian chant" in the west.

[2] Greg. Nyss.: *In laudem Basilii*, Greg. Naz.: *oratio xliii*, 34–36.

[3] A number of St Basil's homilies were preached at this time, as their titles show, Hom. viii, *At the time of drought and famine*; Hom. vi, *On the words: I will destroy their barns and build greater ones. See* also Hom. vii and ix, etc.

6. Basil metropolitan of Cæsarea (370-379)

We have seen our Saint as a student, scholar and monk. We now come to the last phase in which he is a great Prince of the Church, one of the greatest of that younger generation of Catholic bishops who carried on the fight that Athanasius had fought and finally stamped out the Arian heresy. Cæsarea in Cappadocia, his birthplace of which he now became bishop, was one of the greatest metropolitan sees, after the three patriarchates. Before Constantinople and Jerusalem had become patriarchal sees, after Antioch came Ephesus, Cæsarea and Heraclea. The bishops of these places were more than metropolitans, they had metropolitans under them. They are sometimes called *Exarchs*, and no doubt all three would have kept that intermediate rank between patriarchs and ordinary metropolitans,[1] had not the unhappy ambition of Constantinople eventually swallowed them up into its patriarchate. But in St Basil's time no one dreamed of the future grandeur of Constantinople.[2] Cæsarea was an apostolic see[3] from which the great Church of Armenia had been founded.[4] The primate (Katholikos) of Armenia always was ordained at Cæsarea, till Armenia became Monophysite in the fifth century. And the Exarch of Cæsarea ruled over all northern and central Asia Minor, over Cappadocia, Pontus, Galatia and

[1] The organization of bishops, never quite consistently nor perfectly carried out, is: 1, The Pope; 2, Patriarchs; 3, Exarchs (=Primates); 4, Metropolitans (=Archbishops); 5, Bishops; 6, Chorepiscopi (something like our Auxiliary Bishops).

[2] The first step in its advance was at the second general Council, in 381.

[3] Acts ii, 9.; I Peter, i, 1.

[4] By St Gregory the Illuminator in the third century.

Pisidia. His boundaries touched the patriarchate of Antioch to the south (Cilicia belonged to Antioch) and the other exarchate of Ephesus to the west (the Roman province of Asia and Phrygia were under Ephesus). And he had jurisdiction over the great Church of Armenia to the east.

During the nine years (370–379) till his death, in which St Basil ruled this great province, he upheld the dignity of his see and was recognized throughout the Christian Church as one of her mightiest bishops. And when he died he left in his own name the chief glory of the see of Cæsarea. It is a dirty little Turkish town now; but of the few people who brave the hideously uncomfortable journey of five days' hard riding from Angora to *Kaisari*, most do so because it was the city of Basil. He was consecrated by the old bishop of Nazianzos, the father of his friend Gregory,[1] to the joy of all Catholics, to the great annoyance of Valens and the Arians. From distant Alexandria came a warm letter of congratulation from the old hero of the faith, Athanasius, who before he died (in 373) had the joy of seeing the work of his life taken up by that valiant band of younger men, of whom Basil was, perhaps, the chief.

Very soon after the beginning of Basil's reign began one of the last efforts of Arianism, a violent persecution that was really the dying gasp of the great heresy. Domitius Modestus, the Pretorian Prefect, came to Cæsarea to force every one to turn Arian. He summoned Basil, and in a long interview[2] threatened him with confiscation, exile, torture and death unless he would accept the Cæsar's (Valens) religion. Basil withstood him so

---

[1] The father was also named Gregory.
[2] Reported by Greg. Naz.: *Oratio xliii.*

firmly that he said in astonishment: "No one has
ever yet spoken to me so freely." "Perhaps," said
Basil, "you have not yet had much conversation
with a Catholic bishop." Then Valens came himself. The fame of Basil was so great throughout the
empire that Valens wanted to see this man. So he
went to the holy liturgy in the Catholic church on
the Epiphany of the year 372. There he saw the
saint sitting on his throne facing the people, as
eastern bishops do. The Cæsar was so impressed
by his dignity that when the offertory came he
brought up his gift with the other people. And to
every one's astonishment Basil took it, which
shows that he could be conciliatory as well as firm.
Two stories are told of this visit of Valens to
Cæsarea. One is that his only son, Galatos, was
dying and that his wife, Dominica, implored him
to send for Basil to heal him. Valens, wishing to
try every chance, did so. Basil came, cured him at
once, but warned the Cæsar that God only allowed
this miracle on condition that the boy be baptized
by a Catholic. However, as soon as the boy was
well, Valens went back to his usual friends, and had
him baptized by an Arian, with the result that
Galatos at once died. The other story is that he prepared a sentence of banishment against Basil, and
three times as he took up the pen to sign it his
hand was paralysed and the reed broke. So then in
great fear he tore up the parchment.[1] Another time
Valens engaged in a great theological discussion with
the saint, and his cook kept chiming in and sup-
porting the Cæsar's arguments. Basil made them all
very angry by laughing at the cook's bad gram-

[1] Greg. Naz.: *Oratio xliii*, 54, Theodoret, H.E. iv, 16. Both
stories are told in the second nocturn of St Basil's office in the
Roman breviary (June 14). It seems rather hard on Galatos
to be killed for his father's sin.

mar.[1] Valens eventually learnt to respect the
Saint, since these interviews at Cæsarea, and so
during Basil's campaign against the Arians as
bishop he was not again troubled by the government.

7. The affairs of the province. Basil's friends

During his reign St Basil was constantly occupied not only with fighting Arianism[2] but also with
various questions of secular and ecclesiastical
politics. He was the natural protector of his fellow
citizens, and they turned to him in their difficulties. One or two of these cases shall be described
here. The government at that time was everlastingly cutting up provinces and making new ones,
to the great hurt of stable administration. So
Valens in 371 proposed to divide Cappadocia and
form a new province in it, with a wretched little
town called *Potanda*—a place no one had heard of
before—as capital.[3] The people of Cæsarea were in
despair at a proposal that would nearly ruin their
city. They implored Basil to prevent this arrangement, so he wrote to the government and pointed
out the arguments against it very reasonably. "If
you cut a horse in two," he says, "you will not
make two horses."[4] He could not prevent the
division, however, and the only effect of his letter
was that they made *Tyana* (about sixty miles
south-west of Cæsarea) the new capital instead of
Potanda. This led to further complications.
Anthimos, the Bishop of Tyana, hitherto a

[1]Greg. Nyss: *Contra Eunomium*, I. Theodoret, H.E., iv, 16.
[2]His writings against the Arians are quoted below, p. 80.
[3]The same thing was going on all over the empire. It was
really a roundabout way of getting more taxes out of the people.
[4]Ep. 74.

humble suffragan of Cæsarea, now thought that
as his city had become a capital equal to Cæsarea
he ought to be a metropolitan equal to Basil.[1] So
he filched a great part of Cappadocia to make himself a province, and when Basil with his friend
Gregory (of Nazianzos) went to levy their dues from
a monastery near his city he fell upon their caravan,
and there was a regular fight, in which Basil,
Gregory and Anthimos all joined. The end of it was
that Basil and Gregory got through, but Anthimos
captured a string of mules laden with provisions.[2]
In order to withstand this truculent person Basil
then persuaded Gregory to accept the diocese of
Sasima in the debatable land. He ordained him
himself. He also ordained his younger brother
Gregory to be Bishop of Nyssa, hoping that both
would help him to put down Anthimos. But out of
this double ordination arose a serious quarrel that
for a time interrupted the life-long friendship of
the three great Cappadocians.[3] Eventually Basil
and Anthimos became friends again; it seems that
Basil in the interest of peace gave up many of his
rights and allowed Anthimos to keep some of his
ill-gotten province. The saint then sternly put
down a preposterous deacon named Glykeros, who
went about dressed like a patriarch, singing hymns
with a choir of young ladies.[4] But he was not a
stern father. One of his chorepiscopi[5] named

---

[1] It is one more case of the fatal tendency of eastern bishops
to alter ecclesiastical administration according to the changes
of secular politics. The rise of Constantinople and nearly all
the troubles of eastern Christendom to this day come from
this misguided principle. [2] Greg. Naz.: Oratio xliii, 58; Ep. 48.

[3] See pp. 74. 97.

[4] Ep. 169, 170, 171.

[5] A chorepiscopus was a person who shared some of the
bishop's work without having any jurisdiction—something
like our rural deans. They appear sometimes to have had
bishop's and sometimes only priest's orders.

Timothy had mixed himself up in politics, and Basil's letter to him contains only the most delicate reproach mixed with the kindest advice and the most affectionate interest in his affairs.[1] He refused to use torture—the common punishment in those days—and continually, when a robber was brought to him, sent him away with a sermon instead of punishing him.[2] He writes constantly to defend an innocent person who had been accused unjustly to the magistrate, to plead for a remission of taxes in favour of poor people, to intercede for a slave with his master, to persuade the governor to build a bridge that the people want, to soften the heart of a pagan father whose son has become a Christian.[3] The great collection of the saint's letters shows him always in the same light, stern and unflinching before people in high places, gentle and merciful to the poor. It is from these letters that we know him best, and in them that we see the qualities that make St Basil one of the most attractive and charming of all the fathers.

He had naturally many friends. We have seen how closely he was allied to Gregory of Nazianzos. Eusebeios, Bishop of Samosata on the Euphrates (in Kommagene), was also a dear friend to whom he wrote a number of letters; Amphilochios, Bishop of Ikonion, was a disciple to whom he dedicated his treatise on the Holy Ghost (p. 80). Once St Ephrem († c. 379) came from far Syria to visit the great metropolitan at Cæsarea. He could speak no Greek and Basil no Syriac; when Ephrem came to the church at Cæsarea Basil saw him during the office and came up to him afterwards with an interpreter to say: "Are you Ephrem who have taken

---

[1] Ep. 291. [2] Ep. 286.
[3] Ep. 96, 107, 108, 109, 73, 276, 305, etc.

the yoke of salvation so excellently well upon yourself?" "I am Ephrem," he answers, "who walk so
unworthily in the way of salvation." And they
kissed each other, and Ephrem said: "Father,
defend me against laziness and sloth, lead me in
the right way, pierce my evil heart." They talked
for a long time. Ephrem, when he went home never
forgot Basil, and long afterwards wrote a panegyric
about him. And Basil, too, remembered the Syrian
deacon who had come all that way to see him.[1]
"From my youth to old age," St Basil writes, "I
have had many friends."[2] And again: "I have
never sinned against friendship."[3] But one of
these friends gave him great trouble. Eustathios of
Sebaste in Armenia had been intimate with him for
years. Basil loved Eustathios and at first all went
well. Then Eustathios, always shifty and uncertain,
gradually went over to the Arians and repaid
Basil's friendship with calumnies and accusations
during three years. Basil spoke no evil of him, but
always tried to make it up and to bring his old
friend back to the faith. Only in the case of one
flagrant calumny did he justify himself in a letter
to the monks of his diocese.[4] Eustathios died an
open heretic in 380; and Basil's brother Peter succeeded him as Bishop of Sebaste. The saint had
continual relations with western bishops, too.
When Valens was persecuting the Catholics Basil
sent to Pope Damasus (366–384), asking him to
use his authority to make peace in the east. "The
only remedy for these evils," he says, "is a visita-
tion from your mercy."[5] He knew quite well that
the Roman Bishop has jurisdiction over the whole
Church of Christ. He writes at the same time to

---

[1] Sozomenos, H.E., iii, 16.   [2] Ep. 272.   [3] *Ib*.   [4] Ep. 226.
[5] Ep. 70.

St Athanasius: "We thought it expedient to write to the Bishop of Rome that he should examine our affairs and to advise him, since it would be difficult to send anyone thence by the common decree of a synod, to use his lawful authority in the matter, choosing men fit to bear the fatigue of a journey and also fit to correct all perverse people in our parts gently and firmly."[1] During all this time he was treating with Damasus, continually imploring him to send over to help the Eastern Church, and showing in every letter how well he understood that Catholic bishops turn to Rome in time of great trouble. He was angry when he found that all the western bishops took the side of Paulinos in the schism at Antioch, whereas he, as all the easterns, was for Meletios. In one letter he quotes Homer to express his annoyance at Western pride.[2] But his annoyance passed away, and later he shows again how great a regard he has for his distant Latin brothers.[3] He was delighted at the election of St Ambrose at Milan (374), the western father whose character is most like his own. When Ambrose wrote to ask him to send the relics of Dionysius of Milan (who had died in exile for the faith in Cappadocia) back, he does so at once and writes him a charming letter full of praise of the Milanese priests who had come to fetch Dionysius' relics, and full of admiration for the bishop who had sent them. "Man of God," he says, "it is not from men that you have learned the Gospel of Christ; it is God himself who took you from the seat of the Roman magistrates to place you on the throne of the apostles. Fight the good fight. Heal the sickness of Arianism among your people. Renew the old paths of the fathers, and do

[1]Ep. 69.   [2]Ep. 239.   Ep. 265.

not forget to write often to me, so that our friendship many never become weak. So shall we always
be neighbours in spirit although a great distance
divides us on earth.''[1] One remembers these
courteous and friendly relations between the two
great fathers at Cæsarea and Milan as one of the
pleasantest examples of the old good feeling
between eastern and western Christendom. How
little either Basil or Ambrose foresaw that for
eleven centuries a bitter schism could divide their
successors.

During these years of Basil's reign as metropolitan then we see in him from every point of view the
perfect model of a great Catholic bishop. Standing
out valiantly for the faith against the Arians,
ruling his province firmly and wisely, leader of his
people, proudly conscious of the liberty of the
Church against the State, gentle and kind to the
poor, courteous, friendly and charming to his
friends, best and most entertaining of letter-
writers, submitting his difficulties to his rightful
chief at Rome, from far Cappadocia he has left an
example that any bishop in any land may pray to
be worthy to follow.

8. St Gregory of Nyssa (c.331-c.395)

Since we left Basil's younger brother Gregory at
home as a young man not very fond of prayers, we
have almost lost sight of him. His life is too much
overshadowed by that of his great brother for him
to have a chapter to himself. One paragraph will
be enough to give a short outline of his career. He,
as well as the other brother Peter, had been educated chiefly by Basil, whom he speaks of as his

[1]Ep. 197.

"father and master."[1] His friends wanted him to be
a priest, but at first he preferred the career of an
Orator, so that Gregory of Nazianzos says rather
unkindly and unfairly that he "liked the name of
orator better than that of Christian."[2] There is
really no reason why an orator should not be as
good a Christian as anyone else. At the same time,
Gregory married a lady named Theosebeia.[3] She
did not die till 381. He had, however, already
served in church as a Reader.[4] Eventually he made
up his mind to forsake the world and leave his wife.[5]
He went to be a monk, apparently at Basil's
settlement at Annesos. In 371 Basil ordained him
Bishop of Nyssa, very much against his will, he
says.[6] Nyssa was a little town in Cappadocia on the
river Halys, about forty miles west of Cæsarea.
He was, therefore, a suffragan of his brother. Basil
thought he would find in him a valuable help in the
affairs of the province. But, on the whole, it was
rather a disappointment. No one questioned Gregory's virtues or good intentions; but his brother
did not think him a success as a bishop. Basil has
to complain of his "unwise and uncandid interference"[7]; he says that by his "simplicity" he gave
a great deal of trouble[8] and that he was "altogether
without experience in ecclesiastical affairs."[9] It
would seem, then, that Gregory was a pious and
irreproachable person, who was not, however,
specially fitted to rule a diocese. It is his writings
that give him a right to be remembered. However
he had the honour of suffering for the faith. In 375

[1]*De hominis opif.* 1 (M.P. Gr. xliv, 125).   [2]Ep. xi.
[3]Greg. Naz. Ep. 197.   [4]Greg. Naz. Ep. 11.
[5]She seems to have joined him again later and to have lived
with him like a sister (Greg. Naz. Ep. 197).
[6]Basil, Ep. 225 and 345.   [7]Ep. 58 and 60.
[8]Ep. 100.   [9]Ep. 215.

the Governor, Demosthenes—an Arian, of course,
under Valens—deposed him as a Homoüsian and
set up an Arian anti-bishop at Nyssa. Gregory of
Nazianzos wrote to comfort him.[1] For years he
then wandered about, "like a log floating on the
water," says the other Gregory.[2] When Valens
died (378) he came back to Nyssa. The next year
he was at a synod at Antioch that tried to settle
the great schism there (of Meletios). He outlived
Basil, and was present at the second general
Council (Constantinople I in 381). He was well-
known as a staunch Catholic, so much so that the
Emperor Theodosius (379–395) ordered that the
test of being a Catholic bishop in Pontus was to be
in communion with three persons, Helladios of
Cæsarea (Basil's successor), Otreios of Melitene in
Armenia and Gregory of Nyssa. We hear of him
last at a Synod of Constantinople in 394 under the
Patriarch Nektarios (381–397). Then he disappears; he died probably soon after. His last years
were troubled by a quarrel with his metropolitan
Helladios.[3] For the writings that give him an important place among the Greek fathers see pp. 83-85.

9. St Basil's death (Jan. 1, 379)

There is little more to tell of Basil but his death
and burial. During his last years he had the pain
of seeing the Roman arms defeated in a series of
bloody battles with the Goths.[4] On the other hand,
the cause he had fought for all his life, that of the
Nicene faith against the Arians, triumphed com-

[1]Greg. Naz. Ep. 72.　　[2]Ep. 81.　　[3]Greg. Nyss. Ep. 1.
[4]Valens allowed the Goths to settle in the empire in 376.
But they soon began to fight. In 377 they defeated the Romans,
and again in 378 at Adrianople. Valens himself was killed at
this battle, but Gratian and Theodosius restored the honour of
the Roman arms and drove back the barbarians for a time.

pletely under Theodosius. He just lived to see this triumph. In 378, only forty-nine years old, but worn out with austerities and the ill-health from which he had suffered all his life, he lay on his death-bed. The whole city was moved by the news of his sickness, and thousands besieged his house to speak to him once more. At the very end they told him that certain persons, who should have been ordained deacon and priest, had waited over-long because of his sickness, so he roused himself once more and held a great ordination. Then he went back to die. On January 1, 379, he spoke the words with which we all hope to end our lives: "Into thy hands, O Lord, I commend my spirit," and went to his reward.[1]

Gregory of Nyssa buried his brother with such pomp as had never been seen before at Cæsarea. The whole city accompanied their great bishop to the grave, and every one tried to touch the hem of his vestments as his body was borne on an open bier through the streets. Strangers, Jews and pagans lamented him as much as his own Catholics.[2] His life-long friend, Gregory of Nazianzos, was too sick himself to be able to come; but two years later (in 381) he preached a great panegyric that is one of the chief authorities for Basil's life and a classical example of this kind of sermon. He remembers the days long ago when they had sat on the same bench as young students: "O home of our friendship, beautiful Athens, where we loved each other in the comradeship of that really divine life!"[3] He wrote a beautiful letter to his namesake of Nyssa: "So I have lived to see the death of Basil and the departure of that blessed soul to the presence of God, to whom he had

[1]Greg. Naz. Or. 43.   [2]Greg. Naz. Or. 43.
[3]Epitaph 119.

prayed all through his life."[1] "How great now," he says, "is the solitude of the Church that has lost his glory on earth, that is no longer adorned with his crown."[2] And Gregory of Nyssa, however inexperienced he may have been as bishop, during all the rest of his life never ceased honouring the memory of his great brother. He, too, preached a great panegyric about him; and soon afterwards he went out to Annesos, where Makrine still lived as a nun. He found her very sick; they talked about Basil. He could not help weeping when he spoke of him, but she, more firm, gloried in his memory, spoke with pride of his life and would not mourn the brother she was soon to see again before the throne of God. She died very soon after.

One would like to have a picture of so great a father as was St Basil. Gregory of Nazianzos describes him as tall, pale and thin, with a long beard; he was always absorbed in his thoughts and very shy.[3]

The great Church he defended during his life has not forgotten him after death. Every year in east and west the memory is kept of the saint whom we agree to call Basil the Great. His own Byzantine Church keeps his feast on the day of his death, January 1. On that day the monks who look to him as their founder, the bishops who count him as a chief glory of their order, sing: "The Lord of all receives Circumcision, the Master of Life mercifully receives the wound and gives salvation to the world. And the high Priest of the Creator rejoices in heaven, the light-bearer and divine Bishop of Christ, Basil."[4] They have another feast of St Basil, with all his holy relations, the two Makrines,

[1]Ep. 76.   [2]Ib.   [3]Greg. Naz. Or. 43.
[4]Horologion, Jan. 1. Echos of the Feast, 3.

Emmelia, Gregory of Nyssa and Peter of Sebaste, on May 30[1]; and they honour him again together with St Gregory of Nazianzos and St John Chrysostom on January 30. Nor have his Latin cousins forgotten him. On June 14, the day of his consecration, the Roman Martyrology remembers: "At Cæsarea in Cappadocia the ordination of St Basil, Bishop, who, at the time of the emperor Valens, shone with wonderful wisdom and knowledge, was adorned with all virtues, and defended the Church with unchanging constancy against the Arians and Macedonians." And before our altars, white-robed for a Confessor Pontiff, we say on that day the Mass of a Doctor of the Church: *In medio Ecclesiæ aperuit os eius; et implevit eum Dominus spiritu sapientiæ et intellectus: stolam gloriæ induit eum.*

10. Table of dates

330. *St Basil born.*

c. 331. St Gregory of Nyssa born.

c. 345–355. Basil student at Cæsarea, Constantinople, Athens.

355. Back home at Neocæsarea in Pontus.

355–357. Professor of rhetoric at Cappadocia.

357. *Baptized* by Dianeios of Cæsarea.

357–358. Journey to monasteries in Egypt, Palestine, Syria.

358–364. Head of monastic community at Annesos.

361–363. Julian emperor.

362. Dianeios of Cæsarea †. Eusebeios succeeds him. Julian punishes the city.

364. *Basil ordained deacon and priest* by Eusebeios. He goes back to Annesos.

[1]This is a Uniate feast. The Roman Martyrology commemorates his relations on the same day (Nilles: *Kal. Man.* Innsbruck, Ed. 2, 1896, I, 167, 168).

364–378. Valens Cæsar in the east.

365–370. Priest at Cæsarea.

367–368. Famine in Cappadocia.

370. *Basil Metropolitan of Cæsarea.* Domitius
Modestus threatens to banish him.

371. Cappadocia divided into two civil provinces. Gregory ordained Bishop of Nyssa.

372 (Epiphany). Valens at Cæsarea.

374. St Ambrose Archbishop of Milan.

375. Gregory of Nyssa banished.

378. Valens †.

379–395. Theodosius I Cæsar in the east (394–
395 emperor).

379 (Jan. 1). *Death of St Basil.*

c. 395. Death of St Gregory of Nyssa.

11. St Basil's works

If Basil is famous as a saint, as the organizer of
eastern monasticism and a great Catholic bishop,
he has a further title to fame as one of the chief
classical writers of the fourth century. His language and style are immeasurably better than
those of St Athanasius. Athanasius was hardly a
stylist at all; but Basil had studied in the best
school in the world and had been a famous teacher
of rhetoric before he went to be a monk. His
writing is less ornate than that of St John Chrysostom; perhaps for that reason it is more attractive
to modern people. Through all his many works,
especially in his sermons and letters, there is a
restrained eloquence, a fire controlled by a very
dignified and reticent self-command, that makes
them, the most sympathetic and pleasant to
read of all the works of Greek fathers. He uses,
of course, the language of his time. The dual and
optative mood had disappeared long ago. It would

have been an absurd affectation to revive them in the fourth century. Nevertheless, his writing is the best answer to the old idea that Greek letters were dead in the first Christian centuries.

His works were first published in Greek at Basel in 1532, in three folio volumes, reprinted at Venice in 1535 and at Basel in 1551. A learned Jesuit, Fronton le Duc,[1] edited them and this edition was published by the Dominican F. Combefis at Paris in 1679, in two volumes. The best edition is still that of the Benedictines of St Maur, three folios at Paris, 1721–1730. L. de Sinners reprinted it at Paris in 1839. In Migne's collection (Patrologia Græca) his works fill four volumes, XXIX–XXXII (Paris, 1857). H. Hurter, S.J., has published a Latin version of the *De Spiritu sancto* in his *SS. Patrum opusc. sel.* XXXI (Innsbruck, 1875). Various works have been translated into many languages. Rufinus of Aquileia (†410) did ten sermons and both monastic rules into Latin. There is an old English version of the *Hexaemeron* (H. W. Norman: *The Anglo-Saxon version of the Hexaemeron of St Basil*, London, 1848). G. Lewis: *The treatise of St Basil on the Holy Spirit* (London, 1888).

DOGMATIC WORKS. The *Answer to the Apology of impious Eunomios* (ἀνατρεπτικὸς τοῦ ἀπολογητικοῦ τοῦ δυσσεβοῦς Εὐνομίου, Libri V, quibus impii Eunomii apologeticus evertitur, M. P. Gr. XXIX, 497–773) was written about the year 363 or 364. It is his chief work against extreme Arianism. *Of the Holy Ghost* (περὶ τοῦ ἁγίου πνεύματ , De Spiritu sancto, XXXII, 67–218), written in 375 and dedicated to his pupil Amphilochios of Ikonion, contains thirty chapters. It is a defence of the equality

---

[1] *Fronto Ducceus* in Latin.

and consubstantial nature of God the Holy Ghost
against the later Arians, who had begun to apply
their theories about God the Son to the third
Person of the Blessed Trinity (the Pneumatomachians). It has always been the standard work on
the subject.

EXEGESIS. His most famous exegetical books are
the nine Homilies on the *Hexaemeron* (ἐξαήμερον,
XXIX, 3–208), that is, on the six days of creation.
St Ambrose's Hexaemeron (M. P. L. XIV, 123–
274) is practically a compilation from this and
from a work of Origenes with the same title. Basil
explains the creation with the strangest theories
of physics and many edifying applications. He
also wrote fifty Homilies on the *Psalms* (XXIX–XXX)
some of which, however, are doubtfully authentic.
A commentary on *Isaias*, I-XVI (XXX) is very
doubtful.

ASCETIC WORKS. His two *Monastic Rules* have the
first place here. There is a longer Rule of fifty-five
chapters (ὅροι κατὰ πλάτος) and a shorter one of
313 chapters (ὅροι κατ᾽ ἐπιτομήν. Both in XXXI,
Regulæ fusius tractatæ, Regulæ brevius tractatæ).
The longer rule was written at Annesos, the shorter
one—an epitome—later, at Cæsarea. He wrote a
number of other treatises about the *Life of Monks*
(βίος τῶν μοναχῶν), de vita monachorum, XXXI), the
Judgment of God (περὶ κρίματος θεοῦ, de iudicio Dei,
XXXI), *Rules of Morals* (τὰ ἠθικά, ethica), eighty
principles of virtuous life (ὅροι, principia), etc., all
of which are collected under the general name,
Ascetica (ἀσκητικά) in M. P. G. XXXI, 619–1428.

HOMILIES. A number of St Basil's sermons,
preached on various occasions, have been preserved. The best known are the ones *Against
Usurers* (κατὰ τοκιζόντων, Contra usuriarios, XXIX,

263–280), and at the time of the *famine in Cappadocia* (367–368, p. 64). Twenty-four others (XXXI, 163–618) treat of various questions of dogma, morals and exegesis, or celebrate various saints and martyrs.

LETTERS. No one really knows St Basil who has not read his letters. There are 365 altogether (XXXII 219–1110), in which he writes of every kind of subject, details of his own life and events in the history of his time, dogma, polemic, practical advice and controversy. Sometimes he consoles some one for a loss, sometimes he asks a favour or thanks his correspondent for a favour already received. We find in them politics, discussions of points of scholarship, anecdotes of every kind. He corresponded with all sorts of persons from the Pope to heretics; he writes to governors, officers, monks, nuns, bishops, to the great Athanasius, his own relations, his clergy; most of all to Gregory of Nazianzos; even to Apollinaris of Laodicea, of unhappy memory. Sometimes he is angry and complains, sometimes he describes the country where he is; he constantly makes quiet fun. In his own time these letters were famous; Gregory of Nazianzos began collecting them at once after his death.[1] There is certainly no collection of Greek letters so entertaining as these.[2]

LITURGY. The *Liturgy of St Basil* (XXXI, 1629–1678) is used throughout the eastern world, from Kiew to Alexandria and from Dalmatia to Japan. It is printed first in all the Orthodox and Melkite

[1]Greg. Naz. Ep. 53.
[2]They make a perfect parallel to the Latin letters of St Jerome (†420) both in their interest, humour and pleasantness, and in their beautiful style. For St Jerome, in spite of the shocks he sometimes gives us in the Vulgate, could write most beautiful Latin when he chose.

Euchologia. It is not the oftenest used, but the foundation of the Byzantine rite (p. 64 n. 1). Liturgically, it occurs in thirteen translations besides the original Greek. How far it is really the saint's own composition is a question that will probably never be settled.

12. St Gregory Nyssene's works

St Basil's brother was a prolific writer, though none of his works reach the level of those of Basil. He is a philosopher and an ardent admirer and faithful disciple of Origenes († 254), whom he follows exactly in his interpretation of Scripture. His most characteristic work is philosophical speculation about the Holy Trinity, the immortality of the soul, and so on. Needless to say, as a disciple of Origenes he is Neoplatonic.

The Jesuit Fronton le Duc, first edited his works in two folio volumes at Paris in 1615; J. Gretser, S.J., published an additional volume of works omitted by le Duc in 1618. The next edition (complete with Gretser's additions) was at Paris in 1638, three volumes. Other works have been discovered by various people since, notably seven more letters by J. Caracciolo (Florence, 1731). Gregory of Nyssa fills three volumes of Migne (Patr. Gr. XLIV–XLVI, Paris, 1858). The *Oxford Select Library of Nicene and Postnicene Fathers* contains a selection of his works in English (Ser. II, vol. v).

EXEGESIS. He wrote a *Defence of the Hexaemeron* (ἀπολογητικὸς περὶ τῆς ἑξαημέρου, Explicatio apologetica in hexaemeron, XLIV, 61–124), a vindication and completion of his brother's work, and thirty chapters *Of the creation of man* (περὶ κατασκευῆς ἀνθρώπου, De hominis opificio, XLIV, 125–256). We have also from him a *Life of Moses* (περὶ τοῦ βίου Μωυσέως τοῦ νομοθέτου, De vita Moysis, seu de virtutis perfectione, XLIV, 297–430), in which he fills up the Biblical account with allegorical interpretations. The point of the life is that Moses should be a model to a friend of Gregory named Kaisarios. Further, an allegorical treatise *On the Inscriptions of the Psalms* (εἰς τὴν ἐπιγραφὴν τῶν ψαλμῶν, In psalmorum inscriptionem, libri II, XLIV, 432–608), a Commentary on *Ecclesiastes* (XLIV, 616–753), in the form of eight homilies, twenty-five Homilies on the *Song of Songs* (XLIV, 756–1120), five on the Lord's Prayer (XLIV, 1120–1193) and eight on the *Beatitudes* (XLIV, 1193–1301).

DOGMATIC WORKS. The most important is his *Great Catechism* (λόγος κατηχητικὸς ὁ μέγας, Oratio catechetica magna, forty chapters, XLV, 9–105), a defence of the Catholic faith against pagans, Jews and Arians. Then the *Twelve Books against Eunomios* (πρὸς Εὐνόμιον ἀντιρρητικοὶ λόγοι, Libri XII, contra Eunomium, XLV, 237–1121). Eunomios had answered St Basil's work against him (p. 80) after that saint's death; this is a refutation of the answer. His *Refutation of Apollinaris* (ἀντιρρητικός πρὸς τὰ Ἀπολλιναρίου, Antirrheticus adv. Apollinarem, fifty-nine chapters, XLV, 1124–1269) and the sequel, *Against Apollinaris*, dedicated to Theophilos of Alexandria (κατ᾿ Ἀπολλιναρίου, Adv. Apollinarem ad Theophilum, XLV, 1269–1277), are important authorities for the life and teaching of that heretic.[1] Then there are many shorter treatises

[1] Apollinaris (Apollinarios), Bishop of Laodicea in Syria (†c.392), was a famous heretic who, accepting the Neoplatonic theory that man consists of three elements, *body*, *soul* and *spirit*, taught that in our Lord the Divinity (the *Logos*, Word of God), took the place of this third element, the spirit. So he was not perfect man; he lacked one element of our nature, the

on various dogmas, such as the Blessed Trinity, the Immortality of the soul and Fate.

ASCETIC WORKS. He wrote a treatise on *Virginity* περὶ παρθενίας, de virginitate, XLVI, 317–416), Letters to monks and short treatises on the End of man, the Life of a Christian, and so on, also a treatise *Against those who put off their baptism* (XLVI).

HOMILIES. Many of the works we have already noted are written in the form of sermons. There are others preached at Nyssa and Constantinople, Panegyrics of saints, among which we note those on St Gregory Thaumaturgos, St Basil his brother, St Makrine his sister, and the Funeral orations of the princess Pulcheria and the empress Flaccilla. His sermons are very ornate and full of flowers of rhetoric. They cannot be compared to those of St Basil. All are contained in M. P. Gr. XLVI.

LETTERS. Migne (P. Gr. XLVI) contains twenty-six letters. The second letter about *pilgrimages to Jerusalem* gives a vivid picture of the abuses and scandals that even then accompanied visits to the holy land. Gregory thinks that if people behave so badly when they get to Jerusalem they had better stay at home. This letter was often used by Protestants in the sixteenth century as an argument against all pilgrimages; a purpose that would have annoyed its author, since he made a very pious pilgrimage to the holy places himself. He is not the only Catholic who has been distressed at the quarrels that go on round our Lord's tomb.

human spirit. Apollinaris then was a kind of forerunner of the Monophysites. Nearly all the fathers of this time wrote at least one treatise against him. Harnack thinks he was the only reasonable theologian of the fourth century, and he has become a quite appalling obsession to J. Dräseke. *See* my article s.v. *Apollinarism* in Hastings' *Dictionary of Religion and Ethics* (T. and T. Clarke, vol. I.).

13. Literature

St. Basil. C. Klose: *Basilius der Grosse* (Stralsund, 1835). F. Böhringer: *Basilius von Cäsarea* (Stuttgart, 1875, in *Die Kirche Christi und ihre Zeugen*, vii). E. Fialon: *Étude historique et Littéraire sur St Basile* (Paris, 1869). P. Allard: *Saint Basile* (Paris, 1899, in *Les Saints*, V. Lecoffre). H. Weiss: *Die grossen Kappadocier als Exegeten* (Braunsberg, 1872). A. Bayle: *St Basile, archévêque de Césarée* (Avignon, 1878). H. Doergens: *Der hl. Basilius u.die classischen Studien* (Leipzig, 1857). E. Scholl: *Die Lehre des hl. Basilius von der Gnade* (Freiburg, 1881).

St Gregory of Nyssa. J. Rupp: *Gregors, des Bischofs von Nyssa, Leben u. Meinungen* (Leipzig, 1834). Fr. Böhringer: *Gregor von Nyssa* (Stuttgart, 1876, *op. cit.*). H. Weiss, *op. cit.* Fr. Hilt: *Des hl. Gregor von Nyssa Lehre vom Menschen systematisch dargestellt* (Köln, 1890). W. Meyer: *Die Gotteslehre des Gregor von Nyssa* (Leipzig, 1894). J. Bauer: *Die Trostreden des Gregorios von Nyssa in ihrem Verhältniss zur antiken Rhetorik* (Marburg, 1892).

CHAPTER III

ST GREGORY OF NAZIANZOS (330–390)

GREGORY OF NAZIANZOS, the intimate friend and companion of St Basil, fills a more important place in the consciousness of the eastern Churches than he does with us in the west. We should hardly name him among the very greatest fathers, but in the east his writings are considered so important and so valuable that he is to the descendants of his own people the "Theologian" in a special and proper sense. That is his surname among them; they hardly ever speak of him as Nazianzene; when a Greek says "Gregory the Theologian" (Γρηγόριος ὁ θεολόγος) he means this saint. The Theologian was one of the three friends who redeemed the once not well-sounding name of Cappadocia.[1] He was not only a theologian but a philosopher, poet and a man of public political life as well. He had a chequered career and several unpleasant adventures before he at last settled down in peace to end his days in his own town. Less great than Basil, more so than Gregory of Nyssa, he has left the memory of an irreproachable, but not always very prudent saint, and of a voluminous, orthodox and edifying writer.[2]

[1] The three great Cappadocians are St Basil, St Gregory of Nazianzos and St Gregory of Nyssa (Basil's younger brother).

[2] Most saints who were bishops are named after their dioceses; thus we speak of St Hilary of Poitiers, St Augustine of Canterbury, St Hugh of Lincoln. This saint is an exception. He was Bishop of Sasima, but is always called after his native town, Nazianzos.

1. Early years (330-*c*.345)

Gregory was born in 330 at Arianzos, a property belonging to his father near Nazianzos. *Nazianzos* (Ναζιανζός), or *Diocæsarea*, in Cappadocia, was a small town about sixty-five miles south-west of the capital, Cæsarea.[1] And of this city his father, also called Gregory, was bishop. His mother, Nonna, was a saint, who brought her son up as carefully and as piously as St Emmelia was bringing up her son Basil at the same time.

The fact that Gregory's father was a bishop, and a very holy and orthodox bishop, which confronts us at the beginning of this life, will surprise most people, whether Catholic or Orthodox. How, one asks, could a bishop have a wife and family? And how could a bishop's wife be a saint?

The principle that is at the root of the law of celibacy certainly goes back to the time of the Apostles. St Paul tells us plainly that he considers virginity to be the higher state (1 Cor. vii, 28, 32–34, 40), and our Lord himself had taught the same thing (Matt. xix, 12). Inevitably, then, the Christian Church looked upon celibacy as a more holy thing. If anyone is to follow this higher and more austere path, surely it should be, in the first place, the clergy who are called to minister more closely to God. So clerks, as a general rule, prefer to remain unmarried; then nearly all do so. It begins to be looked upon as unedifying if one does marry; then as almost, eventually as quite scandalous. It is a typical case of a law obtaining force by prescription.[2] But the law crystallized into different

[1] Now a village, *Nenizi*.
[2] Even in the old law a temporary celibacy was required of priests before they sacrificed (Ex. xix, 15).

forms in east and west. In the west, at any rate since the fourth century,[1] the law is celibacy for all clerks in major orders. In the east deacons and priests may keep their wives if they are already married, but bishops must be celibate.[2] There is no reason to suppose that the Bishop of Nazianzos ceased being a married man when he was ordained; on the contrary, our St Gregory had a younger brother, Kaisarios, who must have been born afterwards. We must conclude then from this case that, at any rate in Cappadocia, celibacy was not yet considered a binding law for bishops, although in the fourth century the general feeling on the subject had already very nearly produced a law. The bishops, who took a foremost place at that time, the saints and fathers such as Gregory the son, Basil, Chrysostom, and so on, were celibate as a matter of course.

The elder Gregory was a well-known man, too, in a way. He had been a pagan and a statesman. His wife, St Nonna, converted him; he was bap-

[1] The first case of a definite law in the west seems to be the letter of Pope Siricius (384–399) to Himerius of Tarracona (Ep. I, c. 7, in the C.I.C. dist. lxxxii), Innocent I (401–417) repeats it (dist. xxxi) and from that time a number of councils (e. gr., second Council of Carthage in 390, fifth Council of Carthage in 401) down to the first Lateran Council in 1123 (can. 21) and the second Lateran Council in 1139 (can. 40) form our present law.

[2] Obviously monks and nuns everywhere have always been bound by the same law. A solemn vow of chastity was always the essence of monastic life. The first Council of Nicæa (325) already maintains the "ancient custom" that forbids marriage after ordination. The Council of Constantinople in 692 (the *Quinisextum*, Trullanum II) insists on this law and forbids Bishops to be married. There has always been a strong feeling against bigamy for any clerks. *Bigamy* in Canon Law means not only having two wives at once (bigamia simultanea), but having two, one after another (bigamia successiva). This is always an impediment against Holy Orders. To marry a widow is a form of bigamy (bigamia interpretativa).

tized in 328 or 329. Soon after he became Bishop
of Nazianzos, succeeding his baptizer, and was a
valiant defender of the Catholic faith against the
Arians. His son in after years constantly refers to
him with great veneration.[1] Our saint was apparently the eldest child, then came a sister, Gorgonia
and the brother, Kaisarios. The family lived chiefly
at *Arianzos*, on their estate, a few miles south of
Nazianzos on the road to Tyana. But they had a
house in the city, too, and young Gregory began
his education at school there. His mother, Nonna,
easily formed his mind to love the Christian faith
and the example of Christian saints. The boy was
naturally docile and pious from the beginning.
When he was quite little he had a dream that two
beautiful ladies came to him; their names were
Temperance and Virginity.[2] And to these two
ladies he promised to be true all his life, a promise
he very faithfully kept.

2. Education at Cæsarea and Athens (345?-357)

As soon as they were old enough Gregory and
Kaisarios go to Cæsarea, the capital of Cappadocia, to have a better education than could be
got in so small a country town as Nazianzos.[3] At
Cæsarea they meet St Basil for the first time:
Gregory formed a friendship with him than only
one quarrel was to interrupt (p. 97) during all
their lives. The friends parted for a time, and
Gregory went on to Palestine and Alexandria.
Then he sailed to Athens. On the way there was a
frightful storm in which he was nearly drowned.

[1] In the Or. xviii especially.
[2] Greg. Naz. Carm. i, 45.
[3] Sokrates (H.E. iv, 26, 13) says that Nazianzos was quite a
small place of no importance,

He says afterwards in what terror he was then at the thought that he was still unbaptized; the memory of that danger made Gregory, too, one of the most strenuous opponents of the dangerous custom of putting off baptism till a man is grown up.[1] At Athens he met Basil again. Gregory remembered their years of friendship and study at "golden Athens" with as much pleasure as did Basil.[2] Years afterwards, when his friend was dead and he preached his funeral sermon, Gregory recalls the distant days when they had shared the same lodging, the same studies, the same ideas.[3] He was the older of the two and had arrived at Athens first, so he was able to help his friend with advice about life at a University and to defend him from the practical jokes of the other students.[4] There was an amusing quarrel with the Armenians. Cappadocians and Armenians, being neighbours of different races, naturally did not like each other. The Armenians set various traps for these new Cappadocians, out of which Gregory assures us that they came victoriously. And he adds (on the word of a Cappadocian) that "the Armenian nation is not noble nor frank; they are all sly and vicious."[5] After four or five years, in 357, Basil went back home to Cappadocia; Gregory stayed and continued

---

[1] *Carm. de se ipso*, i, 324–326; xi, 162–174, etc.

[2] *See* p. 53.

[3] Oratio xliii, *in laudem Basilii* (xxxvi, 493–605).

[4] Rough practical jokes on a freshman seem to be an inevitable element of a University everywhere. At Athens the most brilliant pleasantry was to seize your man and to throw him into the water (Greg. Naz. Oratio xliii, 16). It is also characteristic that the men should form themselves into companies (Student-envereine) according to their nationalities. There were the Cappadocians, Armenians, Syrians, etc.

[5] (Or. xliii). So many people would say still. It is one of the tragedies of that unhappy people that everyone seems to hate them, not only Kurds and Turks, but all other Christian

his studies at Athens. But soon after he, too, left the University and started back for home.

This time, remembering the perils of the seas, he preferred a long journey by land round by Constantinople. Here he found his brother Kaisarios, who had studied medicine and was now making a fortune as a doctor in the capital. Gregory seems to have been all too eager to make every one flee the world, as he himself was about to do. So he persuades his brother to leave his practice and to come back to Cappadocia with him to be a monk. Kaisarios let himself be persuaded at first, but he never really wanted to change his life. We should say that he obviously had no vocation. So after a short time he went back to Constantinople and looked up his patients again. Gregory was disappointed; his disappointment turned into indignation when he heard that his brother still went on with his career under the pagan emperor Julian (361–363). Did not this inevitably mean at least a tacit apostasy? His suspicion was quite unjust. Kaisarios was a perfectly loyal Christian always, and when he found that by staying at the capital his faith was in real danger he again left his practice and went to Cappadocia. The end of Kaisarios was that he came back to Constantinople after Julian's death, became a government official under Valens (364–378), was baptized and died an edifying death soon after 368. He is an example of an entirely satisfactory Christian in the world. Gregory's everlasting girding that he should be a monk and his attitude of shocked surprise that his brother should choose rather to be a doctor are

nations in those parts too. When a Syrian's donkey won't go, the Syrian beats him and calls him a Jew; if he still won't go he beats him again and calls him an Armenian.

unreasonable and intolerant. Not every one has a
vocation to the "angelic life."[1]

3. Gregory's baptism, ordination and flight (357-*c.*372).

Meanwhile Gregory, who knew his own mind
better than that of his brother, as soon as he came
home to Cappadocia (357), began to see about
being a monk himself. His father, the bishop, was
now an old man, so for a time he stayed with him
and looked after the estate at Arianzos. But each
day he spent certain fixed hours in prayer and
meditation. He was now twenty-seven years old,
and it was quite time for him to be baptized, especially as he had not forgotten his narrow escape of
death by shipwreck. So he was baptized, apparently
by his father,[2] soon after he came home.

Meanwhile Basil was travelling about and learning
from monks how to copy their life.[3] Soon after the
community at Annesos in Pontus had been formed
(358)[4] Gregory went to join it. He describes this
first visit as a short one in which he only just
tasted the sweetness of the ascetic life.[5] As his
father still wanted him at home, he soon went back
to Nazianzos. Then happened one of those curious
cases of an ordination by force of which we often
hear at this time. The people of Nazianzos wanted
the bishop's son to be a priest. The father agreed,
but Gregory himself was entirely against the plan.

[1] For the story of Kaisarios *see* Greg. Naz. Orat. vii, Ep. vii,
and Carm. ii.

[2] According to our Canon Law a man ought not to baptize
his own son, except in case of necessity. But there is no such
principle in the east. Besides, our Canon Law does not provide
for bishops having sons.

[3] *See* p. 57.

[4] p. 58.

[5] Or. II. 6.

He wanted to be a monk with Basil, and monks were not priests. To be a priest meant to go on living in the world at Nazianzos. He felt unworthy and unfit for so high and difficult a life. To flee the world, to meditate in silence and sing hymns at Annesos was easier and safer. So he resisted the proposal with all his might. In spite of his resistance his father took him and ordained him priest by force, apparently on Christmas Day in 361.[1]

The question of these ordinations in which the subject resists and is made a priest by force is a curious one. We should say that a grown-up person cannot receive a sacrament (except, perhaps, the holy Eucharist) validly, unless he has the intention of doing so. These fathers never seem to think of that. We must suppose that, in spite of his resistance, Gregory had, at any rate, that very vague and implicit intention that is needed for the sacrament to be valid.[2] And in any case it is a question of moral force only.

---

[1]But was Christmas (December 25) kept in Cappadocia in the middle of the fourth century? In 385 it was still unknown at Jerusalem; St Ephrem (†379) does not know it, nor was it yet introduced into Armenia or Mesopotamia. Kellner (*Heortologie*, Freiburg i./Br. 1901) thinks that Christmas was kept in Cappadocia first in 382 (pp. 84–85). St John Chrys. announces it as a new feast at Antioch in 388 (Hom. *in nat. Christi*, xlix, 351). Before that the memory of our Lord's birth was kept on the Epiphany (January 6). Bardenhewer (*Patrologie*, Freiburg i./Br. 1894), who gives Christmas, 361, as the date of this ordination, must mean the Epiphany. *See* Usener: *Religionsgesch. Untersuchungen* i, 1889).

[2]People who are not theologians never seem to understand how little *intention* is wanted for a sacrament (the point applies equally to minister and subject). The "implicit intention of doing what Christ instituted" means so vague and small a thing that one can hardly help having it—unless one deliberately excludes it. At the time when every one was talking about Anglican orders, numbers of Catholics confused *intention* with *faith*. Faith is not wanted. It is heresy to say that it is (this was the error of St Cyprian and Firmilian against which

As soon as the ordination was over Gregory, still very indignant and determined not to work as a priest even if he had been made one, ran away to Pontus to join Basil again.[1] But by Easter, 362, Basil persuaded him that since he had been ordained he should go back to the world and help his father in the diocese.[2] He came back then to Nazianzos and was soon able to put an end to a serious disturbance there. His father, the bishop, was always really Catholic and Homoüsian. Only, he had given way once in a moment of weakness, like so many other good and well-meaning bishops in that time of persecution and hopeless confusion, when synods and anti-synods were everlastingly drawing up new formulas of various shades of Arianism, when the government was everlastingly demanding the acceptance of some new profession. The formula that Constantius (337–361) had forced on the great Synod of Ariminium (359) was semi-Arian. The emperor insisted that every bishop should sign it. There were very few confessors who had the courage to hold out still, after years of this sort of thing—it was the time of which St Jerome said that "the whole world groaned and shuddered to find itself Arian."[3] And old Gregory at Nazianzos gave way like the others and signed. At once there was great commotion in the diocese. The Catholics,

Pope Stephen I, 254–257 protested). A man may have utterly wrong, heretical and blasphemous views about a sacrament and yet confer or receive it quite validly.

[1]His *Apology for his Flight* (p. 106) was written in excuse and explanation of this flight to Pontus after his ordination.

[2]The conviction of all these fathers that a man simply cannot be both a monk and a priest, that one state necessarily excludes the other, is very curious as showing what monasticism meant in the first stage of its development. *See* above, p. 57.

[3]*c. Luciferianos*, 19.

and especially the monks, broke off all relations
with a semi-Arian bishop (363). Gregory, the son,
persuaded his father to retract his false step by a
public confession of the Catholic faith (Homoü-
sianism); he then brought all the diocese back to
its normal state of obedience. The dates of these
events are not certain. Some think that this schism
and pacification took place before his ordination
and flight.[1] During this first time, perhaps while
they were both at Annesos, Gregory and Basil
composed a selection from the works of Origenes
(† 254) that they called the *Philokalia* (φιλοκαλία
=Love of beauty).[2] Then for about nine or ten
years (362–372?) Gregory stayed at Nazianzos as
a priest under his father. In 370 the father ordained
Basil Metropolitan of Cæsarea[3] and the son
assisted him, though he does not seem to have been
too well pleased at his friend's promotion.[4] He had
an invincible dread of the responsibility and
dangers of such positions. But a very serious
breach between the friends came when Basil made
Gregory a bishop too.

4. Bishop of Sasima. His hermitage at Seleucia (372-379)

Basil had great difficulties with his rebellious
suffragan, Anthimos of Tyana.[5] In order to resist
this person he thought it a good plan to make his
two staunchest supporters bishops of dioceses on

---

[1] So Bardenhewer (*Patrologie*, p. 264) and Loofs in the Prot.
Realencyklopädie (1899, vii, 142). Ph. Clemencet (editor of the
Benedictine edition of Greg. Naz. *See* p. 107) adopts the order I
have given.
[2] Ep. 115, Clemencet: *Vita Greg.* 65.
[3] *See* above, p. 66.
[4] *Carmen de Seipso*, 398 *seq.*
[5] pp. 68, 69.

the frontier of Tyana. So he ordained his own
brother Bishop of Nyssa[1] and then wanted
Gregory of Nazianzos to be Bishop of Sasima, a few
miles south-east of Nazianzos. If Gregory had disliked the idea of being a priest, he was still more
opposed to that of being bishop. So he refused
absolutely. In spite of that Basil took him and
ordained him (it is another of these astonishing
cases of forced ordinations), apparently in 372.
Gregory's indignation knew no bounds this time.
He absolutely refused to go near Sasima. He
describes it as the most odious place in the world,
barren, solitary, ugly and generally detestable.[2] He
had never been there. Indeed, it is more than
doubtful if he ever went to his diocese at all. So
he ran away again to be a monk somewhere in the
mountains, away from Basil and his father and
Sasima.[3] He seems to have specially disliked the
idea of being set up in a forepost to fight Anthimos, although he was so far loyal to Basil that he
would not listen to Anthimos' arguments against
the metropolitan.[4] For seven years he bore a
grudge against his old friend for this ordination
and the plan of sending him to Sasima. It seems
that Basil certainly made a mistake in ordaining
Gregory against his will and that he expected too
much from his friend. On the other hand, it cannot
be said that Gregory behaved well in this affair.
The old father was very much annoyed at the
whole business. He did not at all want his son to
be Bishop of Sasima, but he did not want him to
be a monk with useless bishop's orders either. He
had been very glad to have him at Nazianzos, and
now he wanted him back there to help in the

[1]p. 74. [2]*Carmen*, 386–485, Ep. 48 and 50.
[3]*Carm.* 490 *seq.*; 529 *seq.* [4]Ep. 48 and 50.

7

affairs of that diocese. So he wrote and implored his son to come, not to Sasima, but to Nazianzos. He was a very old man now. If Basil had not taken this hasty step, he had hoped that his son might gradually undertake all the work at Nazianzos and eventually succeed him as bishop there. Gregory then gave way to his father and came out of his hiding-place. Although he was still very angry with Basil and still refused to go to Sasima, he came back to Nazianzos and administered the diocese for his father. Old Gregory died in 374; St Nonna soon followed him to the grave. Our Gregory then went on taking care of the diocese. But he was still considered bishop of Sasima; this connexion with a place he had never even seen was a trouble to him all his life. Soon afterwards, in 375, the neighbouring bishops began to see about finding a successor to the dead bishop. His son, who had so long administered the diocese, was obviously the right man. But he was bishop of Sasima. They were persuading the metropolitan, Basil, who now recognized his mistake, to accept his resignation of Sasima and to acknowledge him as Bishop of Nazianzos, when Gregory fled again, this time to Seleucia in Isauria. He must have had an invincible repugnance to be the Ordinary of any place, and he had not yet forgiven Basil. He stayed at Seleucia as a hermit for four years. While he was there he heard the news of his old friend's death (St Basil, † Jan. 1, 379). Death ends all quarrels. Gregory now forgot his grievance; all the rest of his life he was the most ardent defender of Basil's memory. He made the first collection of the great metropolitan's letters,[1] and later, in 381, he preached a splendid panegyric, in which he passes

[1] p. 82.

over the trouble about Sasima and remembers only
the happy years they had spent together at "golden
Athens."[1] This generous forgetting of his grievance
is the pleasantest incident in Gregory's life. If
Saints do quarrel sometimes, they make it up
again afterwards.

5. Gregory at Constantinople (379-381)

If Gregory had made anything clear so far it
was that he did not want to be a bishop. He seems
to have been quite happy at Seleucia and only
anxious to be let alone. But events now again
brought him out of his hermitage and called him to
use his orders at the capital. Under the Cæsar
Valens (364–378) the Arians had had it all their
own way, especially at Constantinople. The
Catholics were reduced to a little handful, who
rejected the communion of the Arian bishop
Demophilos (369–379). But when Theodosius I
(379–395) succeeded as emperor the situation
changed. Theodosius was a determined Catholic
always. So the faithful Homoüsians in 379 sent to
Gregory, asking him to come and take charge of
their community, at any rate till a regular bishop
could be appointed. He was obviously just the
person they wanted. He was a bishop who could
use any episcopal function, and he was not engaged
at any diocese. He could not resist this appeal,
himself one of the first champions of the Nicene
faith in eastern Christendom. So again he gave
up his ideal of leading a monk's life and came to
take charge of the Catholics at Constantinople (379).
Here he arranged everything, restored order,
ordained and fulfilled all a bishop's duties till a
bishop should be elected in the usual way.

[1] p. 91.

For so far, at any rate, he did not consider himself, was not considered by anyone, to be bishop of Constantinople, but rather still titular of Sasima. He also preached; his sermons were so famous that St Jerome († 410), already an old man, came to the capital to hear them. Theodosius came to Constantinople in 380 and at once restored to the Catholics the chief church of the city (either the Holy Wisdom or the church of the Apostles) that the Arians had seized. Meanwhile the Egyptians— always disturbers of the peace in the Church of Constantinople—irregularly ordained one of themselves, a certain Maximos, as Ordinary. The greater number of the Catholics refused to acknowledge this person and wanted Gregory to formally resign the see he had never even visited and to accept an election as Ordinary in the capital. He seems to have been disposed to do so; for a time now he apparently claimed to be Bishop of Constantinople.

6. The second general Council (381)

At this time came the meeting of bishops at Constantinople that was eventually recognized as the second general Council. Out of the great Arian movement, then dying out fast, two new heresies had grown. Some Arians applied their theories about God the Son to the Holy Ghost too, saying that he, too, is a creature, less than God the Father. These people are the *Pneumatomachians* (πνευματόμαχοι=fighters against the Spirit). The semi-Arian Bishop of Constantinople, Makedonios (344–348, 350–360), who had been driven out and had come back, was their chief leader; with him a monk, named Marathonios, defended this heresy.[1]

[1]From these two people the heretics are also called *Macedonians* or *Marathonians*.

The Pneumatomachians had been condemned by
an Alexandrine synod in 362; soon afterwards they
themselves held one at Zele in Pontus,[1] in which
they separated themselves from both Catholics
and Arians to form a sect of their own. They were
now disposed to admit the Divinity of our Lord
and his equality with God the Father; but they
transferred all the Arians' ideas about him to the
Holy Ghost. Several Fathers, Didymos the Blind,[2]
our Gregory[3] and others had already written
against this heresy. As a result of the opposition
to Arianism the famous *Apollinaris*, Bishop of
Laodicea in Syria, had evolved his system, according to which our Lord had a human body and soul,
but no human spirit, since the Word took its place.[4]
In 381 Theodosius summoned all the bishops of
the empire to a council at Constantinople, to
declare the faith on these points and once more
to wipe out whatever was left of Arianism. Only
150 eastern bishops came. There were no Latins
and no legates from Rome. This is the council,
œcumenic neither in its summons nor its sessions,
to which the ratification of the Roman See and of
the Church long afterwards gave the right of being
numbered among the Œcumenical synods.[5] At

[1] Its date is uncertain.

[2] *Didymos* (310–395), a layman, was the leader of the Cate-
chetic school at Alexandria. He had become blind when four
years old, but was nevertheless one of the most famous
scholars of his time, and an ardent Origenist. St Jerome,
Rufinus, and other fathers learnt from him. His works in
M.P.G. xxxix, 131–1818. Against the Pneumatomachians he
wrote *On the Holy Ghost*. Of this work only St Jerome's Latin
translation has been preserved (M.P.L. xxiii, 101–154).

[3] In his fifth theological oration (thirty-first Oration).

[4] *See* above, p. 84, n. 1.

[5] That is as far as its dogmatic definitions are concerned. Its
four canons were never received in the west. Its third canon
is the first step in the advance of Constantinople to patriarchal
rank (*see Orth. Eastern Church*, pp. 32–33).

first Meletios of Antioch[1] presided; he died during
the council, and our Gregory of Nazianzos then took
his place. If the addition to the Nicene creed was
made by this council[2] it shows its condemnation
of the Pneumatomachians in the clause about the
Holy Ghost, "the Lord and Lifegiver, who proceeds from the Father, who, together with the
Father and Son, is adored and glorified, who
spoke by the Prophets." The synod refused to
acknowledge Maximos at Constantinople, and took
the side of Meletios at Antioch. Both decisions gave
offence to Rome and the west.[3] The fathers of
Constantinople then recognized Gregory as bishop
of that city. So he must for a short time be considered Ordinary of Constantinople. But his enemies,
especially the Egyptians, still used their old argument against him. He was Bishop of Sasima, and
no one can hold two sees at once. By this time
Gregory must have loathed the very name of that
barren and detestable town that he had never even
seen. Still no doubt there was something in their
argument. He does not seem to have ever formally
resigned his old see, or perhaps the Metropolitan of
Cæsarea (where Helladios had succeeded St Basil)
had not accepted his resignation.[4] No other bishop

[1] The famous bishop about whom the Meletian Schism arose
(*op. cit.*, pp. 90–92).

[2] Mgr Duchesne (*Églises séparées*, Paris, 1905, pp. 77–80) and
others doubt this. If they are right, the second general Council
did nothing at all.

[3] Rome acknowledged Paulinos, Meletios' rival at Antioch.
As for Maximos, she was disposed to acknowledge him too. It
is another case of that alliance between Rome and Egypt that
influences all eastern Church history for centuries (*Orth.
Eastern Church*, p. 92). If ever a philosophical account of ecclesiastical politics in the east is written, the alliance between
Rome and Alexandria as against Antioch and Constantinople
will be seen to be an important factor throughout.

[4] As a matter of fact translations from one see to another

of Sasima had been appointed, if that see had an
Ordinary at all it was Gregory.

The saint was further annoyed by the action of the
council with regard to the Antiochene affair. He
had hoped to arrange matters peaceably now that
Meletios was dead; but the extravagant partisanship
of most of the fathers led to the appointment of
Flavian as a successor in the Meletian line, whereby
the trouble was continued and the friction with the
west increased. So Gregory is now only anxious
to leave Constantinople and the council. He felt,
no doubt, himself the force of the argument
against his position there; perhaps he had never
really meant to become permanently bishop of the
capital. Nektarios was chosen bishop peacefully
and canonically (381–397) and Gregory retired.
Before he left the council he preached a sermon to
the fathers in which he bade them farewell and
gave them good advice as to their duties. Then,
tired of all these disputes and wishing only to end
his days in peace, he went home to Nazianzos.

7. Last years and death (381-390)

He ended his days quietly by the city where he
had spent his first years. Since his father's death no
successor had been appointed at Nazianzos. Our
saint did not consider himself to be that successor—he still bore the burden of that title of
Sasima—but he declared that he would administer

were the rarest things at that time. There was for many
centuries an idea that the symbolic marriage of a bishop to his
see should be as indissoluble as a real marriage—till the see
was widowed by his death. The analogy recurs in all kinds of
forms. To usurp another man's diocese was adultery. So even
in the case of the highest sees, the patriarchates, Rome itself,
a vacancy was filled, not by translating a bishop from somewhere else, but by ordaining a priest or deacon of the diocese.

the diocese till an Ordinary should be elected. He did so for two years. Then by his advice a certain Eulalios was chosen canonically and consecrated in 383. Gregory then lived in retirement on the estate he had inherited at Arianzos. Here again he was able to realize his old ideal of living like a monk, being as much a monk as a bishop could be. He spent the last seven years of his life in prayer and great mortification, and found a relaxation in writing poetry. Besides various hymns and poems written for edification he composed a long *Song of his life* (p. 106). He died in peace in 390 (others think it was in 389).

We have seen that he fills a larger place in the memory of eastern Churches than he does with us. To them he is by a special title the *Theologian*. We remember him chiefly as St Basil's friend and as a man of strangely uncertain character whose want of consistent purpose was caused mainly by the fact that all his life he could never do as he wanted. It was Basil's ill-considered impulse about Sasima that ruined his life. He is the patron saint of people who do not want to be bishops. The Byzantine Church keeps his feast on Jan. 25, again on Jan. 30 with SS. Basil and John Chrysostom,[1] the Syrian Uniates and Jacobites on Jan. 25 and the Latins on May 9. He is a Doctor of the Church.

8. Table of dates

330. *Gregory born at Arianzos* by Nazianzos in Cappadocia.

c.345.(?). Student at Cæsarea, then at Athens with St Basil.

[1] These three are the "three holy Hierarchs and Œcumenical Doctors." This feast dates from 1081 or 1084, when it was instituted by the emperor Alexios Komnenos (1081–1118). cfr. Nilles: *Kalendarium manuale* (ed. 2, Innsbruck, 1896), p. 87.

357. Baptized at Nazianzos. Monk at Annesos.
361. *Ordained priest* at Nazianzos. He escapes to Annesos.
362. Priest at Nazianzos.
363. Schism at Nazianzos.
372. *Ordained Bishop of Sasima.* He escapes again. Back at Nazianzos.
374. Gregory the father †.
375–379. At Seleucia in Isauria.
379–381. *Administers the See of Constantinople.*
381. SECOND GENERAL COUNCIL (First C. of Constantinople). Gregory goes back to Nazianzos.
383. Eulalios Bishop of Nazianzos. Gregory at Arianzos.
390 (or 389). *Gregory* †.

9. Works

J. Billius and F. Morellus edited the works of St Gregory Nazianzene in two folio volumes at Paris in 1609–1611. The Benedictine edition was begun before the French Revolution (vol. 1 by Ph. Clemencet, Paris, 1778) and finished after it (ed. A. B. Caillau, Paris, 1840). In Migne's *Patrol. græca* his works fill four volumes (XXXV–XXXVIII). All these editions are in Greek and Latin. J. Goldhorn published selections of St Greg. Naz. with St Basil in the *Bibl. Patrum Græca dogmatica*, Vol. II (*S. Basilii et S. Greg. Naz. opera dogm. selecta*, Leipzig, 1854). E. Dronke edited some of his poems (*Carmina Selecta S. Greg. Naz.*) at Göttingen in 1840; another selection in W. Christ and M. Paranikas: *Anthologia græca carminum christianorum*, pp. 23–32 (Leipzig, 1871). The *Oratio apologetica de fuga sua* was published separately by J. Alzog in 1868 (Freiburg); the *Oratio in fratrem Cæsarium*

(Paris, 1885), and *Or. in laudem Machabæorum*, by E. Sommer (Paris, 1891). Hurter's *SS. Patrum opuscula selecta* (Innsbruck) contain Latin versions of the five *Orationes theologicæ* (XXIX) and the *Or. de fuga sua* (XL). Rufinus of Aquileia had already translated some of his sermons into Latin (publ. at Strassburg in 1508). The two Orations *against Julian* in an English version by C. W. King (*Julian the Emperor*, London, 1888).

ORATIONS. There are forty-five Orations or sermons spoken by St Gregory Nazianzene on various occasions (XXXV–XXXVI). Of these the numbers 27–31 form a group apart, that he himself describes as *Theological Orations* (οἱ τῆς θεολογίας λόγοι, in Or. 28, 1). These are often numbered apart, 1–5 (as by Hurter, above). They were preached at Constantinople in 379 and 381 to defend the Catholic faith about the holy Trinity against Arians and Pneumatomachians. Among the others the most important are Nos. 4 and 5, two *Accusations against Julian* (λόγοι στηλιτευτικοὶ κατὰ Ἰουλιανόν), prudently held after the emperor's death; also No. 20, *On the Appointment of bishops*, and No. 32, *On Moderation in dispute*. No. 2, the famous *Apology for his flight* (ἀπολογητικὸς τῆς εἰς τὸν Πόντον φυγῆς ἕνεκεν, Oratio apologetica de fuga sua), is not properly an Oration but a treatise. It is his most valuable work. Written about the year 362 as a justification of his flight after he was ordained priest (p. 95) it contains a very ideal and splendid description of the priesthood; it was probably the model on which St John Chrysostom formed his treatise.

POEMS. The longest poem is the *Song of his own life* (ᾆσμα περὶ τοῦ βίου ἑαυτοῦ, Carmen de vita sua, XXXVII, 1029–1166). In this he tells the story of his life in a succession of lines in every kind of metre, hexametres, pentametres, trimetres, iambic and anacreontic, with many lines that do not scan at all. It is the chief source for his biography. Some of his shorter poems approach nearer to poetry. The *Evening Hymn* and *Exhortation to Virgins* (XXXVII, 511–514, 632–640) are in rhythmical prose. In the poem, *About his verses* (XXXVII, 1329–1336) he gives his reasons for writing in this form. The tragedy, *Christ Suffering* (Χριστὸς πασχών, Christus patiens, XXXVIII, 133–138) once attributed to him is a late medieval composition.[1]

LETTERS. Of these 243 are preserved, most of them written at the end of his life at Arianzos (383–390). He began making a collection of them himself for a friend named Nikobolos (Ep. 52, 53, XXXVII). They are contained in Migne, P. Gr. XXXVII. Nearly all are very carefully written, and many are evidently meant to be read by others besides the person to whom they are addressed. They treat of events in his life, and in that of his friends, or they discuss points of theology.

10. Literature

Ph. Clemencet wrote a life of Gregory as an introduction to his edition of the works. C. Ullmann: *Gregorius von Nazianz* (Darmstadt, 1825) is still the standard work. Fr Böhringer includes Greg. Naz. in *Die Kirche Christi u. ihre Zeugen* (Bd. VIII, Stuttgart, 1876). A. Benoît: *S. Gregoire de Nazianze* (Paris, 1885). L. Montant: *Revue critique de quelques questions historiques se rapportant à S. Grég. de Naz. et à son siècle* (Paris, 1878).

[1]Of the eleventh or twelfth cent. (Krumbacher: *Gesch. der Byzant. litt.* p. 746 *seq.*). Naturally Dräseke attributes it to Apollinaris, as he does every doubtful work in Greek.

H. Weiss: *Die grossen Kappadocier* (Braunsberg, 1872). J. Dräseke: *Gregorios von Naz. und sein Verhältnis zum Apollinarismus* (in the *Theol. Studien und Kritiken*, LXV, 1892). F. K. Hümmer: *Des h. Gregor von Naz. Lehre von der Gnade* (Kempten, 1890). J. Hergenröther: *Die Lehre von der göttlichen Dreieinigkeit nach dem Gregor von Nazianz* (Regensburg, 1850).

CHAPTER IV

ST JOHN CHRYSOSTOM (344–407)

JOHN of Constantinople, to whom by universal consent has been given the surname of Chrysostom,[1] "Golden-mouthed," is, perhaps, of all Greek fathers the best known in the west. He is (together with Photius) the most famous Patriarch of Constantinople, one of the only three saints[2] who sat on that soul-endangering throne. He suffered persecution and exile, not for the faith, but for the equally sacred cause of morality; he is remembered by his own people as the author of the liturgy they commonly use, and by every one as the most eloquent and perfect orator of the Christian Church. To Catholics as to the Orthodox he remains for all time the great model and patron of preachers.

[1] Χρυσόστομος (χρυσοῦν στόμα), Chrysóstomus (proparoxytone in both Greek and Latin). So much has this name been joined to his original one, that his is almost the only case in which a surname occurs in our liturgy. As a rule saints are called by their Christian name only in prayers. Thus we speak of St John Damascene, St Thomas Aquinas, St Francis de Sales; but in their collects they are only "Johannes," "Thomas," "Franciscus." On the other hand on January 27 we pray God to increase by grace his Church "quam beati Johannis Chrysostomi, confessoris tui atque pontificis illustrare voluisti gloriosis meritis et doctrinis." So again in the secret and post-communion. The only other case of a surname in the text of the Roman Missal is that of St Peter Chrysologus (Golden-speeched) Archbishop of Ravenna (†450), the western counterpart of our saint (December 4).

[2] The others are St Gregory Nazianzene (390) and St Ignatius of Constantinople (†877), the lawful patriarch when Photius was intruded.

1. Early years (344-369)

St John was born about the year 344 in the city which was the centre of the first half of his life, Antioch on the Orontes, the capital of Syria. Antioch in the fourth century was still one of the greatest cities of the empire. Before Constantinople arose it had been one of the three chief towns, with Rome and Alexandria. Founded in 301 B.C. by Seleukos I (Nikator), the first of the line of Seleucid Kings of Syria[1] and named by him after his father Antiochos,[2] under the Romans it still kept its natural place as the head of Syria. It was an enormous city; the great colonnade from the eastern to the western gate was over five miles long. About fifteen miles to the west was the harbour Seleucia; four miles further down the Orontes was the sacred grove of Daphne, to which pilgrims came from every part of the empire to the oracle of the far-darting Apollo. But Antioch became a great centre of Christianity too. St Paul and St Barnabas here "stayed the whole year in the Church and taught a great crowd; so that at Antioch the disciples were first called Christians" (Acts, xi, 26). At the time of St John Chrysostom, of its 200,000 inhabitants half were Christians. The Antiochene school of theology was very famous, although suspect as unsafe in doctrine, and the

[1]The empire of Alexander the Great (B.C. 336–323) broke up after his death, and was divided among his generals (the διάδοχοι = successors). Of these successors the chief were Ptolemaios in Egypt, who founded the kingdom of the Ptolemies with Alexandria as capital, and this Seleukos in Syria. Both lines were of course Greek, and their capitals were outposts of Hellenism among barbarians. The Romans conquered Syria in 64 B.C., and Egypt in 30 B.C.

[2]Ἀντιόχεια, Antiochîa.

bishop of Antioch was one of the three older
patriarchs.

The splendour of the great Seleucid capital has
gone now. You may ride from the port of Iskanderun
to *Antakiye* in a day, and you will find a little town,
half Turkish, half Arab, that does not fill up a tenth
part of the space enclosed in the old walls. Among
the thick olive-woods around it you will see broken
columns, by the mosque in the chief street ruins of
the old colonnade. Going out through the Mohammedan tombs you come to the grove of Daphne.
Her laurels still tremble in the cool winds as if she
feared the god; but Apollo has gone long ago. Even
the Christian memories hardly linger here; of the
five persons who bear the splendid title of Patriarch
of Antioch not one now lives here.[1] From the tombs
across the river you see the town with its minarets
and the great wheels that churn up the brown water
under the mountains on which you may trace the
ruins of the old walls against the sky. You may
try to call up the old glory of the "great and God-
protected city" in which Chrysostom preached.
While the distant wail of the Mu'ezzin tells you
that there is no god but Allah and Mohammed is
the prophet of Allah, you will think that here we
first got our name of Christians.

Our saint's family was very wealthy and powerful. His father, Secundus, died young, soon after
John's birth, so that the child was educated by his
mother, Anthusa. St Anthusa is one of the great
Christian mothers who brought up their sons to be
famous saints. As we who honour St Augustine
remember St Monica, as the glory of St Gregory

---

[1] The Orthodox and Melkite patriarchs live at Damascus,
the Maronite at Bkerki in the Lebanon, the Jacobite at Diar-
bekr on the Tigris, the titular Latin patriarch at Rome.

Nazianzene is bound up with that of St Nonna, so does Anthusa share the honour of Chrysostom. He remembered always what he owed to her, and later he quotes the words said to him by one of his pagan teachers: "What wonderful women these Christians have!" Then John went to hear the professors who made Antioch famous as a centre of education. Of his masters the most famous was Libanios, one of the last of the old pagan philosophers and orators, and one of the greatest. Libanios, a worthy and excellent person, who was one of Julian's special friends, still clung to the worship of the dying gods. He shared the feeling of those last Hellenes that this new religion, that glorified asceticism and dreaded the world, would mean the death of everything that is beautiful and pleasant. They could not understand the worship of a crucified God; all the fasting and flagellations, the black gowns and downcast faces of monks, poverty, chastity and obedience seemed dismal and horrible to them. They loved Hellas and sunlight, the pleasant old feasts that scattered roses over the steps of temples while the glorious statues gleamed in the clear light. And they wanted the old gods, Apollo and Aphrodite and Artemis, the ideals of perfect beauty, and the dear homely gods of wood and fountain and roadside that were so easily pleased and so content to see their children happy. One is not surprised that the mystic glory of the Lord who reigns from the cross, the strange joy of pain for Christ's sake, the silent love of the good Shepherd, were as much beyond them as the awful majesty of the Lord of Hosts reigning alone above the distant heavens. And yet they were not all intolerant, these last pagans, who still pitifully burnt their incense before the dead gods. Some of

them, at any rate, seem to have lived fairly peacefully among the growing crowd of Galileans. Even
poor Julian, who would have persecuted had he
dared, seems sometimes to be reaching out blindly
towards the Stranger who draws all things to himself.

And Julian's friend, Libanios, was so little prejudiced that it is said that when he saw the genius
of his pupil he wanted to resign his chair in favour
of John. The story shows, at any rate, that our
saint already then was looked upon as the most
distinguished student at Antioch. During this
time he made friends with a certain Basil, who was,
perhaps, the future Bishop of Raphaneia.[1] Afterwards he began his famous treatise on the Priesthood by saying: "I have had many friends both
true and dear, who kept the laws of friendship very
exactly. But there was one of these who was as
much dearer to me than the others as they were
dearer than mere acquaintances." This one is Basil.
"We followed the same studies," he goes on, "and
heard the same masters. We shared the same
enthusiasm for our studies, the same cares, the
same life in everything."[2] During these first years
then he acquired that skill in oratory that made
him so famous; he learned to use the most perfect
language in the world as a skilful workman uses
a pliant tool, to persuade, frighten, amuse or rouse
enthusiasm. He learned, too, to read the Greek
classics, as his later allusions, especially to Plato,
show. But John, who is the master of late Greek
eloquence, was by no means an unstinted admirer
of rhetoric. Later he has very severe things to say
against the art of speaking for its own sake,[3] and

---

[1] In any case not to be confused with St Basil the Great of
Cæsarea.
[2] de Sacerd. i, 1.   [3] In Joannem i, In Genesin 22, etc.

8

on one occasion at least he even ventures to attack Homer.[1]

During these years in the world his religious education was not neglected either. At first this was the care of his mother, Anthusa. Later he came very much under the influence of two famous bishops. The first of these was the man whose name is connected with a great and lamentable schism—Meletios of Antioch. It would take too long to tell the whole story of the Meletian schism here.[2] The Arians had banished Eustathios, the lawful bishop of Antioch, in 330 and had set up a certain Eudoxios as Arian bishop. Eustathios died in 337, so the Catholics were left without a lawful pastor. When Eudoxios also died, in 360, the Arians chose Meletios, Bishop of Sebaste in Armenia, to succeed him. But he turned out to be a Catholic, so they deposed him and set up a real Arian Euzoios instead. Meletios came back claiming to be the real bishop, and no doubt all the Catholics would have acknowledged him, had not Lucifer of Calaris (in Sicily) ordained Paulinos as successor to Eustathios. There were then two Catholic bishops, Paulinos and Meletios; after their deaths the rival lines were continued for eighty-five years. Rome and Alexandria were on the side of the line of Paulinos; most of the Greek fathers stood by Meletios and his successors. But this did not produce any really bad feeling; eventually it was our St John Chrysostom who arranged a reconciliation between the Meletian line and the Pope, after the Eustathian succes-

---

[1] *In Ep. ad Ephes.* 21.
[2] The best account of it is F. Cavallera: *Le Schisme de Mélèce* (Paris, Picard, 1906). The author takes Meletios' side throughout.

sion had died out.[1] Meletios was undoubtedly a
very good and holy person: the Roman Church
has admitted him to her Canon of saints. And he
was the first teacher and always the devoted friend
of Chrysostom. The other master was Diodore,
afterwards Bishop of Tarsos (378–394), one of
the founders of the famous theological school of
Antioch. John's writings, and especially his commentaries on the Bible, show how much he was
influenced by Diodore.

Our saint had no period of worldliness to regret
in after years. On the contrary, from the beginning he was very pious and exact in his duties, and
already in these first years he felt strongly drawn
to join one of the communities of monks that were
set up all over Syria. It was his mother, Anthusa,
who persuaded him not to leave her "doubly a
widow"[2] as long as she lived. John may then have
contemplated the career of an orator at first,
though it is more likely that he was only waiting
till Anthusa died to leave the world and be a monk.
And all this time he was, according to the strange
and dangerous practice of that time, not yet baptized. In later years he, too, like all the Greek
fathers, protested against the custom of putting
off baptism till a man was grown up.[3]

2. Baptism. Life as a monk (369-380)

In 369, when he was about twenty-five years
old, he was baptized by Meletios, who ordained
him Reader (ἀναγνώστης) soon after. A certain

[1] St John and Theophilos of Alexandria arranged that Flavian,
the Meletian bishop, should send an embassy to Pope Siricius
(384–399) under Akakios of Berrhoea in 398 and that the Pope
should acknowledge him (Sozomenos, viii, 3; Sokrates v, 15;
Theodoretos v, 23).

[2] *de sac.* i, 5.   [3] *In Act. Ap.* i, *In Ep. ad Hebr.* 13.

Karterios at that time had a kind of monastery at Antioch itself.[1] Diodore was one of the leaders of this congregation. John was influenced by these holy men, too, and confirmed in his wish to flee the world. Then Anthusa died, apparently about the year 373. At the same time there was a proposal to make both friends, John and Basil, bishops. This scheme led to a quarrel between them. John thought that Basil would make a very good bishop, but was diffident about his own worth. So he let Basil think that he fell in with the scheme and then, as soon as Basil was ordained, John ran away and hid in the mountains.[2] Basil was very much annoyed, thinking that his friend had played an unworthy trick on him.[3] They made up the quarrel eventually, and St John's treatise *on the Priesthood* was written as an excuse for what he had done, and dedicated to Basil as an apology.

He was then able to realize his old wish to be a monk. For four years he lived in a community somewhere in the mountains not far from Antioch; then he retired still more and spent two years as a hermit quite alone in a cave. During all the rest of his life he suffered from ill-health as the result of his over-great mortifications during this time. But he was not destined to remain a monk always. On the contrary, he was to fill a very important place in the world. These six years must be considered as a time of preparation for the great career that was to follow. In about 380 he came back to Antioch,

[1] Sozomenos, H.E.viii, 2. It would hardly be considered a real monastery since one of the first principles of monasticism then was literally to go away from the world to some place in the desert. And Karterios' establishment was in the middle of the city. At any rate it was a school of perfection in which people lived like monks.

[2] *de sac.* i, 6.   [3] *Ib.,* i, 7.

either because his health could not stand a hermit's life or because he understood that he had a work to do in the Church. He has now conquered his former fear of being ordained and takes his place as the most important priest in his own city, till he leaves it to be Patriarch of Constantinople.

3. Ordination. Preacher at Antioch (381-397)

In 381 Meletios ordained John deacon. In 386 Flavian, successor of Meletios († 386) in that line, ordains him priest. He was then about forty years old. Some of his earliest works, notably his treatise *on Virginity* (p. 146) were written before he was known, during the very first years of his career as a deacon and priest. Then Flavian gives him a special mission as preacher, and for twelve years, till he goes to Constantinople in 398, he is the most famous Christian orator of Antioch, gradually becoming the most famous preacher in the world. He preached once a week on Sundays, sometimes on Saturdays too. His sermons were held in all the churches of the city, but especially in the great Golden Church built by Constantine.[1] During this time then, especially, he earned his name of "Golden-mouthed." And the Antiochenes, eager lovers of eloquence like all Greeks, were in raptures about their preacher. We have a long series of homilies on different books of the Bible from these years at Antioch, catechisms addressed

[1] This Golden Church was the chief pride of Christian Antioch; it was a round, or rather eight-sided building, looked upon as the most splendid church in the empire. The Patriarchs of Antioch still bear a representation of it as their arms. Eastern bishops have no cathedrals in our sense; or rather every church is their cathedral. Each has a permanent bishop's throne against the south side of the Ikonostasis, facing the people.

during Lent to the "competentes," who were to be baptized on Easter eve, and sermons preached on special occasions, of which the most famous is that about the Statues. Gradually he felt his power, and he did not hesitate to allude to it. Every one knew that his sermons were the great events of the week. "You wait for my words like little swallows looking for food from their mother," he says,[1] and another time, when he had been away for a short time, he says that it has seemed long to him and he is quite sure it has seemed long to them too.[2] It would take much space to tell in detail all the qualities of his eloquence. In splendid and sonorous Greek he produces his effect each time irresistibly. His flow of words is amazing; he adorns his speech with every ornament of rhetoric. Sometimes he is majestic and splendid, and then he suddenly comes down to pleasant familiarity. He is indignant, and the sentences roll like thunder; he is pathetic, and it is all tears and woe. Or he argues subtly, persuasively, he pleads tenderly, he threatens awfully. He weaves chains of argument or paints pictures, teaches, exhorts and carries every one with him up to some crashing climax. One is not surprised that every Greek preacher down to our own time tries to model himself on Chrysostom and that still, on the rare occasions when you may hear a sermon in an Orthodox church, you are surprised to notice that the homely language of the preacher suddenly stops, and that under the low cupolas rolls a splendid sentence, pompous and magnificent, that he has learned by heart from Chrysostom. We are told that our saint, in order to have more opportunity for his effects, in order to be seen by every one, instead of standing in the

[1] In. *Hoc autem scitote.*   [2] In. *In facie ei restiti.*

usual place in the presbytery before the Ikonostasis went up into the ambo. This ambo, degraded from its original use as the place from which the readings are made, has become our modern pulpit.

His most famous sermons of all are about the Statues.

4. The affair of the statues (387)

In 387 happened one of the riots against the government that continually disturbed the Syrian towns, especially Antioch. These Syrians, like the Egyptians, were never very loyal to the empire into which they had been forced. Later, Syria and Egypt fell away at once when the Moslem came (637 and 641). This time it was some grievance about the taxes—probably a very real one—that made the people commit a mad offence. They rushed to the agora, burnt down a part of the town and knocked over the statues of the Emperor Theodosius (379–395), his wife and sons. Now as for burning down houses, that mattered less, but to upset the emperor's statue! Theodosius was not a man to pass over *lèse-majesté* lightly. It was sheer high treason. As soon as the people had done so, they seem to have realized their danger. A few years later Theodosius killed every man, woman and child in Thessalonica for a sedition of this kind,[1] and the Antiochenes seem to have known their master's character. So they go to their bishop's house and implore him to set out at once for Constantinople to intercede for them. Flavian, the patriarch, was a very old man, but he did not hesitate to do as they wished. Meanwhile the governor, the "Count of the East," began to apply the

[1] It was for this crime that St Ambrose made him do public penance.

punishment. All the members of the Senate who had not fled were at once put in gaol, and awful threats were heard of what Cæsar would do to people who upset his statue. To lose their rights as citizens for ever, to have Antioch reduced to a village, and long prison for all the leaders was the very least they could expect. They would be lucky if a troop of soldiers was not sent to hang and burn them.

During the Lent of 387, while Flavian was away and every one trembled at their danger, John preached his twenty-one homilies *on the affair of the statues*. He begins by reminding them that he had already complained of their unruly habits. He says that many citizens are decent, law-abiding folk, but that a crowd of lazy riotous strangers has long disturbed the city, and now they see the result. "If to-day we are all in such fear, it is the fault of these people. If we had driven them out or made them behave decently, we should not now be in this danger. I know quite well that good manners are practised here, but these strangers,[1] a crew lost to all shame, who have long given up trying to save their souls—these are the people who have brought about all this trouble. You suffer for their crimes, and now God has allowed this insult to the emperor in order to punish us for our carelessness."[2] But all through that Lent he comforts the people, tells them to bear whatever may happen as a punishment for their sins, but to hope for the best, and, above all, to trust in God.

[1] The strangers are the barbarous Syrians from the country round, the decent citizens are the Greeks of the city like himself. No Greek, not even a Greek saint, could ever stand the native population of the place where he is. This passage is amusingly like the way Macedonian Greeks talk of Bulgars and Serbs and Vlachs.

[2] Hom. i, *de Statuis*.

And then at Easter came the most glorious news.
Flavian had seen the emperor and had persuaded
him to forgive the rebellion. The commissioners,
who had already started to inflict a most awful
punishment on the city, were recalled; the affair
would be passed over this time. The messengers
from Flavian arrive as the first dawn of the Easter
sun lightens the sky; he himself is on his way back
and will arrive very soon. So on that Easter morn-
ing St John went up into his ambo and preached
the *Homily on the return of Flavian*. One would
like to quote nearly all of what is the most perfect
example of his eloquence and from every point of
view his most famous sermon. "With the word with
which I began to speak to you during the time of
danger I begin again to-day, and I say with you:
Blessed be God. Blessed be God who allows us to
keep this holy feast with so great joy and delight,
who gives the shepherd (Flavian) back to his
sheep, the master to his disciples, the bishop to
his priests. Blessed be God who has done more
than we either asked or even hoped."[1] " Who
would have thought," he says, "that our father
in so short a time would be able to see the emperor,
take away all danger and come back to keep the
holy Pasch with us?" "God has used this danger
to give greater honour to the city, to the bishop,
and to the prince." He develops these three points.
The city has acquired honour by the patience and
courage of the citizens in so great a danger and
because they sought comfort from God. "When
those who are in prison heard on all sides that the
emperor's fury was growing, that he would destroy
the city from top to bottom, they still kept up
their courage. They said: 'We trust not in man,

[1] *In reditum Flav.* i.

but in Almighty God. We are sure that all will end
well, for it cannot be that this hope be in vain.' "
Then comes glowing praise of the bishop who in his
great age put aside every fear to try to save his
people, as Moses offered himself for the Jews. And
the emperor, too, has acquired undying honour.
"What has happened gives him more glory than his
diadem, for he has shown that he will listen to a
bishop where he would not hear any one else, and
he has at once forgiven so great an injury and has
silenced his own just anger."[1] Then comes an
account of Flavian's interview with Theodosius,
how he pleaded and how the emperor forgave.
And Theodosius, by his noble generosity, has built
himself a monument in the hearts of the people of
Antioch that no riot can ever overturn, his mercy is
mightier than his armies, more precious than his
treasures. Never again will the citizens of this great
city forget what they owe to so noble a prince. The
emperor had told Flavian to hurry back with the
good news. "Go," he said, "at once and reassure
them. I know that they are frightened. When they
see you again they will forget the storm. And pray
for me that all these wars and troubles may come to
an end, and some day I will come to visit Antioch
myself." "Let the heathen," says the preacher,
"be confounded, or, rather, let them be instructed,
now that prince and bishop have shown them
what our philosophy is."[2] "Now let Antioch adorn
her squares with garlands, let torches blaze and
green boughs wave throughout the city, rejoice
as if it had been founded again!" "Teach this
story to your children, and let them tell it to future
generations, that all may know for all time how
great is the mercy of God to this city." "And let us

[1] *Ib.* 3. [2] *Ib.* 16.

always give thanks to God the Lover of men[1] both
for our safety now and for the danger he allowed,
since we know that he ordains all things for our
good. And may we always taste of his mercy in
this world and come at last to the kingdom of
Heaven through Jesus Christ our Lord, to whom
be glory and power for ever. Amen."[2]

5. Chrysostom's theology

During the next ten years St John went on with
his office as preacher, and in a long series of sermons developed his ideas on every part of the life
of a Christian. He preached continually on the duty
of *helping the poor*, he is indignant at the luxury of
the rich. He tells his people to be ashamed of property that they have amassed by pettifogging
traffic, by buying cheap and selling dear, or, worse
still, by lending out money at usury.[3] He has no
tolerance for social distinctions; God gave us all
the same father, Adam.[4] Rich people are worse
than wild beasts. "Weep," he says to those who
are down in the world, "weep as I do, not for your-
selves, but for those who despoil you. Their lot is
worse than yours."[5] He wants people who are well
off to keep a permanent guest-house for poor
travellers. "Have at least such a place by your
stables. Christ comes to you in the form of the poor.
Let Christ, at least, use your stable. You shudder
at such an idea. It is still worse not to receive him
at all."[6] He does not like *slavery*, though no one
then thought it absolutely incompatible with

[1] ὁ θεὸς ὁ φιλάνθρωπος is a favourite expression with Chrysostom; it continually occurs in his liturgy.
[2] *Ib.*, the end.
[3] E. gr., *In Ep. i, ad Thess.* 10; *In Ep. i, ad Cor.* 39; *In
Matth.* 56.
[4] *In Ep. ad Cor.* 34.   [5] *In Ep. i, ad Tim.* 12.   [6] *In Act. Ap.* 45.

Christianity. At least persons must treat their slaves justly and kindly. As for the crowd of useless servants who hang round a rich man's house, " teach them a trade by which they can earn their living honestly and buy their freedom."[1]

He has much to say about the *sanctity of marriage* and about the duties of parents towards their children. Marriage should not be put off till too late, because of the danger of such a course to young people. He insists on the equality of husband and wife. Infidelity is just as bad, just as disgraceful in a man as in a woman.[2] He thinks that each have their proper duties. "God has not given the same life to men as to women. The house for the wife, the public square for the husband. The man works in the field, the woman weaves her children's clothes."[3] He thinks that a man's wife must have great influence over him; the husband will listen to her when he will not take advice from a stranger. She must use this influence in the right way.[4] But he has great and splendid things to say of *celibacy* and of the higher path of those who give up all these things to live only for God. He wrote, besides his treatise *on Virginity*, another *Against those who attack the monastic life* (p. 146). He is indignant against the old *pagan customs* that still survived at marriages and funerals, and for *funerals* especially he explains exactly what rites are really Christian, and how people may show their grief without mourning like them that have no hope.[5] He preached very strongly against *theatres* and *circuses*. It should be added that both at that time were still at the level of the

---

[1] *In Ep. i, ad Cor.* 40. [2] *ad Stagirum.* ii.
[3] *In Ep. i, ad Cor.* 34. [4] *In Joann.* 61.
[5] *De dormientibus*, passim, etc.

late Roman performances, in which the place of
the old Greek poetry and skill was taken by luxu-
rious extravagance and gross indecency. St John's
homily *on Shows*,[1] even if one allows a margin for
rhetoric, contains descriptions of a quite shameless
state of things. He sees in the theatre the source of
idleness, dissatisfaction with real life and especially
immorality. One can then understand how indignant he was when on one occasion he found his
church almost empty because every one had gone
to the circus.[2] St John is one of the most enthu-
siastic admirers of the *Bible*. By far the greater
number of his sermons are explanations of parts of
it; taken together, they form a complete commentary on the chief books, from the sixty-seven
homilies on Genesis to the thirty-four on Hebrews.
In the middle ages his exposition of the Psalms,
and especially the thirty-two sermons on Romans,
were the most admired. Isidore of Pelusium
(† c. 440) says of these: "Had St Paul himself
explained his ideas in Attic Greek, he would not
have used other language than this."[3] Chrysostom
had a special devotion to St Paul; it was he who
made the saying that became a proverb, "The
heart of Paul was the heart of Christ."[4]

Most of the Doctors of the Church have some
one point of the faith of which they are the
classic exponers; thus, St Athanasius is the doctor
of the Divinity of Christ, St Augustine is the
"Mouth of the Church about Grace." By universal
consent, St John Chrysostom is looked upon as the
great defender of the *holy Eucharist*. He is the

[1] *Contra circenses ludos et theatra* (lvi, 263–270).
[2] Hom. vi, *in Gen.*
[3] Isid. Pelus. *Ep.* v, 32. MPL, lxxviii, 1348.
[4] *Cor Pauli cor Christi erat* is constantly quoted in the
Middle Ages.

Doctor Eucharisticus. The blessed Sacrament and
the Real Presence are the subjects to which he
turns most often; his writings on this question form
a complete defence and exposition of the teaching
of the Catholic Church about her most sacred inheritance. In his Homilies on the *sixth chapter of
St John* he develops the ideas that our Lord has
given us "Bread from Heaven, that he who eats
it may not perish," that he himself is the "Living
Bread that came down from heaven," that we are to
"eat his Body and drink his Blood." "We must
listen," says Chrysostom, "to this teaching with fear,
because what we have to say to-day is very awful."[1]
He points to the altar and says, "Christ lies there
sacrificed,"[2] "His Body lies before us,"[3] "That
which is there in the chalice is what flowed from
the side of Christ. What is the Bread? The Body of
Christ."[4] "Think, man, what sacrifice you receive
in your hand (people took the blessed Sacrament
in their right hands), what altar you approach.
Consider that you, dust and ashes, receive the
Body and Blood of Christ."[5] We not only see the
Lord, "we take him in our hand, eat, our teeth
pierce his flesh, that we may be closely joined to
him."[6] "What he did not allow on the cross, that
he allows now at the Liturgy; for your sake he is
broken, that all may receive."[7] "It is not a man
who causes the Offering to become the Body and
Blood of Christ, but he himself who died for us.
The priest stands there as his minister when he

---

[1] Hom., xlvii, 1.
[2] Hom. i *de prod. Judce.* (xlix, 381).
[3] Hom. L *in Matth.* n. 2. (lviii, 507).
[4] Hom. xxiv in 1 *Cor.* 1,2 (lxi, 200).
[5] Hom. *in nat. D.N.I. ch.* 7 (xlix, 361).
[6] Hom. xlvi *in Joh.* 3 (lix, 260).
[7] Hom. xxiv *in* i *Cor.* 2 (lxi, 200).

speaks the words, but the power and grace come
from the Lord. This is my Body, he says. This word
changes the Offering."[1] "With confidence we
receive your gift," he says in a prayer, "and
because of your word we firmly believe that we
receive a pledge of eternal life, because you say so,
Lord, Son of God, who live with the Father in
eternal life."[2]

In other points of the faith Chrysostom stands
where we should expect an orthodox and Catholic
father of the fourth century to stand. One need
hardly say that he is uncompromisingly *Homoüsian*
and that he anathematizes the Arian heresy, which
indeed was dying out fast in his time. He was a
friend of Theodore of Mopsuestia († 428), who
afterwards was looked upon as the father of the
Nestorian heresy, but there is no trace of Nestorianism in Chrysostom. He believed that our Lord
had two natures as firmly as that he was one person. "When I say one Christ, I mean a union, not
a mixture, so that one nature was not absorbed
in the other, but was united to it."[3] One could not
wish for a more accurate statement. The two chief
heresies in his time were *Marcionism* and *Manicheism*, and against both he preached continually.
He spoke very strongly against pagan superstitions,
amulets, auguries, omens and so on. He honoured
saints[4] and *relics* and gave *absolution* from sins.

[1] Hom. 1 and 2 *de prod. Judce.* 6 (xlix, 380 and 389). This text
shows plainly that St John believed that the words of Institu-
tion and not the Epiklesis consecrate.

[2] Hom. xlvii *in Joh. See* also Hom. xxiv *in* 1 *Cor.* 1; *De
Sacerd.* iii, 4 ("'You see the Lord lying sacrificed and the priest
offering and praying, and the tongue reddened with the
Precious Blood"—a favourite expression with Chrysostom),
Hom. lxxxii *in Matth.* Catech. ii, 2, etc., etc.

[3] Hom. vii *in Phil.* 2, 3 (lxii, 231, 232).

[4] For instance in his sermon on SS Berenice and Prosdoce:

When he was accused at the Oak-tree Synod
(p. 136) one charge was that he was even too lax in
teaching the ease with which sins can be forgiven.
"If you sin again," he is reported to have said, "do
penance again; as often as you sin come to me and
I will heal you." Only on one point does he sometimes use doubtful expressions. He knew nothing
of the Pelagian heresy, which did not begin (411)
till after his death. He always spoke strongly
against the Manichees, who said that all matter is
bad, and in his zeal to defend the holiness of
nature he sometimes uses expressions that seem
to exalt it at the cost of grace.[1] Julian of Eclanum,
the Pelagian, afterwards quoted such passages, so
as to claim Chrysostom for his side. To whom
St Augustine opposes texts from the same saint
that prove the contrary, and says very truly:
"What is the good of scrutinizing the works of
persons who had no need of caution in this difficult
question, since they wrote before the heresy had
begun. Certainly they would have been more
careful if they had been obliged to answer objec-
tions in this matter."[2]

"Not only on this their feast, but on other days too, let us
cling to them, pray to them, beg them to be our patrons. For
not only living but also dead they have great favour with God,
indeed even greater favour now that they are dead. For now they
bear wounds suffered for Christ, and by showing these there is
nothing that they cannot obtain of the King." (Hom. *de
SS Berenice et Prosdoce*, 7).

[1] Hom. *in Rom.* v, Hom. xii *in Hebr.* Hom. xlii *in Gen.* i. I
have quoted some such passages in the *Orth. Eastern Church*,
p. 109.

[2] *De prædest. SS.* xiv, 27. He quotes as anti-Pelagian passages
in Chrysostom Ep. iii, *ad Olymp. De Resurr. Lazari*, Hom.
ix *in Gen.* Hom. *de Baptizatis.* Hom. x *in Rom.* It is curious to
note that Chrysostom, the Eucharistic Doctor, has some
doubtful passages about Grace, and that Augustine, the
Doctor of Grace, has some inaccurate places about the
Eucharist.

That St John believed in the *Primacy* and universal jurisdiction of the Pope of Rome, he showed very plainly when his own trouble came and he appealed to the Holy See to judge between him and his enemies (below, p. 139). On one point especially his ideas will please a modern reader. He was on the whole tolerant, much more so than anyone else at that time. "Least of all," he writes, "should Christians try to convert sinners by force. Judges punish criminals and make them change their ways, even if unwillingly. But we must call such people to better things, not by force but by persuasion. The law gives us no right to punish, and even if it did we might not use such a right, because God will not reward people who are compelled to change their lives, but only those who freely do so from conviction."[1]

So John spent eleven years preaching as a priest at Antioch. Then came the great change in his life when he was called away to fill what was already practically the chief place in eastern Christendom.

6. Patriarch of Constantinople (398)

In 397 Nektarios of Constantinople died. There were several candidates for the succession. Theophilos of Alexandria, representing the former chief eastern see that had been reduced in rank by the advance of New Rome, who, like all the Egyptians, was jealous of the new patriarchate of Constantinople, had a candidate of his own, through whom he hoped to rule over that see as well as over his own. But John of Antioch was already a very famous man throughout the east. The news of his wonderful power as orator, of his

[1] *de Sac.* ii, 3. He did not always quite act up to these principles.

holiness and unquestioned orthodoxy, had long
reached the capital; so he was elected by the clergy
to fill the place Nektarios had left. Theophilos
concealed his annoyance and himself ordained
the new bishop on Feb. 26, 398. So popular was
John at Antioch that they had to smuggle him
away in secret, lest the people should make a rebellion rather than lose him. It is curious that the two
people concerned in his appointment at Constantinople, Theophilos, who ordained him, and the
Eunuch Eutropios, the favourite of the Emperor
Arcadius, were the very two men who became his
chief enemies afterwards.

As Patriarch of Constantinople[1] John continued
his work as preacher. He preached here, too, constantly; but from this moment the main interest of
his life is no longer in his sermons, but in the grave
political troubles that led to his two banishments.
Theodosius the Great (379–395) was dead. The
empire was divided between his two sons;
Arcadius (395–408) ruled in the east, Honorius
(395–423) in the west. Theodosius was the last
emperor who ruled the whole empire; this
division of east and west, first made by Diocletian (284–305), joined together again by Constantine (323–337), now becomes a permanent state of
things. The two halves were never united again.[2]

[1] The title *Patriarch* was used loosely for a long time (*Orth.
Eastern Ch.*, p. 8). Constantinople did not, perhaps, become
strictly what we should call a patriarchal see till the Council
of Chalcedon (451, Can. 28; which even then was not recognized
by Rome). But it was already (since Canon 3 of the second
general Council, 381) practically the chief see in the east,
"having the primacy of honour after Rome." It does not appear
that St John ever spoke of himself as Patriarch.

[2] The western half of the empire came to an end with
Romulus Augustulus in 476. The right over the whole then fell
back on the eastern line at Constantinople. But, in spite of
Justinian I (527–565)'s heroic efforts, the emperors never got

There is not much good to be said of Arcadius.
He was at the mercy of a succession of court
favourites; and his wife Eudoxia, who was tho-
roughly bad, gradually got hold of the administration. This Eudoxia became the great enemy of the
patriarch.

7. Eutropios's disgrace (399)

The first trouble was the affair of the eunuch
Eutropios. He was the all-powerful favourite.
In 399 he made the emperor name him Consul, and
for a time he practically ruled the empire. Like all
such court favourites, he ruled abominably badly.
He sold offices and justice, robbed the public
funds and was an example of every kind of shameless immorality. The patriarch was not likely to
bear with such a person, even if he were a Consul;
so soon after John's ordination we find him alluding
plainly to these scandals in his sermons.[1] He remon-
strated with Eutropios personally, but that only
led to a greater quarrel. The Consul especially
found the right of sanctuary inconvenient. At
that time, as still in many eastern lands, certain
places of refuge were allowed, so that criminals
who could reach them were safe. These sanctuaries
had been the temples; then naturally churches
took their place. The right was recognized by the
government; how far such a chance of escape for
criminals would be an advantage to society in a
well-ordered state is another question. At any rate,
in a troubled and violent time it gave a man a
chance of escaping the first burst of rage against

back any real authority in the west, except intermittently in
Southern Italy and Sicily. And in 800 with Charles the Great
begins a permanent rival line of emperors in the west.

[1] In the vii Hom. *in Ep. ad Coloss.* and the second *in Ep. ad
Philipp.*

him. He could take sanctuary, prepare his defence at leisure and then, if he were judged innocent, come out. The right of taking sanctuary existed in the west, too, all through the middle ages. To violate sanctuary and drag a man away from his refuge in the church was a specially heinous form of sacrilege.[1] St John then stood out for this right; on several occasions people attacked by Eutropios managed to escape him by taking sanctuary. So Eutropios found the law inconvenient and persuaded Arcadius to abolish it. The patriarch refused to recognize its abolition and the question further embittered the Consul against him. Now comes the dramatic moment of this story. Suddenly Eutropios fell, as such favourites do fall. He had offended the empress, the court gave him up and all the long list of his crimes were on his head— treason, bribery, evil administration, robbery, corruption, injustice, violence and murder. He had no chance for his life, except one. He fled from the guards who sought him and took sanctuary in John's church. And the patriarch, true to his principles, in this case, too, defended the right in favour of the man who had abolished it. The soldiers surrounded the church and clamoured for Eutropios; they did not dare break in. John refused to give him up and protected him till he could get away to Cyprus. The picture of the fallen eunuch, who had abolished sanctuary, cowering at the altar and Chrysostom, his enemy, standing over him and protecting him, is one of the vivid scenes that has taken hold of the imagination of people in those parts.[2] Nor did the saint fail to

[1] Among the forms of *sacrilegium locale* in the old books of law will be found *violatio asyli*.

[2] I have seen boys at a Greek school playing at this scene; it is constantly reproduced in pictures.

improve the occasion in two Homilies *on the fall of Eutropios.*

8. The Synod at the oak tree and first exile (403)

A more serious trouble was the quarrel between the patriarch and the empress. Eudoxia offended the saint in many ways. She was vain and frivolous; she set the fashion of wearing false hair, painting cheeks and aping the manners of a young girl among matrons. These were the very vanities that had long moved the saint's indignation at Antioch. He did not abate a jot of his denunciation of them at Constantinople, in spite of the danger of offending the empress. Worse still, she misgoverned the empire. She had robbed a widow of her field; there were other cases of tyranny and injustice committed by her. Against all these things the patriarch spoke openly. So very soon he knew that he had to count this lady as his enemy. She hated him and began to consider how she could get rid of him. Then came a great quarrel with Theophilos of Alexandria. We have seen that Theophilos had had other plans for the succession at Constantinople. Although he had pretended to give in and had himself ordained John, he was always secretly his enemy. Now his enmity breaks out openly.

Origenes († 254), the greatest scholar of the eastern Church, perhaps the most wonderful genius of all Christian writers, was destined to be the source of endless disputes for centuries after his death. He is the father of the fathers of the Church. Every school had learned from him; but, on the other hand, he was more than suspect of various heretical opinions. He had been a Subordinationist[1] and a Chiliast,[2] and had taught the pre-existence of souls. So for centuries the fathers were divided between his ardent admirers, who forgave or ignored these errors, and his enemies, who looked upon him as the father of all heresies.[3] This question, then, was the immediate ostensible cause of the quarrel between Theophilos of Alexandria and John of Constantinople. Theophilos had in his patriarchate many monks, and monks were nearly always Origenists. Chief among these Origenist monks were four who were called by the strange name of the "Tall Brothers."[4] The

---

[1] That is that he taught that the Son of God was less great than the Father; Subordinationism was the forerunner of Arianism.

[2] *Chiliasm* (=Millennialism) was the belief in the end of all evil, a reign of Christ for 1,000 years on earth, the conversion of the devil, and all evil spirits, the end of hell, and a final restoration of all things in God.

[3] The question of Origenes comes up again and again, and continually severs the best friends. Gregory Thaumaturgos (†270), Pamphilos of Berytos (†309) and Dionysios the Great (of Alexandria, †264) were his most devoted disciples and admirers. In a less degree Basil (†379), Gregory of Nazianzos (†390), Gregory of Nyssa (†c.395), our John Chrysostom (†407) were counted Origenists, so was the whole school of Antioch, and countless monks everywhere. Among his uncompromising enemies were Methodios of Olympios (†c.312), Theophilos, this Patriarch of Alexandria (†412), most of the Alexandrine school, and many Latins. St Jerome (†420) had been an Origenist, but became a violent partisan of the other side, and had a tremendous quarrel with Rufinus (†410) about this question. Origenes comes up again all through the troubles of the sixth century, and once more the burning question was whether he should be considered a heretic or a father of the Church. Eventually the fifth general Council (Constantinople II in 553) declared against him (Can. 11). For all that Origenes' influence, on eastern theology especially, has been enormous; all their metaphysic and still more their exegesis can be traced back to him. Even the men who most attacked him (including St. Jerome) owed far more to him than they would ever confess.

[4] Οἱ μακροὶ ἀδελφοί. Their real names were Dioskuros, Ammonios, Eusebios and Euthymios.

patriarch held a synod in 399, condemned Origenes and forbade his writings. The Tall Brothers
then refused to accept his decision. They were
joined by a priest named Isidore, who had quar-
relled with Theophilos. The brothers and Isidore
escape from Egypt, where their patriarch meant
to punish them, come to Constantinople and beg
John to protect them. St John behaved very
prudently. When he had heard their tale he
allowed them to lodge in a monastery, but would
not admit them to communion till he had heard
from their own bishop. So he writes to Theophilos
asking him what it is all about. Meanwhile there
was already a strong party in his own city against
him. The leader was the empress. She was furious
because she had heard the patriarch in a sermon
speak of Jezebel, and she thought he meant her.
Very likely he did. That she was a Jezebel is abun-
dantly evident. Then there were three bishops,
some monks and a good many ladies who did not
like the patriarch's sermons. The bishops and monks
thought him too severe, and the ladies could not
bear his ideas about wigs and painted faces. Two
deacons whom he had suspended for bad conduct
joined the party. So the empress persuades Theophilos to come to Constantinople, on the strength
of this affair of the Tall Brothers, and to hold a
synod against John. Theophilos came in 403. He
had, of course, no shadow of right to judge the
patriarch of Constantinople; it was an additional
insult to do so in that patriarch's own city. He
brought a number of his Egyptians with him;
joined with the rebellious Byzantines they held a
synod of thirty-six bishops. They sat at Chalcedon,[1] across the water, in a property that pos-

[1] *Chalcedon*, where the fourth General Council was held in

sessed that rare adornment in those parts—a splendid oak tree. This is the famous Oak-Tree Synod (σύνοδος ἐπὶ τὴν δρῦν, Synodus ad quercum) in 403. From the saint's sermon after his return from exile and Photius' collection[1] we know what the case against St John was. The points are so absurdly frivolous that it is quite evident that he was condemned really only because the empress wanted to get rid of him. He was charged with having suspended a deacon who had beaten his slave, with being friendly towards pagans, with squandering Church property in almsgiving, with treating his clergy harshly and saying they were not worth three oboles, with being too easy in forgiving sins, eating honey-cakes, making classical allusions in his sermons, exciting the lower classes and interfering in Theophilos' jurisdiction by receiving the Tall Brothers. This last accusation is a most brazen piece of impudence. He had done nothing of the kind, as we have seen. And if Theophilos was so jealous of patriarchal independence, what was he doing at Chalcedon? Lastly comes the real matter, a vague allusion to treason against the empress. John naturally refused to attend this entirely uncanonical synod. So he was declared contumacious, deposed and sentenced to banishment. When he heard his sentence, he preached a famous sermon. "Tell me, what am I to fear? Death? Christ is my life and death my gain (Phil. i, 21). Banishment? The earth is the Lord's and the fullness thereof (Ps. xxiii, 1). The loss of goods? Naked I came into the world and naked I shall leave it (Job i, 21)." But still, he says, even in exile nothing

451, lies opposite Constantinople across the Bosphorus—now *Qadi Köi* and *Haidar Pasha*. The Baghdad railway starts here.
[1] *Bibliotheca Photii*, 59.

can separate him from the church of which he is
lawful bishop, for "whom God has joined together,
no man can put asunder" (Matt. xix, 6).[1] He
gave himself up to the officer who came to take
him away and a great crowd of his faithful people
accompanied him to the ship on the Bosphorus
that was to carry him to Bithynia.

But this first exile did not last long. Soon after he
was gone there was a great earthquake at Constantinople, and Eudoxia was frightened at what she took
to be a judgment of God. Also the people, faithful to
their patriarch, began to show signs of revolt. So
she sent for him very soon after, inviting him back.
At first John declared that he would not return till
another and greater synod had pronounced his
innocence.[2] But the insistence of the empress, who
was now as anxious to have him back as she had
been to get rid of him, and the rumour of trouble
among the people overcame his scruple. He came
back in triumph (403), Eudoxia herself came down
to the quay to receive him, and this first trouble
was over. As usual, he preached his next sermon
on the subject, the *Homily at his return*.[3] He tells
the whole story of his trial and banishment, and
then praises Eudoxia, for bringing him back, in a
way that seems almost too flattering.

9. The second exile (404-407)

But the reconciliation did not last long. A few

[1]Hom. *ante exilium* (lii, 427–430).
[2]This was in accordance with the decree of the *Synod of
Antioch* in 341, namely, that if a bishop were deposed by a
council, he should not be restored till a larger council had
declared for him (Can. 4 and 12). The law did not apply in this
case really, because it supposes that the first synod was a
canonical one.
[3]Hom. *post reditum* (lii, 443–448).

months afterwards the quarrel broke out again,
and this time, like the old disturbance at Antioch
(pp. 119-120), it was about a statue. Eudoxia had a
silver statue of herself set up just outside the great
church of the Holy Wisdom.[1] The erection of the
statue was celebrated with a great feast, dancing,
racing, drinking and play-acting. The patriarch
had always hated this sort of thing, especially the
acting (p. 124), and now he saw in it, as an additional profanation, a desecration of the church.
People trying to say their prayers inside were
disturbed by ribald choruses and a shouting race-
course mob. So he protested to the prefect of the
city and demanded that the statue should be set
up somewhere else, further from the church door.
Eudoxia saw in this demand a personal offence
against herself and her statue, and was mightily
offended. Already she began to think about sending
the patriarch back into exile. He heard of her plan
and then things came to a climax when he preached
a sermon on St John Baptist. For he began his
homily by saying: "Once again Herodias rages,
once again she screams and dances, again she asks
for the head of *John*."[2] The allusion was obvious,
not only the Baptist was named John. Eudoxia was
furious. She had been called a Jezebel before, and
now she is a Herodias.

So she wrote to Theophilos at Alexandria, to ask
him to come back and hold another synod against
his brother of Constantinople. Theophilos did not
want the trouble of making another long journey,
so he answered that John could be got rid of in a

[1] That is, of course, the older church built by Constantine.
The present Holy Wisdom at Constantinople was built on its
site by Justinian (527–565) after the old church had been
burned down in 532; it was finished in 537.
[2] Sokrates, H.E. vi, 18, Sozomenos, viii, 20.

much simpler way. Let the government invoke
that very Synod of Antioch about which he had
had a scruple[1] and, since he had come back without
having been restored by a synod, his restoration
could be described as unlawful and he could be
sent back into exile at once. Eudoxia took this
advice. Just before Easter in 404 John was arrested
in his own house; all the catechumens who had
assembled for their last preparation for baptism
were driven away by soldiers. The patriarch was
kept a prisoner till after Whitsunday. On June 20
he was again put on a ship and sent away. He was
taken across the Black Sea and Asia Minor to
Cucusus at the extreme end of Cappadocia, near
the Cilician frontier, in little Armenia. A certain
Arsakios was set up as anti-patriarch of Constantinople. St John still had a large following of faithful subjects in the city. These people, the "Joan-
nites," were then fiercely persecuted; but their
lawful bishop kept up relations with them by
letter. Eudoxia died soon after she had succeeded
in finally banishing her enemy (404). Arsakios died
too in the next year; but the government at once
set up another intruder, Attikos (406–425). St John
never came back alive from this second exile.

10. Appeal to the Pope (404)

Like Athanasius in his trouble, and so many
other saints of the eastern Church, Chrysostom
then, finding himself banished and persecuted by
the empire, solemnly and formally appealed to
the great Patriarch at Old Rome, whose rule
stretches over the whole Church of Christ.[2] St

---

[1] *See* above p. 137, n. 2.
[2] Palladios: *Dial.* 9. *Hist. Laus.* 121 (xxxiv, 1233). John's
letter to the Pope in Palladios: *Dial.* 10–22.

Innocent I (401–417), a very great and splendid Pope, then held the keys. The saint's enemies had appealed to him, too, asking him to agree in John's deposition and to acknowledge Arsakios. Innocent, having heard both sides, on this occasion, too, stood out firmly for the lawful patriarch; and this time, too, as in the later affair of Ignatius and Photius (857), when the appeal to Rome went against them, the government and the usurper at Constantinople dragged the eastern Church into formal schism.

Innocent wrote to John comforting him in his trouble and promising to do all he could for him.[1] Then he wrote to Theophilos of Alexandria reproaching him for his uncanonical proceedings at the Oak Tree and saying that a general Council had better be summoned to settle the affair.[2] But the general Council never came about; there were too many difficulties. So the Pope then wrote again to Honorius, the emperor in the west, asking him to remonstrate with his brother Arcadius. Honorius did so, but only got an offensive answer back, in which he was told to mind his own business.[3] There was no possibility of restoring the patriarch by force; so the Pope refused to admit the usurper to his diptychs. Arsakios and then Attikos retorted by breaking communion with the west, and a schism began that lasted eleven years (404–415). Rome then was not able to help St John materially; the incident would be unimportant were it not one more example of the acknowledgment of the Primacy by the eastern fathers and one more case in which the Holy See

[1] *Dial.* 4.
[2] *Dial.* l.c.
[3] Honorius' letter in Baronius, *Annales* ann. 404. §80 *seq.* (Mansi: iii, 1122 *seq.*).

unhesitatingly defended the right side, even at the cost of a schism.[1]

11. Death and final triumph (407, 438)

We now come to the end. From Cucusus the saint was moved to Arabissos near, and then the government sent him on again to the north of Asia Minor. But on the way, worn out with the privations of his exile in a wild and desert country, he stopped at Komanes in Pontus, too sick to go any further. A martyr of the Diocletian persecution, St Basiliskos, was buried here, and when John arrived and spent the night sleeping by the martyr's tomb he saw Basiliskos in a dream who seemed to say to him, "Brother, take comfort, to-morrow we shall be together." The next day Chrysostom rose, vested himself and said the holy Liturgy. After his communion he lay down and died (Sept. 14, 407).[2] His last words have always been remembered by those who honour his memory, *Glory to God for everything, δόξα τῷ θεῷ πάντων ἔνεκεν.*

And then, as in the case of our St Thomas of Canterbury, God allowed the final triumph of his saint after death. Arcadius the persecutor died in 408. His son, Theodosius II (408–450), succeeded him, and Theodosius repented of the harm done by his parents. In 438 he sent for the saint's relics, that they might be brought back to Constantinople. He himself went down to the shore to meet them, with all his court. In the evening of Jan. 27

---

[1]There were four great schisms, making up altogether 203 years, between east and west before the greatest of all under Photius. In each of them Rome was right, without any question; *see* Duchesne: *Eglises Séparées* (Paris, 1905), 163, and *Orth. Eastern Church*, p. 96–97.

[2]Palladios, *Dial.* c. 11.

the procession of boats came up the Golden Horn, lit by blazing torches that gleamed from the Bosphorus to the Propontis. The emperor kneeling before the barge on which the body rested, "asked forgiveness for his parents and for what they had done in ignorance."[1] The waves of the Golden Horn, lit up by the light of the torches, flowing out into the Hellespont and into the great sea beyond, are a symbol of the glory of the golden-mouthed preacher that spread out from his patriarchal city to the ends of the Christian world. For not only in his own country is he honoured. Throughout the great Latin Church, too, across the ocean to lands of which he had never heard, wherever a Catholic priest stands before his people to preach, we remember our patron and example, who spoke in season, out of season, reproved, rebuked, exhorted with all patience and learning.[2] The day on which his relics were brought back (Jan. 27) is his feast among his own Byzantines and to us Latins. They sing: "The holy Church rejoices mystically at the return of thy sacred relics, and receives them as a golden treasure. She never ceases teaching her children to sing of thee, and of the grace obtained by thy prayers, John of the Golden Mouth."[3]

She never does cease. She teaches her Latin children, too, on that day to sing of the "High Priest who in his day pleased God. For there is none other like him who kept the law of the most

[1] Theodoret, H.E. v, 36 (lxxxii, 1268).
[2] II Tim. iv, 1, 2.
[3] *Kontakion* (Echos I) in the Byzantine Horologion, Jan. 27. The Byzantine Church honours St John Chrysostom on Jan. 30, with SS Basil and Gregory Nazianzene (these three are the "three holy Hierarchs"), and by himself on Nov. 13 as well.

High. Blessed is the man who suffered hardship, because when he has been tried he shall receive a crown of victory."[1] And when we sing of Chrysostom in our language while they praise him in theirs,[2] we may look out across the sea and think of his people, his own Byzantines, cut off from the throne that defended him by this lamentable schism, and groaning under the heel of the unbaptized tyrant whose presence still defiles the city of eighty Roman Cæsars. If anything can trouble the peace of the saints, he must be troubled to see his successors rebel against those of Innocent, and to hear the Mu'ezzin cry from the place he would not have defiled by Eudoxia's statue. And if any saint has a special reason to pray to God for the end of these evils it is John who appealed to Old Rome as lawful Bishop of New Rome, who, where Islam is now preached, spoke for the gospel of Christ with his golden mouth.

12. Table of dates

c. 344. St John Chrysostom *born at Antioch*. Educated at Antioch.

  369. Baptism.

  374–380. Monk near Antioch.

  381. Ordained deacon by Meletios.

  386. Ordained priest by Flavian.

  386–397. *Preacher at Antioch.*

  387. Affair of the statues at Antioch.

  398. *Patriarch of Constantinople.*

  399. Eutropios' disgrace.

  403. *Oak Tree Synod.* First exile.

  404–407. Second exile.

[1]Gradual in the Roman Missal, Jan. 27.

[2]It is the same day really, but for the dislocation of the calendar that makes their Jan. 27 come thirteen days after ours.

407 (Sept. 14). *Death at Komanes in Pontus.*
438 (Jan. 27). His relics brought to Constanti-
    nople.

13. Works

St John Chrysostom has left more works than
any other Greek father. Most of these are Homilies
preached at Antioch and Constantinople. Fronton
le Duc (Fronto Duceus) edited the first complete
collection in Greek and Latin in twelve folio
volumes (Paris, 1609–1633). An Anglican, H.
Savile, published an edition in eight volumes
(Greek only) at Eton in 1612, and the Benedictine,
B. de Montfaucon, did so at Paris in thirteen
volumes (Greek and Latin, 1718–1738). The
editions of Le Duc and Montfaucon have often been
reprinted since. The works fill eighteen volumes
of Migne (Patr. Gr. XLVII–LXIV). Separate treatises
have been published on many occasions. Especially
the most read work, *On the Priesthood,* has gone
through countless editions. J. A. Bengel edited it
in Greek and Latin in 1725 (Stuttgart); there is an
edition of the Greek text only published by
Tauchnitz (1825, often reprinted, last in 1887)
and an excellent one in the *Cambridge Patristic
texts* by J. A. Nairn (Cambridge, 1906.)[1] H. Hurter,
S.J., gives a Latin translation of it in the series,
SS. Patrum opuscula selecta, vol. XL (Innsbruck,
1879); W. R. W. Stephens did it into English for
the *Select Library of Nicene and Post-Nicene
Fathers* (Ser. 1, vol. IX, 1892) and T. A. Moxom has
done so for the *Early Church Classics* (S. P. C. K.,
1907). The *Homily on the Return of Flavian* was
edited in Greek by L. de Sinner (Paris, 1842), the

[1]This is the best modern text. There is a little mild Protestantism in the introduction and notes.

one *on Eutropios* by J. G. Beane (Paris, 1893).
Hurter's *SS. Pp. opusc. sel.* also include his treatise
on the Divinity of Christ (quod Christus sit Deus,
vol. XV) and his five *Homilies against the Anomeans*
(de Incomprehensibili, vol. XXIX). Most of the
Homilies on the N. T. were collected and pub-
lished at Oxford in five volumes (1849–1855) by
F. Field. Lastly, useful selections are: *Johannis
Chrys. opera præstantissima,* by F. W. Lomler
(Rudolstadt, 1840, Gr. and Lat.), *S. Joh. Chrys.
opera selecta* by F. Dübner (Paris, 1861, Gr. and
Lat., only one vol. published) and Mary Allies:
Leaves from S. John Chrysostom (Burns and Oates,
1889).

HOMILIES ON THE BIBLE. St John preached long
courses of sermons on various books of the Bible,
so that, taken together, they form a continuous
commentary on most of the books. At Antioch in
388 he preached sixty-seven *Homilies on Genesis*
(LIII–LIV) and nine others *on Genesis,* too (LIV, 581–
630). Various passages in *Kings* are explained by
eight Homilies (LIV, 631–708, at Antioch in 387),
and sixty *Psalms* (LV). The Homilies on *Job* and
Proverbs (LXIV, 503–740) are doubtfully authentic.
In 386 he preached *on the difficulties in the Prophecies* (LVI, 163–192), in 386 and 397 on parts
of *Isaias* (LVI, 11–142). Fragments on *Jeremias*
(LXIV, 739–1038) and *Daniel* (LVI, 193–246) are
collected from Catenas. In the year 390 he explained *St Matthew* in ninety sermons (LVII–LVIII).
Of his commentaries on St Mark and St Luke only
seven Homilies *on the Parable of Lazarus* (LC.,
xvi, 19–31, xlviii, 963–1054) are preserved. Eighty-
eight sermons on *St John* (LIX) were preached in
389. At Constantinople, in 400 or 401, he preached
fifty-five Homilies on the *Acts of the Apostles* (LX)

and he explained all *St Paul's Epistles* in long series of sermons (LX–LXIV).

OTHER SERMONS. The most famous are those *on the Statues* (p. 120, XLIX, 15–222) and on *Eutropios* (p. 133, LII, 391–414). He preached *against the Jews* (eight Homilies. XLVIII, 843–942), *against the Anomeans* (extreme Arians, twelve Homilies, XLVIII, 701–812), *on the Resurrection* (L, 417–432), *on Penance* (nine Hom. XLIX, 277–350), *against Circuses and Theatres* (LVI, 263–270) and on most of the great feasts of the calendar (XLIX, L, LII, LXIV). We have seven sermons *on St Paul* (L, 473–514) and others *on Martyrs* and various saints (L). The sermons *before* and *after his first exile* are famous (LII, 427–430, 443–448).

OTHERWORKS. Although preaching was St John's special vocation, he wrote books too. In 382 he composed a treatise *Against Julian and the Heathen* (κατὰ Ἰουλιανοῦ καί πρὸς ἕλληνας, Adv. Julianum et gentiles, L, 533-572), and in 387 a *Defence of the Divinity of Christ against Jews and Pagans* (πρὸς ἰουδαίους καὶ ἕλληνας ἀπόδειξις ὅτι ἐστὶ θεὸς ὁ Χριστός. Demonstratio qd. Christus sit Deus adv. iudæos et gentiles, XLVIII, 813–838). He defended monasticism in his work *Against those who attack the Monastic Life* (πρὸς τοὺς πολεμοῦντας τοῖς ἐπὶ τὸ μονάζειν ἐνάγουσιν. Adv. oppugnatores vitæ monasticæ, LIII, XLVII, 319–386), written in 376, and wrote ascetic treatises *on Virginity* (περὶ παρθενίας, de virginitate, XLVIII, 533–596) and *on the state of Widows* (περὶ μονανδρίας, de viduis, XLVIII, 533–596). He was rightly indignant against the dangerous and scandalous custom that clerks should live in the same houses as nuns (πρὸς τοὺς ἔχοντας παρθένους συνεισάκτους. de virginibus subintroductis, XLVII, 495–514 and 514–532). But

the most important of all his ascetic works are the
six books *on the Priesthood* (περὶ ἱερωσύνης. de
Sacerdotio libri VI, XLVII, 623–692).[1] We have seen
on what occasion this little treatise was written
(p. 116). It is, with St Gregory I's *Regula Pastoralis*,
the classical work on the dignity of the priesthood
and the responsibility and duties of priests.

LETTERS. Vol. LII of Migne's Greek series contains
238 letters written by Chrysostom to various
people, which give a number of valuable details
about his own life, as well as a lively and interesting picture of society in his time.

LITURGY. The Service of the holy Eucharist used
throughout the Orthodox Church and among the
Catholic Melkites for nearly every day in the year[2]
bears the title: *The divine Liturgy of our father
among the saints John Chrysostom.* It is a shortened
form of the older Liturgy ascribed to St Basil.
How far it is really the work of Chrysostom is a
question that has not yet been settled. We know
that at Antioch our saint was much concerned
about the right celebration of the holy Liturgy and
anxious to make any modifications that would
cause a more reverent attendance.[3] It is also certain that the Liturgy was very long, and that this
form is an abridgement of the older one. As
Patriarch of Constantinople John would naturally
apply the same principles; from the chief church in

---

[1] Ἱερωσύνης (*sacerdotium*) means Bishophood rather than
Priesthood. *Sacerdos* in Latin and ἱερεύς in Greek practically
always mean a bishop in the age of the fathers. But most of
what the saint says about bishops applies equally to priests.

[2] On some days the older use of St Basil is followed (*see*
p. 64, n. 1), and for Lent (except Saturdays and Sundays) they
use the Liturgy of the Presanctified that they ascribe to
St Gregory Dialogos (our Pope Gregory the Great, 590–604).

[3] *In Ep. II ad Thess. In Act. Ap.* 29. *In Ep. I ad Cor.* 36.
In Gen. 4. *In Matth.* 73.

the east his reform would spread very quickly over all those parts. In the Liturgy there are forms and expressions that are evidently his. But whether he really drew up and imposed a complete Liturgy is another question. The first part, the Preparation of the gifts ($\pi\rho\sigma\kappa\omi\delta\eta$), is certainly much later than his time. And for the rest, also, Liturgies are modified too gradually, there are too many influences at work for their final and definite form ever to be really the work of one man.[1]

14. Literature

We have a contemporary life of the saint written by one of his faithful bishops, who refused to acknowledge Arsakios and Attikos, namely, *Palladios* ($\delta\iota\acute{a}\lambda\sigma\gamma\sigma$ $\pi\epsilon\rho\grave{\iota}$ $\tau\sigma\hat{\upsilon}$ $\beta\acute{\iota}\sigma\upsilon$ $\mathrm{'I}\omega\acute{a}\nu\nu\sigma\upsilon$. Dialogus de vita S. Joannis Chrys. XLVII, 5–82). This dialogue, Chrysostom's own works, and references in the contemporary Church historians (Sokrates, Sozomenos, Theodoretos) are the sources from which a very complete account of his life can be drawn up.

J. Stilting: *De S. Joanne Chrys.* (in the Acta SS. IV, Antwerp, 1753). A. Neander: *Der h. Johannes Chrys. u. die Kirche, besonders des Orients, in dessen Zeitalter* (2 vols, Berlin, 1821; still the classical life). F. Böhringer: *Chrysostomus* (*Die Kirche Christi u. ihre Zeugen*, vol. 1, 4, Zürich, 1846). Rochet: *Histoire de S. Jean Chrys.* (2 vols, Paris, 1866). F. Ludwig: *Der h. Joh. Chrys. in seinem Verhältniss zum byzantischenHof* (Braunsberg, 1883). R. W. Busch: *Life and times of Chrysostom* (London, 1885). A. Puech: *Un Réformateur de la société chrétienne au ive siècle* (Paris, 1891) and *S. Jean*

[1] I have given an outline of this Liturgy in the *Orth. Eastern Church*, pp. 412–418.

Chrys. (Paris, 1900, in *Les Saints*, Lecoffre). G.
Marshal: *S. Jean Chrys. à Antioche* (Paris, 1898).
P. Albert: *S. Jean Chrys. considéré comme orateur
populaire* (Paris, 1858). L. Ackermann: *Die
Beredsamkeit des h. Joh. Chrys.* (Würzburg, 1889).
T. Förster: *Chrys. in snem Verhältniss zur Antio-
chenischen Schule* (Gotha, 1869). F. Chase: *Chrysostom, a Study in the history of Biblical Interpretation* (London, 1887).

CHAPTER V

ST CYRIL OF JERUSALEM (c. 315–386)

CYRIL of Jerusalem was one of the many Catholic bishops who suffered persecution and exile for the faith at the time of the Arian troubles. Of the thirty-five years during which he was bishop he spent altogether sixteen in banishment. He was the witness of Julian's attempt to rebuild the temple, and was known to the other Greek fathers of that time as a valiant and steadfast defender of the faith of Nicæa, as well as a zealous and irreproachable bishop; but his chief title to fame is the series of catechisms he held as a priest at the Holy Sepulchre in Jerusalem.

1. First years (*c.* 315-345)

Cyril[1] was born in or near Jerusalem about the year 315. We know nothing of his parents, and for these early years of his life we have only one or two passing references and what can be deduced from allusions in his writings. He was evidently brought up as a Christian, but there is no reference to his baptism anywhere. One may conjecture that he was baptized, probably by Makarios, Bishop of Jerusalem,[2] as a young man. He seems to have lived alone somewhere as a monk for a time; at

[1] Κύριλλος (Cyrillus) is a common Greek name. It means *little Lord* (diminutive of Κύριος).

[2] This Makarios was present at the first general Council (Nicæa I, 325) and received a long letter from Constantine about building the church of the Holy Sepulchre (Euseb · *Vita Constant.* III, 29–32). He died between 335 and 345.

least his repeated references to the monastic life[1]
seem to imply that he had some experience of it.
And he had certainly studied holy Scripture, the
older fathers, Origenes († 254), the teaching of
various heretics (notably of the Manicheans[2]) and
to some extent profane letters. It was probably
his reputation as an austere and virtuous person
and a theologian that induced Makarios to take
him away from his solitude and ordain him deacon
in 334 or 335. For ten years he then served as
deacon in the Church of Jerusalem. Meanwhile
Makarios died and was succeeded by Maximos.

2. Priest and catechist (345-350)

Maximos ordained Cyril priest in 345 and gave
him the important duty of teaching the faith to
the catechumens before their baptism, and then of
preparing them for their first communion. It was
during these five years that Cyril held the series of
catechetical instruction that have made him famous.
He wrote down what he said, and this series of
twenty-three homilies form practically all we have
of his works. They were held during Lent and
Easter week to the people baptized on Easter eve.
In those days the preparation for baptism was a
very long and serious business. Practically every
one was baptized as a grown person. Many were
converts from Jewry or heathendom, and even
people born of Christian parents generally waited
till they were grown up before they applied for
baptism. We have seen how the fathers of just this
time were baptized at a late age themselves, and
how they afterwards protested against that custom.[3]
A person then who wished to be a Christian passed

[1] *E.gr.* Cat. iv, 24, xii, 33, 34, etc.
[2] Catech. vi, 34.   [3] *See* above, pp. 55, 91. 115.

through a long time of preparation, divided into stages by solemn rites, before he was immersed in the font on Easter eve. Of this period of preparation with its rites most curious and interesting traces remain in our present rite of baptism[1] and in our services for Lent and Holy Week. Naturally the arrangements were not everywhere the same. In this matter as in others different churches followed different rites. At Jerusalem, where the use of Antioch prevailed,[2] no doubt many things were different from the Roman practice; but the main outline of the long process of Initiation seems to have been much the same everywhere. The convert was first solemnly admitted to the class of catechumens.[3] This was done by an exorcism, breathing on his face and the sign of the cross.[4] He then remained a member of that class for a long time, often for years. Meanwhile he learned the rudiments of the faith, although everything that belonged to the *discipline of the secret*[5] was still

---

[1] There are two rites of baptism in the Roman ritual. The more primitive one, in which most of the old ceremonies are preserved, is rarely seen now—the *Order of the baptism of adults*. This service, itself a compendium of the old ceremonies for catechumens, is further abbreviated in the *Order of the baptism of infants* that we usually see.

[2] The use of Antioch was itself taken from Jerusalem. The parent-rite of this family of liturgies is that of *St James* in Greek, certainly composed for the city of Jerusalem (*Orth. Eastern Church*, p. 115).

[3] Κατηχούμενος is the Pres. Part. Pass. of κατηχῶ (to resound, then bewitch, then teach) and means *he who is being taught*.

[4] This is the first rite of our baptismal service.

[5] The *Disciplina arcani* was an important element in the teaching of the Church. In order to shield the most sacred mysteries from profanation they were not revealed till just before or just after baptism. The Jews treated their proselytes in the same way, and the mysteries of the heathen sects from the east that flourished during the first centuries (of Mithraism especially) were only revealed gradually to the initiated.

carefully kept from him. When at last the catechumen was considered firmly established in the
faith, had shown that he would live like a Christian
and himself wished to be baptized[1] he was admitted into the next class and became an Elect,
or Competent (competens, φωτιζόμενος, "being enlightened").[2] This was always at the beginning

The Christian discipline reserved the baptismal creed and the
Our Father till just before baptism; and especially the mystery
of the holy Eucharist and the real Presence was not taught till
after baptism. The discipline of the secret seems to have begun
towards the end of the second century. St Justin's (†166) clear
allusions to the holy Eucharist (Apol. i, 65, 66) argue that
he did not know it. But St Irenæus (†202, Adv. hær. iii, 4, 1, 2)
and still more plainly Tertullian (†240, Apol. vii, 1) allude to it.
About the sixth century, when there were practically no more
heathen in the empire, and the whole process of Initiation had
become modified, the practice dies out. Mgr. Batiffol is disposed
to minimize its observance (*La discipline de l'Arcane*, in his
Études d'Histoire et de Theologie positive, Paris, 1902, pp.3—41).
We constantly find that the fathers of the fourth and fifth
centuries, when preaching to mixed congregations of faithful
and catechumens, find that they can only make a mysterious
allusion to the holy Eucharist and add "the initiated understand what I mean"—*norunt initiati*. We have a classical
example in the Roman breviary (in the eighth lesson for the
Finding of the holy Rood, May 3) where St Augustine in his
sermon (*Tract. II in Joannem*) says that if you ask a catechumen whether he eats the Body of the Son of Man and drinks
his Blood the catechumen will not understand what you mean.

[1] To be a catechumen involved fewer responsibilities than
to be baptized and fewer duties; so many people, as notably
Constantine and Constantius the Emperors, preferred to put off
baptism to the end of their lives. *See* Duchesne: *Orig. du Culte
chrétien* (Paris, 1898), chap. ix, *L'Initiation chrétienne*.

[2] Mgr Duchesne (l.c.) and Dr Funk (*Theol. Quartalschr*. Tü-
bingen, 1883, p. 41 *seq.*) show that these were the only two
classes before baptism—those of the catechumens and competents. They were allowed to come to church for the first part
of the Liturgy (the *Missa catechumenorum*), but were dismissed
by the deacon before the offertory. This dismissal is still a
ceremony in all eastern liturgies. In the oldest extant liturgy
(of the *Const. Apost.*) the deacon cries out: "No one of the
catechumens, no one of the hearers (= competents), no one
of the unbelievers, no one of the heretics" (viii, 12). Then
begins the *Missa fidelium.*

of Lent,[1] since baptism was administered on
Easter eve. Half way through Lent came another
service of exorcisms and the first teaching of part
of the discipline of the secret. They learnt and had
to repeat the creed and Our Father.[2] At Rome, at
any rate, the giving of the salt (*sal sapientiæ*, as
they learnt the new wisdom) was part of the rite.[3]
Later came a signing (consignatio) with oil or
saliva, a last profession of faith (Dost thou
renounce Satan? etc.) and an anointing with the
oil of catechumens.[4] At last, during the long
Easter vigil, after the Prophecies had been read[5],
the bishop blessed the font, and the long line of
competents one by one took off their clothes and
went down into the font. They were baptized by a
triple immersion,[6] and then confirmed with
chrism at once.[7] When they came out of the font
they did not put on their old clothes again, but
new white garments. There was a last imposition of

[1] There is a very close connexion between the observance
of Lent and the preparation of the competents for baptism.
See Duchesne, *op. cit.* and Thurston: *Lent and Holy Week*
(Longmans, 1904), pp. 169 *seq.*

[2] This is the *traditio symboli* that forms the second part of our
baptismal service, when the child is brought into the church.

[3] Thurston: *op. cit.* p. 172.

[4] It will be seen, then, that we still carry the child through
all these stages before baptism. We make it a catechumen, then
an elect, and do all the rites that prepare for baptism;
though it is now all done in a few minutes, instead of stretching
over months.

[5] These Prophecies on Holy Saturday are considered by some
people to be the last instruction of the catechumens before
baptism. Father Thurston thinks not (*ib.* pp. 426 *seq.*).

[6] In all eastern churches baptism is still administered only
by immersion.

[7] Certainly at one time in the west too confirmation was
given at once after baptism. Our ritual contains a curious sur-
vival of this in the anointing with chrism that follows baptism.
All eastern churches still confirm immediately after baptism.
The priest confirms as well as the bishop; and we acknowledge
their confirmation as valid.

hands and they received each a burning light. They were now the enlightened (illuminati, φωτισθέντες). For one week they kept their white robes, and meanwhile were taught the last part of the secret discipline—about the holy Eucharist. On Low Sunday they made their first communions and put off their white robes.[1] After this they belonged to the class of the Faithful (fideles, πιστοί) for the rest of their lives, unless through a grave crime, such as especially murder, idolatry or adultery, they fell from it into that of Penitents. It was then to these competents during Lent and then to them again in Easter week when they had become the "enlightened" that Cyril held his catechetical instructions. The first eighteen are for the competents, the last five for the enlightened (p. 167).

3. Was Cyril ever a semi-Arian?

That our saint in later years as bishop was a most steadfast defender of the faith of Nicæa, for which he suffered continual persecution, is a fact that no one denies. It has, however, been suggested that as a priest he conceded so far to the times as to profess one of the many varieties of semi-Arianism, rather than the whole uncompromising Catholic faith. His metropolitan, Akakios of Cæsarea, as we shall see, was a bitter and persistent Arian; and Arianism was the religion of the court under Constantius (337–361). Times were bad for Homoüsians. Did Cyril bend to the storm? Or was it even as a semi-Arian that he succeeded

---

[1] Hence the name *Dominica in albis* (scil. *deponendis*) = *Sunday of the taking off of white robes.* Whatever reasons of sentiment there may be for choosing Corpus Christi or any other feast for the day of general first communion, undoubtedly from the point of view of tradition and antiquity the right day would be Low Sunday.

to the see of Jerusalem when Maximos died? The
reason for this theory is that in his catechisms he
never uses the word *Homoüsios*. The fact cannot
be said to have no significance. That word was the
standard of the Catholic faith. It is undoubtedly
striking that he—evidently purposely—avoids it.
That he did so seems to argue a kind of economy
on his part. But, on the other hand, although he
does not use the term, he teaches what it means
so clearly that no one who heard him could have
the slightest doubt that he was entirely on the side
of the Nicene fathers. He says that Christ our
Lord is "God born of God, Life of Life, Light of
Light, like in all things to his Father."[1] The
allusion to the Nicene symbol is obvious. Again,
our Lord has the same glory as the Father,[2] he
has the "Father's divinity" himself,[3] He is "God
in nature and truth,"[4] born "from eternity," "God
of God, eternal of the eternal Father,"[5] He is
"God born of the virgin,"[6] has the same divine
nature as the Father.[7] "A perfect Father begot a
perfect Son."[8] "From the one perfect Father is one
perfect Son."[9] And Cyril explicitly rejects the
Arian formula: "There was a time when the Son
was not."[10] Whatever reason, then, he may have
had for avoiding the word Homoüsios, however
much one may think that he would have done
better to use it boldly, it is obviously impossible
to doubt that he was as much a Catholic and a
Homoüsian at this time as afterwards as bishop.
Moreover, we may notice that though Akakios of
Cæsarea was an Arian, his own bishop, Maximos,
under whom he taught his catechism, was alto-

[1]Cat. iv, 7, xi, 4.   [2]Cat. vi, 1.   [3]*Ib*. vi, 6.
[4]*Ib*. vii, 5.   [5]*Ib*. xi, 4.   [6]*Ib*. xii, 1.   [7]*Ib*. xi, 18
[8]*Ib*. vii, 5.   [9]*Ib*. xi, 13.   [10]xi, 17–18.

gether correct and Nicene. And if a priest has his bishop on his side he need not much trouble to conciliate a distant metropolitan. Certainly Maximos would not have entrusted this important office of catechist to anyone whose faith was in the least suspect. That he afterwards compromised in order to be ordained bishop is certainly false. The second general Council, that was unswervingly anti-Arian throughout, acknowledged his ordination as lawful and canonical, as we shall see (p. 165), whereas it deposed Arians and semi-Arians.

4. Cyril's theology

With regard to other points of theology, we may note that Cyril very strongly insists on the *Real Presence* and on *Transubstantiation*, of which he gives a most accurate definition: "That which seems bread is not bread but the Body of Christ; that which seems wine is not wine but the Blood of Christ."[1] "It is not ordinary bread (ἄρτος λιτός), but the Body of Christ."[2] "As Christ changed water into wine, so does he change (μεταβάλλει) wine into his Blood."[3] Christians who receive holy communion become "of one Body and of one Blood with Christ" (σύσσωμοι καὶ σύναιμοι Χριστοῦ) and are "Christbearers. (Χριστοφόροι)."[4] Transubstantiation takes place, he says, "by the invocation of the Holy Ghost."[5] The holy Eucharist is a "spiritual sacrifice" and a "sacrifice of atonement."[6]

Like all the Greeks, St Cyril insists very much

[1]Cat. xxii, 9.   [2]*Ib*. xxi, 3.   [3]*Ib*. xxii, 3.   [4]*Ib*. xxii, 3.
[5]*Ib*. xxi, 3. xxii, 6. This would argue his belief that the Epiklesis consecrates: contrast with this St John Chrysostom, p. 127, n. 1.
[6]*Cat*. xxiii, 8. *See also* all xxii and xxiii for the real Presence, or the quotations in Bardenhewer: *Patrologie* (Freiburg i/ Br. 1894), pp. 250–251.

on *Free Will* and the value of good works.[1] But the precious Blood shed on the cross is our Redemption.[2]

5. Bishop of Jerusalem, to Julian's accession (350-361)

Maximos died in 350 and Cyril was at once elected as his successor. In a letter to Constantius he says that soon after he was consecrated a great shining cross was seen in the sky above the holy city and that every one watched it for several hours.[3] The cross was a fit symbol of his reign as bishop. For almost at once he got into trouble with his metropolitan. The first general Council (Nicæa, 325, can. 7) had given to the see of Jerusalem a not clearly defined "succession of honour," meaning, apparently, a place of honour next after the patriarchs, because it is the holy city; but the council had carefully added that the "domestic rights of the metropolis" must be preserved. The metropolitan see over Palestine was Cæsarea (Pal.). It was not till the fourth Council (Chalcedon in 451) that Cyril's successor Juvenal (420-458) succeeded in getting this vague place of honour changed into a real independent patriarchate.[4] Meanwhile the purely titular "succession of honour" inevitably led to friction with Cæsarea. The metropolitan, naturally, was not pleased to see one of his suffragans placed far above himself in dignity, and the bishops of Jerusalem were not always disposed to obey their metropolitan quite so meekly now that they themselves had so high a rank. This difficult position led to a quarrel

[1] *Cat.* ii, 1. iv, 2, 18–19, etc.   [2] ii, 5.
[3] *Ep. ad Const.* M.P.G., xxxiii, 1165–1176.
[4] *Orth. Eastern Church*, pp. 25–27.

between St Cyril and his superior, Akakios of
Cæsarea. A much more important reason for the
quarrel was the question of faith. Cyril was a
Catholic and Akakios was a most pronounced and
determined leader of the Arians. Akakios had succeeded Eusebeios, the father of Church history,
in 340, and had at once distinguished himself by
his opposition to Athanasius and the Homoüsios.
He was present at the Arian Synod of Antioch
in 341 (ἐν ἐγκαινίοις). Later, in 359, he was the
acknowledged head of the forty extreme Arians at
Seleucia.[2] But it was Akakios who here founded a
third party, as a compromise between the Arians
and semi-Arians, on the basis of the word *similar*
only—the Son of God is to be called neither "of
the same" nor "of a different," nor "of a like substance" with the Father, but only "similar
(ὅμοιος)" in general, without any use of the word
"substance" at all. This third party, the Homoians,
are also called Acacians after their founder.

It was then inevitable that there should be trouble
between Akakios and Cyril. In 358 Akakios summoned a synod at Cæsarea, over which he himself
presided. St Cyril refused to go to it, either
because he thought that his "succession of
honour" after the patriarchs gave him a right to

---

[1] Eusebeios (†340) was also an Arian, but of a milder kind;
had he lived he would have joined the semi-Arian party.
Akakios had been his pupil.

[2] Constantius in 358 summoned a synod to Nicæa, and then
to Nikomedia. Eventually two synods met, one for western
bishops at Ariminium (Rimini in Italy) and the other for
easterns at Seleucia in Isauria. Both synods condemned the
Nicene faith. This year, 359, marks the height of the Arian
flood. "Ingemuit totus orbis et se esse arianum miratus est."
(St Jerome, *c. Lucif.* 19). The tide turned almost at once after
this. St Hilary of Poitiers (†366) was present at Seleucia, being
then in exile for the faith.

be judged only by a patriarchal synod,[1] or
because he knew that he had no chance with what
was a purely Arian assembly. So Akakios and his
synod deposed Cyril, in his absence, for these
reasons: that he had in some way disobeyed or
behaved with insubordination towards his metropolitan,[2] that he had sold vestments and vessels
belonging to his church in order to feed the poor
at a time of famine, that he was a Homoüsian.
For these offences he was banished to Cilicia.
Cyril appealed to a greater council, according to
the right given to deposed bishops by the Synod of
Antioch in 341 (can. 4 and 12); meanwhile he was
hospitably received by Silvanus, Bishop of Tarsus.
The next year the situation was reversed. The
Synod of Seleucia, like the twin-assembly at
Ariminium, was semi-Arian, disposed to be conciliatory and opposed to such extreme people as
Akakios. It also made a point of restoring bishops
who had been unjustly deposed.[3] Akakios and
Cyril both attended. Cyril was restored and
Akakios deposed; but Akakios went to Constan-
tinople, where he had the ear of Constantius, held
an entirely Arian synod there in 360, and, by the
emperor's favour, again deposed Cyril.

[1] The canon of Nicæa had left the whole question of the
place of Jerusalem in a confusion. It certainly meant to leave
the canonical rights of Cæsarea exactly where they had been
before. But the bishops of Jerusalem almost inevitably thought
that the situation had changed now that they held so high a
place. The further promotion given at Chalcedon was the inevitable result of Canon 7 of Nicæa.

[2] This is the whole question—which was it? Sozomenos (iv, 25)
says it was because he had disobeyed and refused to acknowledge Cæsarea as his metropolis, in which case he would have
been wrong; Theodoretos (ii, 22) says it was only because he
had taken precedence, which he had a perfect right to do.

[3] It restored St Hilary to Poitiers. The Roman Breviary on
his feast (Jan. 14, *Lectio* v) is not quite fair about the motives of
his restoration.

6. The attempt to build the temple (*c.* 362)

Constantius died just as he had set out to fight his cousin in 361. Julian (361–363) at once proclaimed the restoration of all banished bishops. Like St Athanasius,[1] St Cyril, too, profited by this edict and came back to Jerusalem (361).

The next event in his life was Julian's attempt to restore the temple. Julian, who had been outrageously treated by his Christian cousin,[2] who loathed the endless Arian and semi-Arian quarrels and worshipped the glorious memory of old Greece, spent his short reign in a hopeless attempt to destroy Christianity and restore the old gods. Himself a philosophic pantheist, with a strong tendency towards monotheism in the form of Sun-worship and a taste for the mysteries of the eastern religions[3] as symbols of profound truths, he did us the unwilling honour of trying to revive his synthetic paganism with specifically Christian ideas,[4] while he as nearly persecuted Christians as his magnificent and contemptuous principles of tolerance would allow.[5] But while he hated Chris-

[1]*See* above p. 34.
[2]Constantius had murdered Julian's father, uncle and two brothers. Julian himself spent the early part of his life in a dreary castle in Cappadocia, as a prisoner in daily fear of being murdered himself.
[3]Mithraism especially. He was initiated by the *Taurobolion* in Gaul in 361, just after he had kept the Epiphany in the Christian church at Vienne. Mithra, identified with Apollo and the Sun, was to him the Logos of the Neo-platonists.
[4]*See* the fragment of his letter to a heathen priest in Hertlein's edition (II, 552-555).
[5]For the story of Julian *see* P. Allard: *Julien l'apostat* (Paris: Lecoffre, 1900, 3 vols.—an exhaustive life); G. Negri: *L'Imperatore Giuliano l'apostata* (Milan, Hoepli, 1902), Harnack's admira-

11

tianity, that would allow no rival, he gladly protected all the old national religions that were to
him simply local expressions of the same philosophic truth. The Roman peasant should go on worshipping his Roman nature-gods, the Greek found
in Apollo, Artemis and Aphrodite externally beautiful symbols of the many-sided hidden reality,
the Egyptian inherited from an immense age his
dark mysteries, the Phrygian turned to Attis and
Cybele, the Syrian to Adonis and Astarte, the Persian to Ahura-Mazda and the Babylonian to Marduk.[1] If that were so, why should not the Jew turn
to the God of Israel. Jews had as much right to a
national god as any one else; and although Julian
never concealed his contempt for this barbarous
sect, although he hated their intolerance and still
more the proselytizing spirit of later Judaism, he
undertook to protect them as well as all the other
religions. Only Christians were too utterly intolerant
and arrogant in their claim of being the only

ble summary in Herzog and Hauck's *Realencyklopädie für prot.
Theol. u. Kirche* (3 edition, Leipzig, Hinrichs, ix, 1901, 609–619),
Gibbon's *Decline and Fall*, chap. xxii–xxiv, and the excellent
monograph by Alice Gardner in the *Heroes of the Nations* series
(*Julian, Philosopher and Emperor*, Putnam, 1895).

[1] For a brilliant summary of these eastern religions that
towards the end of paganism had ousted the original Greek
and Roman mythologies *see* F. Cumont: *Les Religions Orientales dans le Paganisme Romain* (Paris, Leroux, 1905) and *Les
Mystères de Mithra* (Paris, Fontemoing, 1902). It should be
remembered that people like Julian who wanted to restore
"Hellenism" were as far removed from the old simple polytheism as their Christian rivals. Philosophy had destroyed the
old beliefs among educated people entirely. Their ideal was
rather pantheism; and the forms of their religion were these
mysteries (Attis, Adonis, Mithra) from Asia that had invaded
Rome and Greece. For Julian's own ideas the sources are his
Or. iv *To King Sun* (πρὸς τὸν βασιλέα ἥλιον, ed. Hertlein, i,
168–205) and *To the Mother of the Gods* (Or. v, εἰς τὴν μητέρα τῶν
θεῶν, i, 206–233).

faith to have any mercy. He wrote a friendly letter
to a Jewish high priest,[1] whom he condescends to
call his "brother," and in another letter he asks for
Jews' prayers and promises to come to Jerusalem
after the Persian war and there to pray to their
god too. A result of this protection to the Jews
was that he ordered the rebuilding of their temple.[2]
He gave large sums of money for this purpose, and
appointed one Alypios of Antioch to superintend
the work. And naturally Jews from every part of the
empire contributed lavishly to the triumph of their
religion. What happened? It is certain that the
whole scheme came to nothing and that strange
portents put an end to the work. Ammianus Mar-
cellinus, the heathen historian, who is, therefore,
not suspect in this matter, says that globes of fire
burst from the ground and killed the workmen.[3]
So the temple was never rebuilt. The Christian
writers[4] naturally saw in this the hand of God
against the attempt to falsify his Son's words.

[1] The priest's name was *Hillel*, which Julian makes into
'Ιουλός.ed. Hertlein, II, 512-514.

[2] Possibly another reason for this scheme was that it would
prove our Lord's words false: "not a stone shall be left upon a
stone" (Mt. xxiv, 2; Mc. xiii, 2; Le. xxi, 6). All the fathers
of this time (Greg. Naz. *Invectiv. c. Jul.* ii, 4; Sokrates iii, 20;
Sozom. v, 22) describe this as his only motive. But none of them
are fair to Julian. S. Gregory Nazianzene's two *Invectives* are
simply unrestrained abuse. Julian is one of the people whom no
one seems able to treat fairly. Till quite lately every Christian
writer poured abuse on the Apostate. Now there is a reaction
(since Gibbon especially) and enemies of Christianity make
him into a fabulously perfect person. Paul Allard (*op. cit.*) has
set an example of a really scientific, moderate and sympathetic treatment of a man who was almost a genius, always
extraordinarily interesting, very ideal in his character and
irreproachable in his morals, rather mad, and in any case
a hopeless failure. If only poor Julian had taken up any
less hopeless cause than that of the gods he would have been
the greatest emperor since Constantine.

[3] Am. Marc. xxiii, 1.   [4] *Loc. cit.*

Sokrates says that St Cyril, when he saw the preparations, foretold exactly what would happen.[1]

7. From Jovian's accession to Cyril's death (363-386)

Julian died fighting valiantly against the Persians in 363. Jovian (363–364), who succeeded him, was a Catholic. Then came Valentinian (364–375), who named his brother Valens (364–378) Cæsar in the east. Valens was an extreme Arian; so he at once ordered that all bishops who had been banished by Constantius and restored by Julian should again go into exile.[2] St Cyril was one of these bishops, so he had to leave Jerusalem in 367. He did not come back for eleven years, when Valens died (378). We do not know where he spent those years of exile. After Valens Gratian (375–383), Valentinian's son, who was already emperor in the west, made Theodosius I (379–395) Cæsar for the east. Gratian and Theodosius were Catholics and they ordered that all Catholic bishops, that is those who were in communion with the Pope and the Bishop of Alexandria,[3] should be restored. Cyril profited by this and came back to his see, where he ended his days in peace. We hear of him once again at the second general Council (Constantinople I, 381),[4] at which he was present.

[1]Sokr. iii, 20. There is an interesting article about this attempt to rebuild the Temple by M. Adler in the *Jewish Quarterly Review* (July, 1893). He thinks that it was never more than a project, and that the whole story of the attempt was made up by Greg. Naz., from whom every one else (including Ammianus!) copied it.

[2]*See* above p. 35.

[3]That is their test of a Catholic: "those who embrace the communion of Damasus and Peter of Alexandria." Theodoretos, v, 2. *cfr* Cod. Theod. xvi, Tit. I, 1, 2.

[4]For this council *see* pp. 100-103.

Akakios of Cæsarea, his old enemy, was dead;
Cyril's own nephew, Gelasios, a firm Catholic, was
now metropolitan. The difficult and delicate situation between the metropolitan and the suffragan
who had a precedence of honour led to no friction
between nephew and uncle. The council acknowledged Cyril's ordination as Bishop of Jerusalem
as canonical, and praised him for his steadfast
opposition to Arianism.[1] That is the last event in
his life of which we know. That he ruled his see as
a zealous and holy Catholic bishop we see from a
letter of St Basil, who says that in his time the
diocese of Jerusalem had greatly flourished.[2]
St Cyril died on March 18, 386. March 18 is his
feast in both rites, Byzantine and Latin.[3] On that
day our Martyrology names: "At Jerusalem St
Cyril, Bishop, who, having suffered many injuries
from the Arians for the faith, and having been
many times driven from his see, at last rested in
peace, illustrious with the glory of holiness; of
whose untarnished faith the second œcumenical
synod, writing to Damasus, gave a splendid
witness." And the collect for his Mass, with its
allusion to the chief subject of his catechism, is
specially beautiful: "Grant us, Almighty God, that
by the prayers of blessed Cyril, the Bishop, we
may so know thee, the only true God, and Jesus
Christ whom thou didst send, that we may
always be counted among the sheep that hear his
voice."

[1]Theodoret v, 9.   [2]Bas. Ep. 4, *ad monach. lapsum.*

[3]Also to the Syrians, both Jacobite and uniate, and the
Maronites. The Armenians keep St Cyril of Jerusalem on the
second Sunday of Lent, the Copts on March 22; the Nestorians
on the fifth Friday after the Epiphany, in a very miscellaneous
collection of "holy Greek Doctors," who include Nestorius
and St Ambrose!

8. Table of dates

c. 315. *Cyril born at Jerusalem.*
    334 or 335. Ordained deacon.
    345–350. Priest and *catechist at Jerusalem.*
    350. *Bishop of Jerusalem.*
    358. Akakios of Cæsarea's synod. Cyril banished.
    358–359. First exile at Tarsus in Cilicia.
    359. Restored by the Synod of Seleucia.
    360. Synod at Constantinople under Akakios. Cyril's second exile.
    361. Restored by Julian.
c. 362. Julian's attempt to build the temple.
    367. Valens banishes Catholic bishops.
    367–378. Third exile.
    378. Restored by Gratian.
    381. Present at the second general Council.
    386 (March 18). *Death at Jerusalem.*

9. Works

St Cyril's complete works were first published by J. Prévot (Paris, 1608, quarto, reprinted 1631 and 1640), then by Th. Milles at Oxford in 1703 (folio). W. Morell had already edited the seven first and the five "mystagogic" catechisms (Paris, 1564). John Grodeck made a Latin translation at Köln (1564). The best edition is that of the Benedictine A. A. Touttée (Paris, 1720, folio, with Grodeck's Latin version). This is reprinted by Migne, Patr. Gr. xxxiii (Paris, 1857). W. K. Reischl and J. Rupp published the works in two 8vo volumes at Munich in 1848–1860, and Photios Alexandrides at Jerusalem in 1867–1868 (two vols, with notes by Dionysios Kleophas). There is a selection in Latin in Hurter's *Opuscula SS. Patrum* (vii, Innsbruck, 1885).

THE CATECHISMS. These are Cyril's only important work. The twenty-three instructions (M. P. G.
XXXIII) were held at Jerusalem to competents
and then to the neophytes between 345 and 350
(see above, pp.151–155). The introductory catechism
(προκατήχησις) is about the great grace his hearers
are about to receive (baptism) and the importance
of this instruction. The first repeats the same
ideas; the second is about sin and repentance, the
third about the effects of baptism; the fourth is a
short compendium of the chief points of the
Christian faith (avoiding all that comes under the
disciplina arcani), and the fifth describes the vir-
tue of faith. Catechisms 6–18 give an exact commentary on the creed, as professed by the Catechumens at their baptism. This is the end of the
first part. On Easter eve his hearers were baptized and confirmed. The last five instructions
(19–23) are addressed to them as neophytes.
There is no longer a disciplina arcani to be
observed, and they have to be prepared for their
first communion on Low Sunday. These five are
called the *Mystagogic Catechisms* (κατηχήσεις
μυσταγωγικαί), because they treat of the Mysteries
(Sacraments). Nos. 19 and 20 explain again the
rite of baptism without any reticence, 21 is about
confirmation, 22 and 23 about the holy Eucharist.

This series of catechisms is famous as the most
complete ordered course of instructions on the
faith we have from the first centuries and as containing incidentally very valuable references to the
rites of Jerusalem in the fourth century.

OTHER WORKS. Besides the catechisms we have
only one complete *sermon* by St Cyril (M. P. Gr.
XXXIII, 1131–1154), on the healing of the man with
palsy at the pool of Bethsaida (Joh., v, 1–9), a

letter to the emperor Constantius (ib. 1165–1176), about the cross that appeared when Cyril was ordained bishop (p. 158), and three short fragments of sermons (1181–1182).

10. Literature

There are two good lives of St Cyril of Jerusalem: G. Delacroix, *S. Cyrille de Jérusalem. Sa vie et ses œuvres* (Paris, 1865), and J. Mader, *Der h. Cyrillus, Bf. von Jerusalem in seinem Leben u. seinen Schriften* (Einsiedeln, 1891). Probst has examined the Liturgy of Jerusalem in the fourth century from Cyril's references, in the *Katholik* (Mainz, 1884, I. 142–, 253–). L. Rochat, *Le catéchuménat au IV siècle d'après les catechésès de S. Cyrille de Jér.* (Geneva, 1875). P. Gonnet, *De S. Cyrilli hieros. archiepiscopi* (he was not an archbishop) *catechesibus* (Paris, 1876). I. Plitt, *De Cyrilli hieros. orationibus quæ exstant catecheticis* (Heidelberg, 1855).

CHAPTER VI

ST CYRIL OF ALEXANDRIA († 444)

CYRIL, after Athanasius the most famous Patriarch of Alexandria, has incurred an undeserved unpopularity chiefly because during his reign a Christian mob murdered Hypatia. He is not the most attractive of the fathers. He had something of the despotic nature of his uncle, Theophilos; he behaved badly to St John Chrysostom, and in his earlier years especially ruled at Alexandria in a way that gave offence to the civil government; but he was a very great theologian and the leader of the Catholics in his time. He is the Doctor of the Church against Nestorianism. In his time again, as in that of St Athanasius, orthodoxy reigned from Alexandria; what Athanasius was in Arian times, that was Cyril against the Nestorians. As the last of the chain of fathers who follow each other since his great predecessor[1] he is called by Greeks the *Seal of the fathers* (σφραγὶς τῶν πατέρων). His name is bound up always with that of the Council of Ephesus. If not exactly lovable, he is a most imposing and princely figure, typical of the great line of "Christian Pharaohs"[2] who held the second place in Christendom and ruled the mighty Church of Egypt from their throne by the sea. And the chief work of his life was not murdering

---

[1] St John Damascene († c.754) comes long afterwards and stands alone in a different age.

[2] This was a common name for the Patriarchs of Alexandria (*Orth. Eastern Church*, p. 13).

Hypatia, but fighting for the person of Christ and the honour of the Mother of God against the Nestorians.

1. St Cyril before he was patriarch (—412)

We do not know in what year Cyril was born. He belonged to one of the greatest of the Greek families in Egypt and he was the nephew of the Patriarch Theophilos, whom we know as St John Chrysostom's enemy.[1] He must have received the education both in sacred and profane letters, of which he made so great use afterwards, at his own city, Alexandria. The Alexandrine schools were still the most famous in the world. During this first period he made friends with St Isidore, Abbot of a great monastery near Pelusium[2] († c. 440). This Isidore had a very salutary influence over Cyril all his life. Cyril calls him his father even when he himself had become patriarch, and it was under Isidore that he spent some years as a monk.[3] The first certain date in our saint's life is 403, and here he appears in no saintly light, for he accompanied his uncle to the Oak-Tree synod and took his part in the deposition of St John Chrysostom.[4] For many years after he still had a grudge against St John. It was not till 417 that Isidore persuaded him to add his former victim's name to the diptychs of Alexandria.[5] This reconciliation after

---

[1] *See* above, pp. 130, 133-137.

[2] Pelusium was a town on the most eastern branch of the Nile, just outside the Delta, near where the Suez Canal now is. Isidore of Pelusium was a disciple of St John Chrysostom and belonged to the Antiochene school. About 2,000 of his letters are preserved in M.P. Gr. xcviii (1273–1312).

[3] Isid. Pel. Ep. i, 310, 323, 324, 370.

[4] *See* p. 136.   [5] Cyr. Alex. Ep. i, 370.

death with Chrysostom is one example of many cases in which Isidore used his influence over Cyril for a good purpose.

2. Patriarch (before Nestorianism, 412-428)

Theophilos died in October, 412. The government wanted a certain Archdeacon Timothy to succeed,[1] but Cyril was elected canonically and became patriarch. The governor of Egypt was Orestes, who pretended to be a Christian to the Christians and talked philosophy to the pagans. And the last remnant of the Hellenism that Julian (361–363) had in vain tried to revive, clustered round the school by the Serapion, where Hypatia taught her Neo-platonism.

Hypatia[2] was the great heathen influence in the city and was believed to be all powerful with Orestes.[3] Very soon after Cyril's consecration there was trouble between him and the governor. Orestes feared the patriarch's masterful disposition—for Cyril was like his uncle in many ways—and was annoyed to see that he, the bishop, and not himself, the governor, was the real master of the city. First Cyril shut up a

[1] Sokr. vii, 7.

[2] Hypatia was the daughter of a philosopher named Theon. "She had acquired so great learning that she was far superior to all philosophers of her time. She had been led by Plotinos to the school of Plato, and she taught all the lessons of philosophy to her hearers. So students of philosophy crowded to her from all sides. Because of the confidence and authority she had acquired by learning she was able to appear even before governors with great effect. Nor was she ashamed to show herself among a crowd of men; for every one reverenced her and honoured her for her great modesty." (Sokr. vii, 15).

[3] "For, since she very often conversed with Orestes, a calumny against her spread among the Christian people to the effect that she hindered a reconciliation between Cyril and Orestes" (ib).

Novatian church at Alexandria and confiscated the goods of the Novatian bishop Theopompos.[1] Then he expelled all Jews from the city, apparently because they had massacred Christians. Orestes protested against this to the emperor (Theodosius II, 408–450), but Cyril got his way. Lastly came the murder of Hypatia. In March, 415, a mob of Christians, led by the Parabolani[2] and by a Reader named Peter, cruelly tore her to pieces on the steps of a church.[3] Various writers have suggested more or less plainly that the patriarch was involved in this crime. Sokrates does not say so plainly, but he implies it, and adds a solemn moral reflection.[4] As a matter of fact, not

---

[1] *Ib*, i, 7. It must be remembered that Sokrates, the authority for all this account, is greatly prejudiced against Cyril. Novatian was an African priest who had made a schism in Rome at the time of Pope Cornelius (251–253). His followers took a line of extreme strictness. They said the Church consists only of the pure, forbade second marriages, and rebaptized all their converts. Novatianism became practically a form of Montanism, of which Tertullian (†240) was the chief defender.

[2] The *Parabolani* ($\pi\alpha\rho\alpha\beta o\lambda\acute\alpha\nu o\iota$) were people who tended the sick, especially in time of plague, thereby endangering their own lives ($\pi\alpha\rho\alpha\beta o\lambda\grave\eta$ $\tau\hat\eta s$ $\psi\upsilon\chi\hat\eta s$). They were counted as forming a minor order, like the *Fossores*, who buried the dead, the *Notarii*, who wrote down acts of martyrs, and other classes that have since disappeared. They were chosen and ordained by the bishop. Being rough and sturdy fellows of a low class they seem to have often filled up the time between plagues by making political disturbances. At one time they were expressly forbidden to attend political meetings. After Justinian's time (527–565) they disappear (*see* Kraus: *Realenz.* II, 582).

[3] "Certain men of fierce character whose leader was a Reader named Peter made a conspiracy and watched the lady. They caught her coming back from some house, tore her from her saddle and dragged her to a church called the *Kaisarion*. Here they stripped her and killed her with broken shells. When they had torn her to pieces they burned her limbs at the place called Kinaron" (Sokr. vii, 15). It will be seen that the Parabolani, as a class, were not nice people.

[4] "This affair brought no small disgrace to both Cyril and

only is there no sort of evidence that he had anything to do with it, there are positive reasons for
knowing that he had not. After the murder a depu-
tation of citizens went to Constantinople to peti-
tion the emperor to prevent such horrors for the
future and to put down the disorderly Parabolani,
and the first means they urge for that purpose is
that the patriarch should stay in the city (Orestes
wanted him banished).[1] Moreover, if ever a man
had bitter enemies it was Cyril. Wilful murder was
considered just as unsuitable conduct for bishops
in the fifth century as it is now. Why, during all
the fierce conflict with the Nestorians, when they
brought every possible charge against him, did no
one think of calling him Hypatia's murderer?
Although to accuse our saint of this horrid story is
a gross calumny, there is no doubt that in other
ways he did give annoyance to the government.
A number of monks from the Nitrian mountains
(Sokrates says 500!) had insulted and wounded
Orestes in the streets of Alexandria.[2] He had their

the Church of Alexandria, for murder and slaughter and all
such things are altogether opposed to the Christian religion"
(*ib.*). Damaskios, a heathen who wrote a life of Isidore the
Philosopher, long afterwards insinuates the same thing (quoted
in the notes of Henri de Valois—Henricus Valesius, on Sokr.
vii, 15. ed. Gul. Reading, Cambridge, 1720, ii, 361). Charles
Kingsley in *Hypatia* repeats the insinuation, and is responsible
for the dislike of St Cyril among many people who have never
heard of him nor of Hypatia, except through that singularly
silly novel (e.gr., the monk's apology of Christianity to the
heroine just before she dies, Raphael's argument against celibacy, Hypatia's philosophic discourse, etc.).

[1] Cod. Theod. *De episc.* xvi, 2 (quoted by Kopallik, *Cyr. v.
Alex.* pp. 20 *seq.*).

[2] They called him a "sacrificer and a pagan (θυτὴρ καὶ ἕλλην)
and many other offensive names." He declared that he was a
Christian, and had been baptized at Constantinople by Attikos.
But the monks would not believe him, and began throwing
stones, one of which wounded him severely on the head
(Sokr. vii, 14).

leader[1] seized and tortured, under which torture
the monk died. Cyril then brought this person's
body to the church and solemnly buried it, while
he preached a panegyric on him, declaring him a
martyr who had died for the faith and "praising
his high soul with many words."[2] "But," says
Sokrates, "even the Christians, or at least the
more reasonable ones, did not approve of Cyril's
enthusiasm for Ammonios, for they understood
that this man had paid the penalty of his own
folly, and had not suffered because he would not
deny Christ. And at last Cyril himself gradually
let the whole matter be buried in silence,"[3] which
was, perhaps, just as well. We hear no more about
St Thaumasios the martyr; but one can understand
that Orestes, who heard of the service and the
sermon while he was nursing his broken head at
home, was annoyed, and that for these various
reasons "between him and Cyril an unrelenting
feud existed."[4]

But the patriarch was not destined to spend his life
in a series of petty quarrels with a shuffling magistrate. Soon a cause arose that was worthy of his high
spirit, and he was able to direct his restless energy
against a danger that threatened the whole Church.

3. Nestorius and his heresy

We have seen that when St John Chrysostom
was banished (404) the government at Constantinople set up first Arsakios (404-405), and after his
death Attikos (406–425) as anti-bishops.[5] After
St John's death (407) Attikos seems to have been
generally accepted as lawful occupier of the see
till he, too, died in 425. Then came one Sisinios

[1] Named Ammonios.
[2] *Ib.* He changed the martyr's name to Thaumasios.
[3] *Ib.*   [4] vii, 13.

(425–427), and after him, not without dispute, Nestorius (Νεστόριος, 428–431),[1] the most important of the many bishops who have left to the Byzantine Church a fame with which their successors would gladly dispense.[2] Nestorius[3] was an Antiochene who had been a monk in a Laura outside the walls of Antioch. He had then been ordained priest and had a great reputation as a preacher. When he became Patriarch of Constantinople the people thought they were to have a second Chrysostom as bishop. In his first sermon preached before the emperor he showed his zeal against heretics, "Give me," he said, "a world free of heretics and I will give you heaven; help me to destroy heretics and I will help you to destroy Persians" (presumably by his prayers).[4] He further showed this pious zeal by shutting up an Arian conventicle, attacking Novatians, Apollinarists, Quartodecimans[5] and all manner of enemies of the true faith. Sokrates says he was a calumniator and a firebrand[6] and that his tongue was unreserved and petulant.[7]

[1] The story of the quarrels as to the succession after Attikos is told by Sokrates, vii, 26–29.

[2] Among the heretics who occupied the see of Constantinople are Makedonios I (344–348, 350–360) the Pneumatomachian, this Nestorius, Akakios (471–489) who made the Acacian schism, the Monotheletes Sergios I (610–638), Pyrrhos (638–641, 652), Paul II (641–652), a number of Iconoclasts in the eighth century and Cyril I (Lukaris) in the seventeenth century. I count only those whom the orthodox too admit to have been heretics.

[3] He is so well known under this Latin form (for Nestorios) that one must leave it for the present.

[4] Sokr. vii, 29—where the early life of Nestorius is described.

[5] The *Quartodecimans* (Quattuordecim = fourteen) were people who, in spite of the decree of the Nicene Council, kept Easter on Nisan 14 instead of waiting till the following Sunday. They made a schism that lasted till the fifth or sixth century.

[6] vii, 29. I conceive that Πυρκαϊά (or Πυρκαιεύς?) means this and not a man who set fire to houses.   [7] *Ib.*

Very soon after his accession Nestorius began to give his favour to the particular heresy that is called after him. At this time Arianism was practically dead and Apollinarism,[1] too, was universally condemned. Every Catholic believed that the Word of God is equal and consubstantial to the Father and that our Lord had a perfect human nature complete with body and soul. There remained the question *how* the Logos, the Word, is joined to this human nature. It was, apparently, as a result of Antiochene theology that Nestorius and his friends defended a *moral* union only.[2] The Logos came down from Heaven and dwelt in the man Jesus Christ, very much as the Spirit of God had filled the prophets. Christ was really and wholly a man (this against the Apollinarists), the Logos was not part of his human nature, but was in some way joined to it. What other way is possible but some close moral connexion, some indwelling of the Divinity that did not affect his person, but made that person its temple? That is the Nestorian heresy. Gradually Nestorius and his party went further, evolved their theory more consistently and so wandered still further from the Catholic faith, as is the way of heretics. Is there any reason for supposing that the Logos dwelt in Christ always? When did the Logos descend into him? Is it not probable that this is what happened at our Lord's baptism when "the Holy Ghost came down on him in the figure of a dove,"[3] and "stayed in him,"[4] so that before his baptism there was no union at all? Nor did they fail to produce arguments for their new theory.

[1] *See* p. 84, n. 1.
[2] Nestorius had been a disciple of Theodore of Mopsuestia, who was, perhaps, the original father of this heresy (p. 193, n. 1).
[3] Lc. iii, 21. [4] Joh. 33.

Christ was born as a little child, grew in wisdom and age and grace,[1] was surprised,[2] wept,[3] suffered pain, died. None of these things can be true of God. In the language of our philosophy, Nestorianism can be put in one very short sentence: there are *two persons in Christ*, a Divine person, the Logos, dwelling in a human person, the man Jesus. The use of the word *Person*, or rather of its Greek equivalents *Hypostasis* (ὑπόστασις) and *Prosopon* (πρόσωπον)[4] was not technically so clear in the fifth century as it became in scholastic times. The Catholic fathers, St Cyril himself, sometimes use the word Hypostasis for what we call nature, and sometimes for person. But the issue is quite clear. The Nestorians divided Christ into two separate beings only joined by a moral tie; the later Monophysites, going to the other extreme, said that Christ's humanity was absorbed and swallowed up by his divinity, so he would not be really man at all. Against both the Catholic faith is that our Lord is really and completely God, really and completely man, and yet he is really, physically, indissolubly *one*. As we say, he is *one person with two natures*, the nature of God and the nature of man.[5] The Nestorians liked the word

---

[1] Lc. ii, 52.   [2] Mt. viii, 10.   [3] Lc. xix, 41.

[4] Since practically the whole controversy was carried on in Greek.

[5] We may as well understand what Nature and Person mean. Our *nature* is what makes us what we are essentially. If you are a man, that is because you have a human nature, a horse has an equine nature, etc. Since it is naturally impossible for anyone to be two essential things at once, we, and all things, have one nature each. An essential change means a change of nature, the old nature goes and a new one comes. A *person* is the individual being who has a rational nature. We do not use the word for beasts nor plants nor stones. But among men (and angels) we are each of us a person complete in himself. I *have* a human nature, I *am* a human person. The person is the real *me*. The

Theophóros (θεοφόρος); it expressed exactly what they meant: the man Christ was "God-bearing"— had God in him. But it was another word that became the standard of either side, according as it was used or rejected, and in this heresy, as on other occasions, the honour of our Lord's mother was the defence of his honour: people who were really attacking him did so by attacking her. What the term Homoüsios had been in Arian times that was the word *Theotókos* (θεοτόκος) now. Theotókos means *Mother of God*, and all Catholics, every one who believes in our Lord's divinity and is not a Nestorian, calls the blessed Virgin so. It follows obviously from the hypostatic union,

person acts and is responsible. You may always substitute the word person for a proper name or a pronoun. "John does so and so," that is: "that person does so and so." "He is wicked" *scil.* "a wicked person." You cannot say that of nature. He is not a wicked nature, though you may say (loosely) that he *has* a wicked nature. Obviously then, since our Lord by the miracle of the hypostatic union is both God and man, he is the only case of two natures in one person. He has both natures, divine and human; but it is the same *he*, the same person. He died (as man) and he (the same person) is almighty and immortal (as God). So far all Catholics have always agreed, from St Irenæus (†201), who says: Jesus, who suffered for us, he himself *is* the Word of God (adv. hær. iii, 16, 1-3), or rather from St John, who says: "the Word *became* (not "took up his abode in") flesh (= man)," and our Lord himself: "I and the Father are one (Joh. x, 30)" and "I (the same I, the same person) spoke openly to the world (Joh. xviii, 20)." Anyone who is not a philosopher says the whole truth quite accurately by the statement: "He is both God and man." It is the same subject (He, therefore one person), and the two predicates express the two natures. It is only when we come to the philosophical terms that we find that they, like all philosophical words, have not always been used in the same sense. Now we say that *substance, essence* (and in Greek φύσις, οὐσία) mean exactly the same thing as *nature.* On the other hand, *suppositum, hypostasis* and πρόσωπον mean *person.* In earlier times the words hypostasis in Greek and substantia in Latin were often ambiguous, meaning sometimes nature and sometimes person.

She is the mother of Christ, the mother of a person and that person is God. The relation of mother and son concerns persons. The mother of a person who is God is just as much mother of God as the mother of a person who is man is mother of man. The title that expresses the great and unique honour of our Lady was not new in the fifth century. It was used by all Catholics, and had been used for centuries.[1] Here, as always, it was the heretics who were the innovators. They began, as we shall see, to preach against this title and to demand that it should be changed into *Christotókos* (χριστοτόκος), mother of Christ, which is non-committal either way. And against them the watchword of all the Catholics, led by St Cyril, was that Mary is the mother of God.[2] We may then

---

[1] Origenes (†252) uses it: *Comm in Ps.* i (Sokr. vii, 32), so also Euseb. (†c.340) *Vita Const.* (iii, 43), Athanasius (†397). *Or. iii adv. Arian.* 14, 29, 33, Cyril of Jer. (†386) Cat. x, 19, Didymos (†c.395): *de Trin.* i, 31, 94; ii, 41, etc. Greg. Naz. (†c.390). Or. xxix, 4, Ep. 101 *ad Cledon.*, etc.

[2] It is curious that most Protestants resent this word, apparently from a general dislike to any honour given to Christ's mother. If they knew anything about it, they would realize that by refusing it they are letting themselves in for Nestorianism as well as their other heresies. I have heard from High-Church Anglicans of that type that loves anything Eastern but hates everything Roman that the word *Theotókos* is right, but not *Mater Dei* or *Mother of God*. Miss I. Hapgood, who has translated a selection of Orthodox services into the funniest mixture of Prayer-book English and American slang (*Service Book of the Holy Orthodox-Catholic Apostolic Græco-Russian Church.* Boston: Houghton, Mifflin and Co., 1906) puts for Theotokos the portentous form: *Birth-giver of God*. Such scruples are superfluous. *Dei Genitrix* is an exact version of θεοτόκος and *genitrix* is simply a *mother*. It is an accident of language that Latin does not lend itself to a compound form so well as Greek in this case. *Deipara* is not pretty. German Catholics translate the word beautifully: *Gottesgebärerin*. On the other hand, in the case of Orthodox who speak a language that does not form compounds, the liturgy puts simply *Mother of God*, as we do. So Arabic:

sum up the Nestorian heresy in these six points:
(1) The man Christ is not God, God is not the man;
but the man is most intimately joined to God.
(2) Therefore the mother of Christ is not mother of
God. (3) The Word in Christ alone can really be
adored; the man receives the name "Only-begotten
Son of God" only in an improper sense, by partici-
pation. (4) God did not himself become our high
priest. (5) God did not suffer nor die. (6) God was
in Christ in the same way as he was in the Prophets (but rather more intimately); God speaks
through Christ. The man Christ is the temple,
organ, instrument of God.

4. Before the Council of Ephesus (428-431)

Having explained the issue we now come back
to the history. Soon after Nestorius had become
patriarch, one of his followers, a priest named
Anastasios, began the fight by preaching a sermon
at Constantinople in which he denied our Lady's
title. "Let no one call Mary mother of God," he
said, "for she was merely a human being and God
cannot be born of a human being." He proposed
the word *Christotokos* instead. Then a bishop,
Dorotheos of Markianopolis in Asia Minor, who
was in the city, preached a sermon of the same kind
and excommunicated every one who called Mary
the Theotokos. Naturally, people were surprised,

wālidat allāh. The Orthodox themselves never conceive the
possibility of there being a difference of meaning between these
two forms. They constantly say: μήτηρ τοῦ θεοῦ in Greek too.
This pretended distinction is like that imagined between
μετουσίωσις and *transsubstantiastio*, a figment of the prejudiced
mind. If Miss Hapgood were a theologian she would not have
troubled about this point, and she would not have put such
appalling heresy as: "did lay aside his godhead" for ἐκένωσε
σεαυτόν (p. 103).

and it was not long before other priests and laymen spoke in defence of the traditional teaching. We notice that at the very beginning, or during the whole time of this dispute, the question turns around our Lady's title of Theotokos. Already people were divided according as they attacked or defended this word. It was when they gave their reasons for what would seem an unimportant detail that the fundamental difference of their views about Christ appeared. Nestorius himself then took the side of his friends Anastasios and Dorotheos and preached a course of sermons against the Theotokos, explaining that it is idolatrous and blasphemous, God cannot have a mother, Mary's son was not the Logos, but a man in whom the Logos dwelled, and so on—in short, explaining and developing the heresy of which from this moment he becomes the champion.[1] On Lady-day, 429, a Catholic bishop, Proklos of Kyzikos, preaching before the patriarch at Constantinople, defended the title that every one was already discussing, and showed that it is only a corollary from the Catholic faith about the hypostatic union. As soon as the sermon was over Nestorius stood up and denied all that Proklos had said. There seems to have been something of the nature of a scene in church. Nestorius further ratified the excommunication against every one who said Theotokos. The quarrel now spread all over the east. In Egypt too people began to discuss it; Egyptian monks read Nestorius's sermons, and some of them said they agreed with him. So St Cyril in his

---

[1] The sermons in Mansi, v, 763: "Has God a mother? Only a pagan (ἕλλην) speaks of the mother of the gods without being reproved. Mary did not give birth to the Divinity (of course not; no one said she did), ... but she gave birth to a man who was the organ of the Divinity."

Paschal letter of 429[1] explained the matter to them and refuted the arguments of the sermons, but without naming Nestorius. Soon after he wrote a long encyclical letter in which he again defends and explains the word Theotokos. Copies of this encyclical got to Constantinople, and the Theotokians there comforted themselves by reading it.[2] Nestorius was very angry and complained of Cyril's interference.[3] Cyril had not interfered at all as yet; both the Paschal letter and the encyclical were addressed only to his own subjects, who were puzzled by the news from Constantinople. But now he writes to Nestorius and remonstrates with him,[4] to which letter Nestorius sends an unconciliatory answer.[5] The champions of the two sides have now taken up their arms. The story of the Nestorian heresy becomes one of a conflict between Cyril and Nestorius, and so, incidentally, between the sees of Alexandria and Constantinople. There is that side to the quarrel too. Apart from the theological question this story is one chapter in what was a long history, the mutual enmity of these two sees.

Alexandria had been—was still canonically—the second see in Christendom, the first in the east. Since the second general Council (381) Constantinople had been scheming and intriguing to get that place herself and to reduce Alexandria to the third rank—a plan in which she finally succeeded, chiefly after the Council of Chalcedon (451) and the

---

[1] The *Paschal letter* of the Alexandrine patriarchs was published each year to announce the day on which Easter would fall; and at the same time they used the opportunity of discussing any question that concerned their patriarchate at the time. *See* above, p. 42.

[2] Cyr. Ep. xi, 4 (M.P. Gr. lxxvii, 81).

[3] Cyr. Ep. ii (*Ib.* p. 81).

[4] Ep. ii (*Ib.* p. 40).

[5] Cyr. Ep. iii (*Ib.* p. 43).

fall of Dioskoros of Alexandria (the Monophysite).[1]
We shall see that Nestorius got sympathy from
other bishops in many cases, not because they cared
about his views but because they were instinctively
on the side of Constantinople against Alexandria.
Next certain excommunicate clerks of Egypt, who
had run away to the capital, stir up feeling there
against their patriarch. Cyril then wrote a second
letter to Nestorius in 430. This is known as his
Dogmatic Letter, in which he more fully explains
the faith;[2] at the same time he wrote sternly to
the rebellious clerks who were calumniating him.[3]
Nestorius wrote to various people too. He tried to
persuade Isidore of Pelusium and John, Patriarch of
Antioch to take his side. In John's case he appealed
of course to the alliance between Constantinople
and Antioch against Alexandria.

Meanwhile the emperor, Theodosius II (408–
450), had heard of the matter. Nestorius at the
court counted on his support. Cyril wrote to
explain the matter to him, to his wife, Eudokia,
and his sister, Pulcheria.[4] The question had now
become so important that both sides, following the
traditional practice of eastern as well as western
Christendom, appeal to the Pope of Rome. It was
St Celestin (422–432) who was called upon to settle
this matter: he fills the same place as judge in

[1] The quarrel between these two sees is an important element
throughout eastern Church history from the fourth century
till the final fall of Alexandria at the Mohammedan conquest
of Egypt in 641. *See The Orth. Eastern Church*, pp. 11–15, and
28–46. Three great incidents in that fight were Theophilos' deposition of St John Chrysostom (*See* above p. 136), Cyril's
deposition of Nestorius, and, later, the deposition of Dioskoros.
In the first and third our sympathies are with Constantinople,
in the second with Alexandria. But they are all parts of one
long rivalry.

[2] Cyr. Ep. iv (M.P.G. lxxvii, pp. 44–50).

[3] Ep. x (*Ib.* p. 64 *seq.*).   [4] M.S. G. lxxvi, 1133–1420.

Nestorian times as does his successor, St Leo I
(440–461) in the later Monophysite disturbance—
in which, however, the positions were reversed,
and Alexandria was wrong. St Cyril then, "compelled," as he says, "by the command of God who
demands vigilance, and by the ancient custom of
the Church," sent a long account of the matter to
Celestin by one of his deacons, Posidonios.[1]
Nestorius also wrote to the Pope, accusing Cyril
of Arianism and Apollinarism.[2] Celestin held a
synod at Rome (August, 430), in which he entirely
approved of Cyril's theology, condemned Nestorius, commanded him to receive back into communion the Theotokians he had excommunicated,
and threatening to excommunicate him unless he
drew up a written retractation of his heresy within
ten days. The Pope also made Cyril his deputy and
legate for the fulfilment of these laws, and sent him
a copy of the acts of this council.[3] It was on this

[1] Ep. xi, ad Cel. (lxxxvii, 80).

[2] Apollinarism was the usual accusation of Nestorians against
their adversaries. Unless you distinguish two persons in Christ,
they said, you confuse his two natures. Just in the same way
the Monophysites later accused their opponents of being Nestorians—unless you identify the two natures you separate his
person into two.

[3] The acts in Mansi, iv, 1017, 1025, 1035, 1047. The fact that
St Cyril was made Papal deputy is important, because it
justifies his interference in the affairs of Constantinople. When
his uncle Theophilos interfered in St John Chrysostom's affair,
it was an unlawful usurpation (above p. 135). But Cyril had
delegate authority from the Pope, which makes all the difference. It has been said that the Pope's attitude is simply
another instance of the hereditary alliance between Rome and
Alexandria as against Constantinople and Antioch. On the
other hand, twenty years later, when Alexandria was heretical
(Monophysite under Dioskoros) Rome took just as determined
a line against her as now against Constantinople. The explanation of the change of ecclesiastical polity is that both times
the Roman Church was concerned, not about alliances, but
about the Catholic faith.

occasion that Celestin and a Roman deacon, Leo (afterwards Pope Leo I), persuaded Abbot Cassian to write his treatise *On the Incarnation of the Lord*.[1] Before Nestorius heard of this Roman synod he wrote again to the Pope describing the whole quarrel as an aggression on Cyril's part and proposing the title *Mother of Christ* (Christotokos) as a compromise between *Mother of God* (Theotokos) and *Mother of man* (Anthropotokos). He also proposed that a general Council should be summoned to settle the question.[2] Meanwhile his friend, John of Antioch, wrote to warn him not to make a schism and to accept the word Theotokos. Obviously the Pope and Cyril would have nothing of his compromise. As a century before, in the case of the semi-Arian *Homoiusios*, Catholics would accept no half-and-half formula. In Nestorius's answer to John of Antioch he dilates on the pride and domineering spirit of "that Egyptian," Cyril (this was always his policy, to enlist sympathy at Antioch), and hopes great things from the council for which he is so anxious. St Cyril, as soon as he got the Pope's letter and the acts of the Roman synod held a synod himself at Alexandria (Nov., 430), in which he drew up twelve Anathemas against the new heresy: Anathema to those who deny that Emmanuel is truly God, and that therefore his

---

[1] *De Incarnatione Domini contra Nestorium* (M.P.L., l, 9–272). John Cassian (Cassianus) was Abbot of a monastery at Massilia (Marseilles). His most famous work is the *Collationes Patrum* (M.P.L. xlix, 477–1328, and in Hurter's *Opusc. selecta*, series altera, iii), xxiv books of conversations, maxims and principles of the fathers of the Egyptian desert, written down for the edification of the monks at Marseilles. But Cassian in the question of Pelagianism conceived a theory of compromise between Pelagius and Augustine, and so became the father of the Semipelagian heresy. He died in 435.

[2] His letter in Garnier: *Præf. histor.* i, 70.

mother is mother of God; Anathema to those who deny that the Logos became man as one Christ; Anathema to those who say that Christ is only a man bearing God (Theophoros), and so on.[1] As soon as Nestorius heard of this, not to be outdone, he promptly drew up twelve Anathemas against the Theotokians, which he sent to John of Antioch as his answer to Cyril's synod, adding: "Thou shalt not wonder greatly at this Egyptian's arrogance, because thou knowest of many such examples already." It is still the idea of representing it all as merely one more case of Egyptian pride against Syria and Greece.[2] Other bishops of those parts, Andrew of Samosata and Theodoret of Cyrus, wrote angrily against Cyril, too. Everything was now ready for a general Council to settle the question finally. The emperor (Theodosius II), urged by both sides, especially by Nestorius, in Nov., 430, sent letters to all metropolitans and bishops of the empire, summoning them to a great synod to be held at Ephesus at Whitsuntide, 431.

5. The Council of Ephesus (June-July, 431)

From Smyrna you may go by the Aidin railway in three hours to the village of Ayasoluk.[3] From here you ride in an hour to the great plain where stand the ruins of Ephesus; they are being very carefully excavated by a commission sent by the Austrian Government. Looking down from the

[1] The twelve Anathemas in Mansi, iv, 1082. The decrees of this synod with those of the Roman one were sent by Cyril to Nestorius, John of Antioch and Juvenal of Jerusalem.

[2] Mansi, iv, 754-756.

[3] *Ayasoluk* is a Turkish attempt at ἅγιος θεολόγος. The "holy theologian" is St John the Evangelist, first Bishop of Ephesus. Fine tobacco grows here.

rising ground (*Panayir Dagh*) to the east you see
the plain stretch out to the sea between the high
mountain (*Bülbül Dagh*—Nightingale hill) and the
river Kaystros. A canal brings the water up to
the great Ephesian harbour. At your feet lies a
glorious and wonderful white Greek city. Standing
out from the long grass, the olive trees and the
carpet of many-coloured flowers, are the columns
of the broad road, the stage of the great library,
the curve of the theatre—temples and baths and
colonnades, broken and ruined now, but still
majestic and splendid in their gleaming white
marble and all eloquent of the rich and mighty
city that was the capital of Asia. It would be
difficult to see without emotion the broad street and
the columns under whose shade St Paul rested, the
pillars and walls that St John knew. Behind, to the
right, is the great *Artemision*, the temple of the
patron-goddess, sunk in water now and neglected,
since no longer great is Diana of the Ephesians.
And over in front you may see the ruin of a later
building, no less impressive than the others. You
will walk across the street and clamber over broken
walls and through thick bushes to stand here, too,
for this is the double church of Ephesus in which
the council was held.

The bishops came in June, 431, from all parts
of the empire. Nestorius arrived first with sixteen of his followers and with armed retainers,
sure of victory because the emperor was on
his side. Memnon of Ephesus had forty suffragans. Cyril arrived with fifty Egyptians. Juvenal
of Jerusalem and his bishops came late, as did
Flavian of Thessalonica with his. Theodosius sent
an Imperial commissioner, Candidian, to keep
order and to prevent strangers and the great crowd

of monks at Ephesus from interfering. And Pope Celestin approved of the summoning of the council and sent his legates, Arcadius and Projectus, both bishops, and a priest Philip, with letters to thank the emperor for having summoned the council. He had already made Cyril his legate for the whole affair: the synod formally recognized Cyril as Papal legate.[1] As legate he presided and the Latins had received instructions from the Pope to acknowledge him as such and in all things to be on his side. They waited some time for stragglers to come in. John of Antioch still did not appear, and it was supposed that he did not wish to be forced to declare himself openly against his old friend Nestorius.[2] At last, on June 22, the synod held its first session in the double church[3] that it was to make famous throughout the world as the place of the third general Council. Candidian, who was Nestorius's friend and apparently hoped that John would come soon and vote for that side, wanted to wait for him still. But they had already waited a fortnight, so Cyril refused to put off the synod any longer.

[1] The "Alexandrine Cyril, who also holds the place of Celestine, the most holy and most blessed Archbishop of the Roman Church . . . . being present." (Mansi, iv, 1280) Arcadius and Projectus are also "the most pious and God-beloved bishops and legates," and Philip is "priest and legate of the Apostolic See" (*Ib.* 1281).

[2] Two of his metropolitans (of Apamea and Hierapolis) gave this reason for his delay. But from the beginning there was something not straight about John of Antioch. He wrote to Cyril saying that he was on his way, had already been travelling thirty days and would arrive in five or six more. He could not possibly have taken really thirty days from Antioch to Ephesus if he had any sort of idea of the way (you have only to keep due north-west all the time). In easy horse-stages of 30–40 miles a day he could have got there in about a fortnight. His letter is in Mansi, iv, 1121.

[3] The double church is a building with two churches one in front of the other.

There were 198 bishops present. Nestorius seems now to have foreseen that things would go against him, so he stayed at home and refused to show himself. In the first session the Catholic faith was declared, the title Theotokos solemnly recognized, Cyril's 12 anathemas confirmed. The next day Nestorius was deposed and excommunicated as contumacious. The second session was held on July 10. The Latin legates, who had not arrived in time for the first, were present at this and confirmed what had passed. It was then that Philip spoke the famous words about the Primacy: "There is no doubt, indeed it is known to all ages, that the holy and most blessed Peter, Prince and Chief of the Apostles, column of the faith and foundation of the Catholic Church, received the keys of the kingdom, and that the power of forgiving and retaining sins was given to him, and that he till the present time, and always, lives and judge in his successors. Therefore his successor and Vicegerent, our holy and most blessed Pope, the Bishop Celestin, has sent us to this synod to take his place."[1] Firmus of Cæsarea in Cappadocia explained that the council had only carried out the Pope's instructions in its first session.

Meanwhile John of Antioch had arrived at Ephesus with his bishops. The council at once sent deputies to him and asked him to come and take his place among the other fathers. But he consulted with Nestorius, and his hatred of "that Egyptian" now conquered his scruples about his friend's orthodoxy; so instead of going to the double church he held a private assembly in his own house. Candidian, who had become more and more sulky with Cyril, went there, too, with a few

[1] Mansi iv, *l.c.*

Nestorian bishops. John, his bishops and these friends of Nestorius, then proceed to excommunicate Cyril, Memnon of Ephesus and all the real council as being Arians, Eunomians and Apollinarists. They depose Cyril and Memnon and want to ordain a new bishop for Ephesus: the Ephesians themselves prevented this. But Candidian sent his account of the matter to his master, so that Theodosius declared himself for John's council and against Cyril's. The fathers of the real council answer the emperor and explain that they have done everything in order and have deposed Nestorius canonically and in accordance with the decision of the Roman Church. The fourth and fifth sessions (July 16 and 17) again invite John of Antioch to come and take his proper place among the fathers, instead of holding a rival sham-synod at home. As he will not do so, his excommunication of Cyril and Memnon is declared null and void and he and his party are, not excommunicated, but suspended for the present. The sixth session (July 22) explained the Nicene creed, and when a member proposed a new semi-Nestorian symbol as a compromise, it forbade any one to change or alter the old one.[1] The seventh and last session arranged some points of discipline, and drew up six canons and an encyclical letter declaring what the council had defined.[2] The people of Ephesus had been on the right side

[1] This is the decree the Orthodox quote against us, because we have added the *Filioque*. As the council had in view the *original* Nicene creed without the enlargement of Constantinople I, its law would fall with as much force on them as on us, if it meant what they said. They are enormously wrong in the whole question of this decree of Ephesus (*Orth. Eastern Church*, pp. 381–384).

[2] The acts of the council are in Mansi, iv–v; a full history of it in Hefele's *Conciliengesch* (Ed. 2) ii, 141 *seq.*

throughout. After the first session they received the decrees, especially the recognition of our Lady's title, with great joy. They accompanied the fathers back to their lodgings [that evening (June 22) with a great torchlight procession. The memory of that procession still clings to the city. The double church was naturally afterwards always called the church of the All-holy Mother of God, the παναγία θεοτόκος. The city, famous already for so many reasons, acquired a new title as the city of the Theotokos. Still the Turkish peasants, who all over the Levant surprise one by their curious memories of local Christian events, have kept a vague consciousness of what was done in the double church,[1] and still as one looks over Ephesus in the evening one seems to see the gleam of the torches move down the great street among the shadows and the ghosts.

6. After the council (431-439)

It was some time before the emperor was persuaded to accept the decrees of the real council. Candidian had poisoned his mind against it, and at first he was disposed to take the side of John and Nestorius. Both synods sent deputies to Constantinople, each accusing the other. Theodosius then thought of a master-stroke and meant to satisfy every one by punishing them all. So he sent his treasurer to Ephesus with a message that he had deposed John and Nestorius, and Cyril and

[1] The *mukari* who went with me and pretended to talk Greek, but couldn't, when we stood in the double church became tremendously excited, and for the first time said something intelligible: μάλιστα, μάλιστα, παναγία θεοτόκος! All the Turks in Asia Minor call our Lady *Panayia*. But he did not know what θεοτόκος means.

Memnon.[1] Then he found that they were still not satisfied, and he further examined the case, having ordered eight representatives from either council to come to him and explain their views. Eventually he was persuaded that Cyril was right, so he allowed him to go back to Egypt, and he let a new Bishop of Constantinople, Maximian (431–434) be ordained on Oct. 25, 431, in place of the deposed Nestorius. St Cyril arrived at Alexandria on Oct. 30, where he was received in triumph as a second Athanasius.

But the bad feeling between Alexandria and Antioch lasted for a long time. John of Antioch had gone home, too, and he was still full of indignation against the Egyptian. In two councils at Tarsus and Antioch the Syrian bishops declared that Nestorius had been unjustly deposed and that Maximian was a schismatical intruder.[2] It was not till 433 that John accepted the legitimate Council of Ephesus and Cyril was able to write to the Pope (Sixtus III, 432–440) that peace was restored between them.

But the Nestorians always kept a strong party in Syria. Their leader, Nestorius himself, retired to a monastery, where he died quietly about the year 439.[3] We hear nothing more of him. But the Syrian

[1] For some time the fathers were kept prisoners at Ephesus.

[2] One expression used by Cyril especially scandalized the Syrians. It was μία φύσις τοῦ θεοῦ σεσαρκωμένη—one incarnate nature of God. This seemed to them patently Apollinarist. It had, however, already been used by St Athanasius (cfr. Mansi, iv, 689). St Cyril himself explained that by φύσις he meant the same thing as ὑπόστασις (Ep. i, ix, etc.; lxxvii, 232, 241, etc.

[3] The latest writer on the subject, J. F. Bethune-Baker (Nestorius and his teaching, Cambridge, 1908), disputes this, and maintains that the heretic lived till the Council of Chalcedon (451), and warmly approved of its teaching. Many modern writers, in Germany especially, deny that Nestorius really meant the heresy of which he was accused.

Schools still taught his heresy, defending it as the teaching of their two chief theologians, Diodore of Tarsus and Theodore of Mopsuestia.[1] They translated the works of Diodore and Theodore into Syriac, Persian and Armenian. These two persons have always been the fathers read and admired by Nestorians.

The centre of Nestorianism was the school of Edessa,[2] under a priest Ibas, who became Bishop of Edessa (435–457). In 489 the emperor Zeno (474–491) closed the school and banished the Nestorians from the empire. They fled across the Persian frontier to Nisibis.[3] Here the bishop, Barsumas (Barsumah, 453–489), became their champion. The Persian king protected them, as being enemies of the Roman empire, and at Nisibis they spread the Nestorian Church that sent missions eastward right across China. Its history forms one of the most curious and romantic, as well as one of the least known, chapters of Church history. There or thereabouts, among the mountains of Kurdistan and in the valley of Urmiah, they still remain, a pitiful

[1]*Diodore*, Bishop of Tarsus (†c.394), was a leader of the Antiochene school, and a defender of the faith against the Arians. He was a Meletian at the time of that schism, and was present at the second General Council. His works in M.P.Gr. xxxiii. His pupil *Theodore* (†c. 428), a friend of St John Chrysostom, became Bishop of Mopsuestia in Cilicia in 392. Both were representative of the Antiochene school that undoubtedly paved the way for Nestorianism (*see* above p. 176). Afterwards they were especially attacked by the Monophysites and for centuries the question of their orthodoxy was the burning one in the east. The condemnation of Theodore was the first of Justinian's *Three Chapters* in 553 (*Orth. Eastern Church* p. 82). Theodore of Mopsuestia is *the Exegete* to the Syrians. His works in M.P.G. lxvi.
[2]Edessa is now *Urfa*, three long days' march north-east of Aleppo. The Moslems say Abraham was born here.
[3]Now Nesibin, five days north-west of Mosul.

remnant,[1] under a Katholikos, who bears the title
of Mar Simeon, calling themselves *Meshihaye*
(people of the Messias), or *Syrians* or *Nasrani*
(Nazarenes).[2] They remember little of the old heresy
that cut them off from the rest of the Christian
world,[3] and only as a general inheritance from
their fathers do they remember in their liturgy,
among the other saints, St Diodore, St Theodore
and St Nestorius.

7. The end of St Cyril (431-444)

Meanwhile, in the great Catholic Church, that is,
the Church of the Roman empire, Nestorianism
soon became a thing of the past. Maximian of Constantinople was recognized by every one, and he
was a determined Theotokian. Our Lady's title
was accepted and used triumphantly in every
liturgy as a continued protest against the dead
heresy, and there is no more trouble about Nestorianism, till the extreme opposite side, the Monophysite party in Egypt, twenty years later
remember it as a convenient accusation against
their opponents.

With the triumph of the Council of Ephesus St
Cyril's work was done. He lived three more years
at Alexandria, the acknowledged hero of the
Catholics. He spent those years in removing the
last traces of the schism and in gradually pacifying
the Syrian bishops who were still sore at what they
looked upon as a triumph of Egypt over Syria. One

[1] There were about 70,000 in 1833 (Smith and Dwight:
Researches in Armenia, Boston, 1833).

[2] They appear to call themselves *Nastoriye* occasionally, too.

[3] But they did not quite forget it. In 1247 in answer to one of
the many attempts at reunion made by the Pope, they sent
a profession of faith to Rome which was quite orthodox, except
that they changed the word Theotokos into Christotokos.

of his last acts was a prudent and charitable one. He stopped an agitation among Catholics to have Theodore of Mopsuestia condemned too. It is true that Theodore had been Nestorius' master and that the root of the heresy can be traced back to him. On the other hand, the cause had triumphed so completely that there was no need further to condemn a dead man, especially as Theodore was so enormously admired by the Syrians that any attack against him would have hurt their feelings very much and would have made their recon-ciliation and acceptance of the council still more difficult. St Cyril died at Alexandria on June 27, 444. He was succeeded by his Archdeacon, Dioskoros. Almost at once the Monophysites trouble began, in which Dioskoros and the Egyptians, pushing the teaching of their hero to an extreme, fell into the opposite heresy.

The Orthodox remember St Cyril of Alexandria as the Seal of the fathers (p. 169). He was the last of the great group that begins with his pre-decessor, St Athanasius; he was also the most syste-matic and complete in his theology. For he not only wrote against Nestorianism; in all theological questions he for the first time drew up an orderly system of dogma, arranging all the points of the faith logically and tersely in a harmonious whole, so that he disputes with St John Damascene the place as systematic theologian among the Greeks that St Thomas Aquinas holds amongst us. The Byzantine Church keeps the memory of "Cyril, Pope of Alexandria,"[1] on June 9, and again with

[1] The Patriarchs of Alexandria very commonly used the title *Pope* (πάπας) as well as the Roman Pontiffs. Another title, still officially used by them (both Orthodox and Copt), is *Judge of the world* (δικαστὴς τοῦ κόσμου), cfr. *Orth. Eastern Church*, pp. 13, n. 2 and 349 n. 3.

the other great Egyptian, Athanasius, on Jan. 18.
He is "the defender of the true and unspotted
faith,"[1] and she remembers him as "a most learned
man and splendid fighter for the Catholic faith,
whom the Supreme Pontiff, Celestin, thought
worthy to take his place as legate at the Council
of Ephesus."[2] Before the Byzantine mitre, which
is shaped like a crown, was worn by all Byzantine
bishops the Patriarch of Alexandria used it as a
special privilege. Greek writers explain this and
that patriarch's titles of Pope and "Judge of the
World" as a legacy from the time when Cyril was
legate of the Roman Pope at Ephesus. So Nike-
phoros Kallistos: "Celestin, the Bishop of Rome,
did not himself come to the synod because of the
difficulty of the journey. So he wrote to Cyril,
telling him to take his place. And it is said that
from that time he (Cyril) received the mitre and
the titles of Pope and Judge of the whole world,
which rights then descended to all the holy bishops
who lawfully occupy the throne of Alexandria."[3]

Pope Leo XIII declared St Cyril of Alexandria
a Doctor of the Church. We keep his feast on
Feb. 9, and he, too, like his namesake of Jerusalem, has a very beautiful collect alluding to the
work of his life: "God, who didst make thy holy
Confessor and Pontiff, Cyril, a victorious defender
of the divine motherhood of the most blessed
Virgin Mary, grant by his prayers that we who
believe her to be really mother of God may be
saved by her protection as our mother." And just
as the memory of Athanasius lives in our churches
each time we say the Nicene creed, so do we echo

[1]So the Council of Chalcedon (451) Act. 3.

[2]*Menaia* for June 9.

[3]Nik. Kall. *Hist. Eccl.* xiv, 34 (M.P.G. cxlvi, cfr. Theodore
Balsamon in Goar: *Euchologion* (Venice, 1720), p. 259.

the voice of Cyril and of the Council of Ephesus
every time we sing in the litany, *Sancta Dei
genitrix*, and every time we say, "Holy Mary,
mother of God, pray for us sinners, now and at the
hour of our death."

8. Table of dates

c. 380 (?). Cyril born.

403. Oak-tree Synod, Cyril present with his
uncle, Theophilos.

412. *Patriarch of Alexandria.*

415. Hypatia murdered.

428–431. Nestorius Patriarch of Constantinople.

429. Beginning of Nestorianism at Constantinople.

429. Cyril's Paschal letter against the heresy.

430. His dogmatic letter to Nestorius.

430. Synod of Rome, Nov., Synod of Alexandria.

431. THIRD GENERAL COUNCIL AT EPHESUS
(June–July).

433. John of Antioch accepts the council.

c. 439. Death of Nestorius (?).

444 (June 27). *Death of St Cyril.*

489. Zeno closes the school of Edessa. The
Nestorians go to Persia.

9. Works

J. Aubert, a Canon of Paris, published the complete text of Cyril of Alexandria in Greek in six
folio volumes (Paris, 1638). This is the only complete edition. It is reprinted with a Latin translation in Migne P. Gr. LXVIII–LXXVII. Cardinal Mai
edited a number of addenda (*Bibl. nova Patrum*)
that are included in Migne. R. P. Smith (*S. Cyr.
Alex. arch. commentarii in Lucae evang. quæ*

supersunt syriace, Oxford, 1858), Ph. E. Pusey
(*S. P. N. Cyr. arch. Alex. in XII Prophetas*, Oxford,
1868, 2 vols; *In D. Joh. Evang. Accedunt fragmenta varia*, Oxford, 1872, 3 vols, and other
works, Oxford, 1877), and C. J. Neumann (*Cyr.
Alex. librorum ctra Julianum fragmenta græca et
syriaca*, in *Juliani imp. librorum ctra Christianos
quæ supersunt*, Leipzig, 1880) have collected
other works and fragments for a future complete
edition.

R. P. Smith translated *A Commentary on the
Gospel acc. to St Luke by S. Cyril* (Oxford, 1859, 2
vols, 8vo), and W. Wright, *Fragments of the
Homilies of Cyril of Alex. on the Gospel of S. Luke,
edited from a Nitrian MS.* (London, 1874, 40),
both from the Syriac. There is an English translation (anonymous) of Cyril's *Commentary on
St John* (London, 1880–1886). H. Hurter includes
the *Encomium in S. Mariam* (the XI homily, fourth
preached at Ephesus) in his series, *SS. Patrum
opuscula selecta* (Innsbruck, 1894, vol. XII: *De
glor. Dei gen. Maria ss. PP. opusc. sel.*, pp. 39–52).

POLEMICAL WORKS. Most of these are written
against Nestorianism. First come two works on the
holy Trinity against the Arians, *The Book of
treasures about the holy and consubstantial Trinity*
(ἡ βίβλος τῶν θησαυρῶν περὶ τῆς ἁγίας καὶ ὁμοουσίου
τριάδος. Thesaurus de scta et consubstantiali
Trinitate, LXXV, 9–656) in thirty-five discourses
(λόγοι), and *Seven dialogues about the holy and consubstantial Trinity* (περὶ ἁγίας τε καὶ ὁμοουσίου
τριάδος λόγοι ἑπτά. De S. et consubst. Trin. dia-
logi VII, LXXV, 657–1124)—dialogues with his
friend Hermias.

The chief anti-Nestorian works are three books
addressed to the emperor Theodosius II, to his

younger sisters, Arkadia and Marina, to his elder sister, Pulcheria, and wife, Eudokia—*Defences of the true faith* (λόγοι προσφωνητικοὶ περὶ τῆς ὀρθῆς πίστεως. De recta fide, LXXVI, 1133–1200, 1201–1336, 1336–1420). Then, *An answer to the blasphemies of Nestorius* (κατὰ τῶν Νεστορίου δυσφημιῶν πεντά βίβλος 'ἀντίρρησις. Contra blasphemias Nestorii l.v., LXXVI, 9–248). He wrote a *Defence of the twelve points*[1] *to the eastern bishops* ('Απολογητικὸς ὑπὲρ τῶν δώδεκα κεφαλάίων πρὸς τοὺς τῆς ἀνατολῆς ἐπισκόπους. Apologia de XII capitibus, LXXXVI, 315–386), and defended them again in his *Letter to Evoptios against the answer of Theodoret*[2] *to the twelve points* ('ἐπιστολὴ πρὸς Εὐόπτιον κ.τ.λ. Ep. ad Evoptium, LXXVI, 385–452) and in a little *Explanation of the Twelve Points* ('ἐπίλυσις τῶν δώδεκα κεφαλάίων. Expositio XII capit. LXXVI, 293–312). After the Council of Ephesus Cyril wrote an *Apology to the emperor Theodosius* (λόγος ἀπολογητικός. Apologia ad Theod. Imp. LXXVI, 453–488), a treatise *On the Incarnation of the Word of God* (περὶ τῆς ἐνανθρωπήσεως τοῦ θεοῦ λόγου. De incarnatione Verbi divini, LXXV, 1413–1420), a work, *That Christ is one* (ὅτι εἷς ὁ χριστός. Quod Christus unus sit, LXXV, 1253–1362), a *Conversation against Nestorius* (διάλεξις πρὸς Νεστόριον. Tract. adv. Nest. LXXVI, 249–256) and a book *Against those who will not call the holy Virgin Mother of God* (κατὰ τῶν μὴ βουλομένων ὁμολογεῖν θεοτόκον τὴν ἁγίαν παρ-

---

[1]That is: of the twelve anathemas (pp. 185-186).

[2]Theodoret (386–458) was a disciple of Theodore of Mopsuestia. He became Bishop of Cyrus (κυρός), two days' journey from Antioch, and for a time defended Nestorius. At the Council of Chalcedon he condemned both Nestorianism and Monophysism and died in the communion of the Church. He was one of the most learned men of his time, and a very good and holy bishop. His best known work is a Church history in five books, a continuation of Eusebeios (from 323 to 428).

θένον. Adv. eos qui nolunt vocare s. virginem genitricem Dei, LXXV, 255-292). Lastly, there is an *Apology for the holy Christian religion against the books of the godless Julian* (ὑπὲρ τῆς τῶν χριστιανῶν εὐαγοῦς θρησκείας πρὸς τὰ τοῦ ἐν ἀθέοις Ἰουλιανοῦ. De scta religione christ. adv. atheum Julianum LXXVI, 503–1064), an answer to Julian's three books *Against the Christians*.

EXEGETICAL WORKS. These take up the most place among Cyril's works. He wrote seventeen books *On the worship and adoration of God in spirit and truth* (περὶ τῆς ἐν πνεύματι καὶ ἀληθείᾳ προσκυνήσεως καὶ λατρείας. De adoratione Dei in spiritu et veritate, LXVIII, 133–1126), in which he explains that, although the letter of the old law is abolished, its spirit remains. Then there are the *Ornaments* (γλαφυρά. Dicta elegantia, LXIX, 9–678) in thirteen books, a commentary on select texts of the *Pentateuch*, commentaries on *Isaias* (LXX, 9–1450), the *Minor Prophets* (LXXI, LXXII, 9–364), and fragments of commentaries on other books of the Old Testament (LXIX-LXX). We have a long commentary on *St John's Gospel* (LXXIII–LXXIV, 9-756), parts of that on *St Matthew* (LXXII, 365–474) and *St Luke* (LXXII, 475–950) and on *Rom.* 1 and 2 *Cor. and Hebr.* (LXXIV, 773–1006).

HOMILIES. Twenty-nine *Paschal letters* are preserved, sermons preached at the Council of Ephesus, of which the fourth (LXXVII, 991–996) on our Lady's title as Theotokos is the most famous, and others preached on various occasions. All are in M. P. Gr. LXXVII.

LETTERS. Vol. LXXVII (9–390) of Migne contains eighty-eight letters written by or to St Cyril. The three addressed to Nestorius (Nos. 2, 4 and 17) were solemnly approved by the Council of Chalcedon.

The thirty-ninth (to John of Antioch), sometimes called the symbol of Ephesus, was approved in the same way.

10. Literature

J. Kopallik, *Cyrillus von Alexandrien* (Mainz, 1881), is the standard life. N. Παγίδας: Κύριλλος ὁ Ἀλεξανδρείας ἀρχιεπίσκοπος, Leipzig, 1884. A. Largent, *St Cyrille d'Alex. et le concile d' Ephèse* (Paris, 1892). J. Kohlhofer, *S. Cyr. Alex. de Sanctificatione* (Würzburg, 1866). The source for the history of the Nestorian heresy is *Liberati breviarium causæ Nestorianorum et Eutychianiorum* (in M. P. L. LXVIII). *See* also Sokrates, VII, 29 *seq.* Theodoret, *Hær.* fab. IV, 12. Hefele, *Conciliensgeschichte* (ed. 2), II, 141 *seq.*

CHAPTER VII
ST JOHN OF DAMASCUS († c. 754)

JOHN of Damascus, surnamed Chrysorroas,[1] monk and priest near Jerusalem, is in most ways unlike any other father of the Church. Unless we count St Bernard († 1153) one, John is the last of the fathers. In any case, he is the last Greek father, coming long after the others, alone in a very different age. He spent all his life under the government of a Mohammedan khalifah. His work as a writer was rather to compile and arrange what the older fathers had said than to add to it. He is the first of the long line of Christian Aristotelians, and one of the two greatest poets of the eastern Church.[2] He was (with St Theodore of Studion) the chief defender of images during the Iconoclast troubles, and he is more than any other author the theologian studied in Orthodox colleges. His treatise *Of the orthodox faith* is the standard text book in their schools still, as St Thomas Aquinas' *Summa theologica* is in ours. And he is to them the last court of appeal in theological ques-

[1]Χρυσορροάς, *Gold-flowing*, is the old Greek name of the chief river of Damascus (in Arabic *Nahr barada*) ; *see* p. 204.

[2]The other poet is Romanos the Singer (ὁ μελῳδός), a deacon of Beirut († c. 565). He wrote 1,000 hymns, of which the Byzantine liturgical books have preserved about eighty. Krumbacher (*Byzant. Litter.*, Munich, 1891, pp. 308–309) thinks that some day Romanos will perhaps be counted greatest of all Christian poets. His most famous hymn is one for Christmas, beginning: *To-day the Virgin* (ἡ παρθένος σήμερον) which was sung very solemnly while the emperor sate at dinner on Christmas day. The Orthodox (and Melkites) keep the feast of St Romanos the Singer on Oct. 1, on which day the Menologion tells his life.

tions. No Orthodox Christian would dare contradict St John Damascene, though occasionally they have to explain what he really meant—as when he writes of the procession of the Holy Ghost from the Father through the Son. We know too little of his life; but to us also he is a very interesting and sympathetic person whose life and times form a singularly picturesque chapter of eastern Church history.

1. The City of Syria

The real eternal city is Damascus, the head of Syria. Centuries before Rome was founded it was great and flourishing, the greatest city of western Asia. When Solomon reigned at Jerusalem Razon, his rival, ruled over a great kingdom at Damascus;[1] even then it was an ancient place, beside which Jerusalem was a city of yesterday. Far back in the days when the Chananæan was in the land, Abraham took with him "this Damascene Eliezer."[2] Josephus says Damascus was founded by Uz, the grandson of Sem.[3] Who can say how old it is? Far back as you can trace into the mists that hang over the first age of Syrian history, through them you always see this gleaming white city by the river, at the head of the caravan roads. Tens of centuries ago Damascus was queen of Asia. Through all the changes since, whatever rulers may reign, whatever religion may be taught, nothing has displaced her. The Egyptian ruled here seventeen centuries before Christ, the Assyrian came and the Chaldee, the Persian, the Macedonian, the Roman and the Arab, and always Damascus was the head of Syria.

To-day still it is the chief town between Constanti-

[1] 3 Kings, xi, 23. [2] Gen. xv, 2. [3] *Ant. Jud.*, i, 6, 4.

nople and Cairo in one direction, between Rome and
Bombay in the other. For whatever else may change,
nothing can affect its superb position. What a great
harbour is, at the point where all ships must pass,
that is Damascus at the head of the great roads of
western Asia. Still, as for untold centuries, it is
from Damascus that the long lines of caravans
start. One great route goes across the Syrian desert
to Baghdad, another, the Pilgrims' way, due south
through Palestine to Mecca; northward the roads
lead to Hama, Aleppo and across Asia Minor to
Stambul, north-east to Mosul and on to the
Caspian Sea; to the west across the Anti-Lebanon
in one day[1] you may reach Beirut and take ship for
any part of the world.

At the edge of the great desert Damascus stands
like a heavenly city. Water is the one thing needful
in these parts, and Damascus has water in abun-
dance. It is the water and its position that explain
how this city must always be the chief place of
western Asia. From the Anti-Lebanon streams flow
down to the gardens of Damascus; there is the
Nahr barada (Cold River), the old Golden Stream
(Chrysorroas) of the Greeks, and countless other
waters that flow round and through the city in a
silver network. One can understand Naaman's
indignant question: "Are not Abana and Pharphar,
rivers of Damascus, better than all the waters of
Israel?"[2] For seven miles these rivers flow through
gardens and orchards around the city. Looking
down from the Salihiye height you may see the
bright green of the apricot groves (rarest sight in
Syria), a broad girdle around the city whose domes
and minarets stand up white and palest gold or
flushed with the faintest red, all iridescent with

[1] In nine hours by the railway now.　　[2] 4 Kings, v, 12.

subtle suggestion of many colours in its gleaming whiteness, like a pearl set in emeralds. To come back to Damascus from the hideous rocks of the Hauran is like going up to the gates of heaven after hell. After the parched sand and burning rocks you walk among green rushes under showers of apricot blossom and hear the water trickling beneath the cool damp banks; and all through the shady bazaars where you look up and see the minarets, pencils of dazzling white against the blue, you hear the fountains plashing in the courts of the houses. No wonder that the Bedawin from their sultry tents look across to the green patch on the horizon and tell you that there certainly is the most beautiful place on earth; no wonder that every Arab poet sings of the glories of the City of Syria; and no wonder that Mohammed the Prophet when he looked over Damascus said he dared not go down into it, since a man only once may enter heaven.

Naturally every one who set out to conquer Syria thought first of taking the City of Syria.[1] Since the khalifahs reigned there splendidly in the first and best age of Islam (A.H. 41–137, A.D. 661–753) people have almost forgotten that Damascus was for centuries a great Christian town. It was on the way to Damascus that St Paul was converted, and in a house in the street that is still called straight at Damascus that he was baptized.[2] From the time the empire became Christian to the Arab conquest of

[1] *Madīnat ash-Shām* (or *Shām* alone) is the name that in Arabic has almost displaced the old Dimishk (Demeshek). Damascus is called *Shām* (Syria), just as Cairo is *Miṣr* (Egypt). To distinguish the city from the land you must say *Madīnat ash-Shām* (city of Syria) and *Bilād ash-Shām* (land of Syria).

[2] Act. Ap. IX, 1–19. The *Sūk at-Tawīle* from the *Bāb Sharkī* (Eastern Gate) by the Melkite patriarchal church, right through the town (east—west) is still called *Darb al-Mustakīm* (Straight Street). Carpets and silk are sold here.

Syria Damascus rivalled with Antioch as the chief town of Christian Syria. It had a great and splendid church, that of St John, in which was kept the Baptist's head.[1] This church, built on the site of a heathen temple, is one of the famous basilicas of Justinian (527–565). The bishop of Damascus took the second place after his patriarch (of Antioch), and the city was an important frontier-fortress of the empire over against the desert. After the battle of Yarmuk (634) at which the Romans lost Syria, 'Omar, the second khalifah (A.H. 11–23, A.D. 632–644) sent Abu-'Ubaida to take Damascus. Since then it has been under Moslem rule. The Crusaders never succeeded in taking it, though in 1126 they came up to its walls.

It was from the time Mu'awiya, the first Ommeyade (A.H. 41–60, A.D. 661–680) set up his capital here till his race was dethroned (A.H. 132, A.D. 750)[2] that Damascus reached its greatest prosperity as centre of the Mohammedan world. The Ommeyade khalifahs spent enormous sums on adorning the city and building mosques. They were neither unjust nor harsh to their Christian subjects. At first they allowed them to keep half of the great church, while the other half was made a mosque;[3] and the Christians had fifteen other churches. Although Syria was then full of Monophysites,[4] the inhabitants of the great cities, who

[1] Now the mosque of the Ommeyades (Jāmi' al-'Umawī). The saint's head is still kept here with great honour, and Damascenes swear by "the head of Yahya," which is what they call St John Baptist.

[2] In 750 Marwan, the last Ommeyade in Syria, was defeated and killed by Abu'l-Abbās, called as-Saffāh, who founded the Abbasside line. As-Saffāh's brother, Abu-Ja'far, called Al-Mansur, removed his capital to Baghdad in A.H. 150, A.D. 753.

[3] Walid (A.H. 86–96, A.C. 705–715) took away their share from the Christians. Since his time the whole church is a mosque.

[4] Since the Council of Chalcedon (451), Monophysism had

were Greek by blood and spoke Greek, were mostly Orthodox.[1] And we find that the tolerance of these khalifahs, though it did not go as far as putting unbelievers on an equal footing with Moslems, allowed both Christians and Jews to fill important places and often to amass great fortunes. The Rayahs had to pay their poll-tax, and to submit to all the other humiliating conditions appointed by Moslem law, of course. But the Commander of the Faithful was glad to make use of their superior skill in most arts, and since his religion taught him perfectly correct principles of justice,[2] if he was an honest and decent person (as many of these Ommeyades certainly were), he paid his servants liberally and allowed them to profit by their service. Jews had a great reputation for medicine, so the khalifah's doctor was nearly always a Jew, and Christians were employed as architects,[3] scribes and administrators. The life of our saint will show us the curious sight of a Christian father of the Church protected from a Christian emperor and able to attack that emperor's heresy without fear, because he lived under a Moslem khalifah.

become a national cause with western Syrians, as was Nestorianism in the eastern part. The real national church of native Syrians is the Jacobite sect.

[1] And, of course, Catholic till the schism of the ninth and eleventh centuries.

[2] It is only fair to remember that the Rayahs were enormously better off than Jews or heretics under mediæval Christian kings. Our complaint now is that whereas Christendom has at last learned tolerance, Mohammedan governments have changed nothing since they began.

[3] A great number of "Saracen" buildings in Syria, Egypt and Spain were, as a matter of fact, built by Christian Rayahs.

2. Before Iconoclasm (*c.* 680-726)

At the end of the seventh Christian century,
during the years 65–86 of the *hijrah* (A.D. 684–705)
Abdul-Malik, son of Marwan, the fifth prince of
the house of 'Ummeyah, reigned at Damascus.
He cleared Syria of his domestic enemies, the
avengers of Hussain,[1] who still rebelled against the
Ommeyades, made himself master of Arabia, Irak,
Chaldea and all Northern Africa. At his court was
a Christian named John "who kept the flower of
piety and the fragrance of Christian knowledge in
the midst of thorns."[2] This John is the father of
our saint. He held an important place under the
Mohammedan government, being the chief officer
in the revenue department. This place seems to
have been hereditary in the family. They were all
good Christians; "God blessed them as he had
blessed Daniel among the Assyrians (he means
Chaldeans) because of his piety and Joseph among
the Egyptians, although they were captives in a
strange and hostile land."[3] The Arabs gave John
an Arabic name, *Al-Mansur*,[4] which seems to have
become a kind of family surname, since our saint,
the son, is commonly called John Mansur too. The
father then was an excellent man who spent all his
money on redeeming Christian captives and other
works of charity. He was very rich and had pro-

[1] Hussain, the younger son of 'Ali Ibn Abu Tālib and grandson of the Prophet, was barbarously killed (680) at Kerbela,
twenty-five miles north-west of Kūfa in Mesopotamia, by
command of Yazid I (A.H. 40–64, A.D. 661–683), the second
khalifah of the Ommeyade line. The story is well-known from
Gibbon, chap. l.

[2] Johannis Hieros, *Vita S. P. N. Joh. Damasc.* v (ed. Lequien,
p. 3). This is the work from which we know the story of St John
Damascene (*see* p. 247). I quote from it throughout.

[3] *Ib.* p. 4.

[4] Meaning: *He who is helped, Adiutus.*

perty all over Judea and Palestine.[1] He was, of
course, a Greek by blood, or, at any rate, his family
had long been completely hellenized. St John
wrote always in Greek.

The saint was born at Damascus towards the end
of the seventh century. We do not know the date of
his birth, and can only conjecture that it was probably between 680 and 690. He was baptized as a
baby,[2] and was carefully educated in all suitable
knowledge. His biographer gives an amusing description of what he did *not* learn: "His father then
took care to teach him, not how to ride horses, not
how to wield a spear, not to shoot arrows, not to
hunt wild beasts and change his natural mildness
into beastly cruelty, as happens to many who commonly lose their tempers (in hunting) and rush about
in a furious rage. John, his father, a second Chiron, did
not teach him all this, but he sought a tutor learned
in all science, skilful in every form of knowledge,
who would produce good words from his heart;
and he handed over his son to him, to be nourished
with this kind of food."[3] Then he was able to pro-
cure another teacher for the boy. The Arabs carried
on plundering excursions along all the Mediter-
ranean coasts and always came back with a number
of prisoners, whom they made slaves. From one
of these raids on the coast of Sicily they brought
back a monk named Cosmas.[4] This monk was
"beautiful in appearance and more beautiful in his
soul."[5] When the Arabs were about to murder
some of the captives who were no good as slaves,

[1] *Vita Joh.* p. 4.
[2] The practice of putting off baptism, of which we have seen
many examples, had altogether come to an end by now.
[3] *Vita*, vii, p. 5.
[4] He was a Greek, of course. Sicily was still part of Greater
Greece.
[5] *Vita*, viii, p. 5.

these martyrs threw themselves at the feet of Cosmas and asked his blessing. The Arabs, seeing this, think he must be a great prince in his own country and ask him what his rank is. Cosmas answers: "I have no worldly dignity, but only that of a priest.[1] Otherwise I am only a useless monk who have studied philosophy, not only our philosophy which consists in the love of God, but also that which makes men in the world wise. " Having said this his eyes were filled with tears,[2] a natural result under the circumstances.

The author of the Life tells us great things of Cosmas's learning. He knew grammar and logic, as much arithmetic as Pythagoras and as much geometry as Euclid; and he had studied music and poetry and astronomy. "Such was Cosmas, but I leave others to praise him. My intention here is to tell the fame of John."[3] The father of our saint bought Cosmas for a great price from the government, and from that time the learned monk becomes his son's tutor and master. They study all these sciences diligently, but especially theology, with such good result as St John's later fame as a theologian shows. While he was learning from the Sicilian monk in his father's house his studies were shared by a friend who seems to have been an adopted son of the older John and an adopted brother of our saint. This friend was also named Cosmas. He eventually accompanied St John to the monastery in which they both became monks, and became a saint and a poet—St Cosmas the Singer[4]—only less famous than St John Damascene.

[1] The old idea that a monk could not be a priest had disappeared by now, and a certain number of monks were regularly ordained to give sacraments to the others. These are the ἱερομόναχοι, that still form a special class in eastern monasteries. [2] *Vita*, viii, p. 5. [3] *Vita*, xi, pp. 7, 8. [4] Κοσμᾶς ὁ μελῳδός.

In spite of his theological training John did not
at first propose for himself any other career than
that of his father. This place as minister of the
revenue department seems to have been hereditary
in the family; so when the father died the son took
his place and served for a time under the khalifah.
In 705 Walid I (A.H. 86–96, A.D. 705–715) succeeded his father, Abdul-Malik. He was the best of
the Ommeyade sovereigns, humane, charitable,
just, and a splendid patron of letters and arts. He
built hospitals, schools and granaries; he enlarged
and beautified the great mosque at Damascus,[1]
the Dome of the Rock[2] at Jerusalem and the mosque
over the Prophet's tomb at Madinah. Since he was
tolerant and just there was no special difficulty for
a Christian in serving his government, and John
already during this first part of his life practised
in a Moslem court all Christian virtues. His
biographer tells of his goodness in general and
specially praises his humility. Although he was
so learned he was not puffed up, "but just as the
branches of a noble tree, when they are laden with
precious fruit, bend down towards the ground, so
he, bearing a great weight of learning and scholarship, bowed down in meekness."[3] The comparison
is a pretty one and suggests the branches heavy
with golden apricots that shade the walls of
Damascus. It seems that St John lived at the
capital and filled his post in the government till
about the year 730. Then he went to be a monk.[4]

[1] This is the old church of St John, from which he finally
expelled the Christians.

[2] *Qubbat as-Sachrah*, the beautiful mosque that stands in the
middle of the place of the old temple. Although it is commonly
called the mosque of 'Omar, it was built by Abdul-Malik,
Walid's father.

[3] *Vita*, xii, p. 8.

[4] The khalifahs under whom he served after Walid's death

But already, before he left the world, he had begun the great work of his life, the refutation of Iconoclasm.

3. The Iconoclasts (726-842)

The Iconoclast heresy was the last of the series of storms that swept over the eastern Church since Arianism. It lasted altogether 116 years, from 726 to 842. Almost immediately after it came the schism of Photius (857) that cut her away from the rest of the Christian world, and left her too dead even for a great heresy.

Iconoclast means an *Image-breaker*.[1] The issue was this. Since the days when they had hidden in catacombs Christians had painted pictures of their mysteries, of our Lord and of his saints. Every one who has seen a catacomb has been shown the rude wall-paintings of scenes in our Lord's life, allegorical representations of the holy Eucharist, pictures of the good Shepherd, of the holy mother with her Child, of the apostles. As soon as the Church was free and more prosperous, naturally these representations became more artistic, richer, more elaborate. It was a difference of taste rather than of principle that led to the greater use of carving and of solid statues in the west, and of flat paintings, mosaics and bass-reliefs in the east. There is no theological difference between a solid representation and a flat one; moreover, the divergence is only a very general one. There were plenty of statues in the east before the Iconoclast troubles.

The Lateran museum contains what is, perhaps, the most beautiful Christian statue ever

are Sulaimān (715–717), 'Omar II, the Pious (*as-Salah*, 717–720), Yazid II (720–724), Hisham (724–743).

[1] εἰκονοκλαστής.

made, a Good Shepherd of the fourth century.[1]
The well-known bronze St Peter in his basilica at
Rome is of the fifth century. Obviously the sign of
the cross was from the beginning the Christian
standard, long before Constantine put it on his
banner.[2] There are numbers of crosses in the catacombs.[3] It was a natural development to add to
the cross a figure of our Lord. The mock-crucifix
on the Palatine shows that the crucifix was known
before Constantine.[4] The first certain evidence we
have of a representation of our Lord's death does
not occur till some time later. In the time of
Justinian (527–565) there was a picture of the
crucifixion in a church at Gaza in South Palestine, and Anastasios Sinaitikos (c. 550) painted one
in a book. Venantius Fortunatus († 603) saw an
embroidered crucifix at Tours and Gregory of
Tours (c. 593) refers to a statue of the crucifix at
Narbonne.[5] It is probably merely by chance that
we do not find a plain reference to it earlier,
though possibly before Constantine the shameful
nature of death by crucifixion may have made
Christians shy of putting such pictures in public,

[1] This statue has been often photographed. A print of it may
be seen on p. 227 of F. X. Kraus: *Gesch. der christl. Kunst I*
(Freiburg, Herder, 1896), and it forms the frontispiece to
S. Beissel, S.J.: *Altchristl. Kunst u. Liturgie in Italian* (Herder,
1899).

[2] Constantine's cross was formed by the monogram of Christ:
XP.   [3] *See* Kraus, *op. cit.* i, pp. 130–133.

[4] The mock-crucifix is a caricature of a man worshipping a
crucified figure with an ass's head, and the inscription, in
Greek: *Alexamenos worships God*. It was scratched by a pagan
soldier on the wall in mockery of a Christian comrade. Its date
is the beginning of the third century. At one time it was disputed whether the thing was meant for Christianity at all:
I believe that practically every one now admits that it was. *See*
Garrucci: *Il crocifisso graffito* (Rome, 1857), Kraus, *op. cit.* i, 172
seq., and his *Das Spottcrucifix vom Palatin* (Freiburg i/Br. 1872).

[5] Kraus, *op. cit.* i, 173.

where pagans could see them. For the same reason,
apparently, our Lord was long represented as alive
on the cross, not dead, generally fully robed and
without any appearance of pain. People insisted
more on the triumph of the cross, the idea expressed by the line, *Regnavit a ligno Deus*, than on
the pathetic and tragic side of Christ's death. In
eastern Christendom a much more popular picture
was that of our Lord enthroned in glory, surrounded by his court of saints and accompanied
by very beautiful and subtle mystic symbols.
So in east and west for centuries pictures and
representations of holy things had formed a normal
and prominent part of Christian life.

Naturally these pictures and statues were treated
with respect. A sign inevitably shares in the honour
of its archetype. No one had ever thought that we
adore these things. Every Christian knew the first
commandment quite well, and when we come to
the first Christian centuries it is rather late to suppose that anyone really believed he could pray to
a painting.[1] On the other hand, paintings and
statues form as right and as natural a visible sign
of things unseen as motions of our body, kneeling,
standing, lifting up hands are of invisible attitudes
of mind. And to insult them is to insult the persons
they represent, to honour the real thing involves a
delegate honour paid to its picture. It was a waste
of time in the eighth century, as it would be now,

[1] The pagans did not adore their statues at that time either.
It is only in a very low state of civilization that anyone can do
so stupid a thing. To suppose that Julian and the Greek philosophers really thought that their statues could hear them is
either a ludicrous error or a gross calumny. To them, too,
statues were signs and types only. What was wrong with pagans
was that their idols were signs of false gods. To honour a
statue of your god is perfectly reasonable, but it must not be a
statue of Apollo nor Athene.

to explain to Catholics that their statues are really
only wood or stone, and that they can neither see
nor hear nor help us.

However, at this time suddenly a storm of persecution burst against holy pictures and all who used
them; and a succession of emperors suddenly discovered that all such pictures were idolatrous and
that the Church must go back to a purer faith and
keep the first commandment. The question at issue
then was not in itself an absolutely essential one.
Pictures and statues are not essential. But it was
naturally one that made more disturbance than
would a greater, but less obvious, controversy.
Simple people might spend their lives in peace and
go to church regularly without ever understanding
much about the mysteries of nature and person in
Christ; but the poorest peasant understood what
was happening when the government sent soldiers
to tear down and break up the holy pictures. And
all Catholics, not only the simple people but
theologians, and philosophers, monks, bishops,
patriarchs and popes, stood out to the end for
the pictures, and martyrs shed their blood for
them. They could not let a venerable and ancient
practice go at the command of a secular tyrant,
they could not admit that the whole Church had
practised idolatry till now, nor even seem to
acknowledge the heretical confusion and calumny
that was the argument against the holy eikons.
Iconoclasm was a heresy because it involved a
heretical argument; and any point of Church discipline is worth dying for, if it is attacked by a
government that claims the right to make laws
for the Church.

The movement against the eikons seems to
have begun through Mohammedan influence. No

Moslem will ever have a picture of any living thing; that is a fundamental point of his law.[1] The khalifahs Yazid I (680–683) and Yazid II (720–724) made a crusade against pictures, considering them to be idols. It seems strange that Christians should have followed the hereditary enemies of their faith in such a matter as this; but there were some who did so. A Nestorian bishop, Xenaias of Hierapolis (Ba'albek in Syria), took up the idea,[2] and gradually a party was formed of people who wanted to do away with all holy pictures. Their arguments were, first that such pictures are idolatrous and forbidden by the first commandment, and secondly that they scandalize and frighten away Jews and Moslems from Christianity. Then the government took up the cause of these people and the Iconoclast persecutions began.

"At that time Leo the Isaurian ruled the Roman empire, who raged like a furious lion against the venerable eikons[3] and against the orthodox congregation of the Church."[4] Leo III, the Isaurian[5]

[1] The Shiahs have modified this, and the Shah of Persia puts his head on stamps. But any sort of picture of a man is still an abomination to the Sunni. In Turkey the Sultan's autograph takes the place of his portrait on coins or stamps; it is treason to have a picture of him. He is the only sovereign who has never been photographed, or, at least, whose photograph no one has ever seen. This hatred of pictures has produced one good effect among Moslems. Since they have strong natural artistic feeling they express it in the only way they may, by writing texts. Most mosques are adorned with superbly beautiful inscriptions, and the artist in Islam is the scribe. So they have always taken that art very seriously and have kept a tradition of beauty in writing that no one else has. The Arab is the only man who can write really beautifully.

[2] Hardouin, *Concil. Coll.* iv, 306.

[3] Eikon (εἰκών) is Greek for an image. It is a convenient word, first because it became a kind of technical name used in Latin too (Icon), and also because it covers both pictures and statues.   [4] *Vita, Joh. Dam.* xiv, p. 9.

[5] Isauria, his birthplace, is in the south of Asia Minor.

(717–741), who is remembered in Church history as the Iconoclast persecutor, was, in spite of that, a very valiant and heroic prince. In his reign for the first time the Moslems came to the gates of Constantinople (717), and Leo drove them back and then carried on a victorious war against the enemies of Christendom, till he utterly routed them at Akroinos in 740. But he was tyrannical to his own subjects. In 722 he wanted to force all Jews in the empire to be baptized, and he cruelly persecuted the remnant of the old Montanist heresy. It is said that the khalifah 'Omar II (717–720) tried to convert him to Islam. He only succeeded up to the point of persuading Leo to abhor eikons. In 726 the emperor made his first proclamation, forbidding anyone to keep or honour an eikon and ordering those in all churches to be destroyed. Outside his palace was a famous miraculous picture of Christ called the "Answering Christ" (Χριστὸς ἀντιφωνητής). This was removed in spite of the open indignation of the people. Germanos I, Patriarch of Constantinople (715–730), steadfastly withstood the tyrant and defended the eikons. He was made to resign and died soon after. Then the emperor wrote to Pope Gregory II (715–731), telling him to destroy all his images, otherwise, says Leo, "I will send an army to break your idols and to take you prisoner." Gregory answered sternly reproaching the emperor for his new law, and expressing his astonishment that the ruler of the Roman world does not yet know the difference between a statue and an idol. In 730 a new edict against eikons appeared and new laws were made against image-worshippers. Gregory III (731–741) excommunicated the emperor in 732.

Constantine V (Kopronymos, 741–775), who succeeded his father Leo, carried on the war. The monks were specially devout to the holy eikons, so they were most persecuted. Their monasteries were burnt down and numbers of them were martyred. John of Monagria and Abbot Stephen are the most famous of these martyrs. In 754 Constantine summoned a pretended œcumenical synod at Constantinople that forbade the use of images. The patriarchs of Rome, Alexandria, Antioch and Jerusalem refused to send legates to it. The great church of the blessed Virgin at Constantinople was stripped of its eikons and painted in a new style, which people said made it look like a birdcage and a fruit shop. Pope Stephen III (768–772) held a synod at the Lateran in 769 and excommunicated the Image-breakers. Under the emperor Leo IV (775–780) the persecution was less sharp; when he died his wife Irene, who became regent for her son Constantine VI (Pophyrogennetos, 780–797), arranged with the patriarch Tarasios of Constantinople (784–806) for the restoration of the eikons.

In 787 the *second Council of Nicæa* (the seventh general Council) met. Pope Adrian I (772–795) and the other patriarchs sent their legates.[1] About 300 bishops were present. They declared accurately the difference between the honour paid to images (προσκύνησις) and adoration (λατρεία), commanded all eikons to be restored and honoured, and they drew up twenty-two canons in defence of them, as well as to arrange other points of discipline.[2] The last session was held at Constan-

[1] The Pope sent an Archpriest Peter and an Abbot Peter of St Sabas' monastery at Rome, Politianos of Alexandria, Theodoretos of Antioch and Elias of Jerusalem were represented by monks.

[2] The Acts of Nicæa II in Mansi, xiii, 442–458. *See also* Hefele: *Conciliengesch.* iii, 460, *seq.*

tinople in the presence of the empress and her son with great pomp; it seemed as if the whole trouble had passed over. It broke out again later, however, under the emperor Leo V (the Armenian, 813–820), who renewed the old laws against the eikons. St Theodore, Abbot of the Studion monastery at Constantinople (†826), was a great defender of the Catholic practice at this time. Michael II (the Stammerer, 820–829) recalled the banished image-worshippers and wanted to make peace. But his son Theophilos (829–842) began the persecution again and ordered fearful punishments against every one who painted an eikon.

At last the final peace was restored to the Church after his death by his widow Theodora, Regent during the minority of her son Michael III (the Drunkard, 842–867).[1] This lady annulled all the Iconoclast laws and declared her acceptance of the second Council of Nicæa. On Feb. 19, 842, the holy eikons were brought back in solemn procession through the streets of Constantinople and set up again in the great church of the Holy Wisdom. It was the first Sunday of Lent. The Byzantine Church still remembers that final triumph and peace after the long storm; every year on the first Sunday of Lent she keeps the *feast of Orthodoxy* on which the eikons are carried in procession round the churches and a hymn (ascribed to St Theodore of Studion) in their honour is sung.[2]

[1] The end of the Iconoclast trouble brings us to the eve of the great schism. It was this Michael III, the Drunkard, who intruded Photius at Constantinople in 857.

[2] κυριακὴ τῆς ὀρθοδοξίας, ἤγουν ἀναστηλώσεως τῶν ἁγίων εἰκόνων. *The Sunday of orthodoxy, that is, of the restitution of the holy eikons.* Both Orthodox and Melkites keep this feast. Because of the name Orthodoxy, that originally referred only to this question (against Iconoclasm) they have gradually made the feast apply to true belief in general, and on

4. Revenue-officer and theologian
(726-730)

St John did not live to see that feast of Orthodoxy, but from the beginning of the trouble till his
death (c. 754) he was the chief defender of the
faith against the image-breakers. No one will dispute that he and Theodore of Studion were the
leaders of the Catholics in their writings, and John
was the greater of the two. So in this case again
we have a father of the Church whose great title
to fame is his opposition to a contemporary heresy;
the name of John of Damascus is always bound
up with the story of Iconoclasm. He did not suffer
for the faith. All the time he was safe from the

it they read a long *Synodikon* containing Anathemas against
a most varied collection of heretics (in Russia they add curses
against revolutionaries) and blessings on defenders of the
faith, from Constantine and Helen to Photius and Cerularius.
The names of heretics are read out and to each the choir
answers "thrice accursed"; to the names of Orthodox heroes
the answer is "thrice eternal memory." The latest development is that Sunday of Orthodoxy has become the great day
for declaring their hatred of Latin heresies. This is very far
from the original idea of keeping the memory of the triumph
of the eikons, which triumph was almost entirely the Pope's
work against the Byzantine court. In Iconoclast days, as so
often before, Rome never swerved, and all the image-worshippers looked to the Pope as their leader (Theodore of Studion especially), while the Patriarchs of Constantinople
wavered backwards and forwards at the emperor's command.
The Melkite *Synodikon* naturally only condemns people that
Catholics consider heretics, and the list of heroes has been
purified. The *Canon* (wrongly) ascribed to St Theodore is a
very splendid poem. It begins: "Let us sing a hymn of thanksgiving to God the giver of all blessing, who has raised up to us
a horn of salvation defending the orthodox faith." A version in
English rhymes by Dr Neale is in his *Hymns of the Eastern
Church*, No. 40 (ed. Hatherly, J. T. Hayes, 1882, p. 102–103).
For Sunday of Orthodoxy and its *Synodikon*, see N. Nilles:
Kalend. Manuale (Innsbruck, 1897), pp. 103–118, and Prince
Max of Saxony: *Prælectiones de Liturgiis orientalibus*, i (Frei-
burg, Herder, 1908), pp. 91–100.

emperor's vengeance under the protection of the khalifah; but from this shelter he wrote the works that became at once what they are still, the classical apology for the use and worship[1] of holy images. As soon as Leo the Isaurian published his first edict against the eikons (726), St John answered it with his first treatise *Against the destroyers of holy eikons* (p. 244); he was probably still at Damascus when he wrote the second treatise (*ib.*).

A story is told by his biographer that forms the fourth lesson of the Roman breviary on his feast. The emperor Leo is said to have tried to punish his opponent by guile, since he could not seize him himself. So he, Leo, forged a letter purporting to be addressed to himself by John, in which the saint tells him that Damascus is ill-defended and that the Romans can easily come and take it, and that the writer is willing to help this invasion by treachery. The emperor then sent this forgery to his enemy the khalifah, adding a note of his own, to the effect that he hates treachery and could not think of breaking the peace he had concluded with the Moslems; so he thinks it best to let his noble ally know how his revenue officer is behaving. It was, indeed, as the life says, "a snake-like wile." The khalifah reads Leo's note and the enclosure, and is, of course, furious. He sends for John Mansur, will listen to no denial, and has his right hand cut off as a

[1]*Worship*, of course, does not mean the adoration paid to God, nor even necessarily the honour paid to saints. It is a general word for reverence of any kind ("with my body I thee worship," in the marriage-service; magistrates and such people are "worshipful"). As long as people understand the right use of common words, *worship* is an accurate rendering of προσκύνησις, and *image-worshipper* is the natural opposite of *image-breaker*.

punishment for such treason. One wonders why he did not have him put to death. So St John is crippled and "the hand that was generally stained with ink as it wrote defences of the holy eikons was now stained with blood."[1] John goes home and then sends a message to the khalifah imploring him not to leave his hand "hung up in the market-place," but to send it to its original owner. The khalifah sees no harm in this, the hand was not much use now, but John may keep it if he likes. The saint receives it and carries it into his private chapel, where he has a picture of the holy Theotokos, prostrates himself and says this prayer in hexametres: "Lady and purest mother, who didst give birth to my God, because of the holy eikons my right hand is cut off. Thou knowest well the cause, that Leo the emperor rages; so help me at once and heal my hand by the power of the Most High, who became man from thee, who works many wonders by thy prayers. May he now heal this hand through thy intercession, and it shall in future always write poetry in thy honour, O Theotokos, and in honour of thy Son made man in thee and for the true faith. Be my advocate, for thou canst do anything, being mother of God."[2] Such was the prayer and the poem that our Lady could not resist. At once his hand was joined again to the arm; he used it first to write a thanksgiving. And "all the barbarians admitted the miracle and were convinced of his innocence," though they do not seem to have been converted to John's religion.[3]

[1] *Vita Joh. Dam.* xvii, p. 11.   [2] *Ib.* xviii, p. 12.
[3] The whole story in the *Vita*, xv–xx, pp. 10–13. Both the Latin religious houses at Damascus are on the sites of great events. The Franciscans near the *Bāb Tumā*, who were there first, show the place where St Paul was baptized in Ananias'

The next step in our saint's life was that he and his foster-brother Cosmas left the radiant city of Syria to be monks in a horrible wilderness near Jerusalem. The khalifah let them go, after a struggle, for he valued his revenue officer. John gave all his goods to the poor and set out for the monastery of St Sabas.

5. Monk at Mar Saba (*c.* 730-*c.* 734)

St Sabas (*Mar Saba*) was then, as now, the chief monastery in Palestine. It had been founded by St Euthymios in the fifth century. His more famous disciple, St Sabas, a Cappadocian and a defender of the faith against the Monophysites († 531) had left his name to the great Laura. His tomb[1] and that of St John Damascene are still its chief treasures.

From Jerusalem you cross the valley of the Cedron and take the road towards the Dead Sea. In about three hours you will have left the green valley and will come out into the burning desert whose barren rocks slope down towards Jericho. And here you find one of the most wonderful sights of Palestine, Mar Saba. The monastery is not well seen from the road, only a great tower and a wall appear. One must go in at the gate, through the court past St Sabas' miraculous palm-tree, down into the *wadi* and along the bed of the dried-up torrent. Here you pick your way among burning rocks and climb up the other side. It is

house. The Jesuits across the road have the next best thing, St John Damascene's house, where this miracle happened. You may see a picture of it in their church; but they represent St John kneeling before a statue, whereas it was certainly a flat picture.

[1] Now empty. The Venetians stole his relics, as they stole St Mark from Alexandria.

from here that, looking back, you may see the strange and wild beauty of Mar Saba.

Against a sky that is at once deep blue and yet glowing with hot light[1] every tint of white and yellow, from dazzling dead white through pearl grey to warm brown, is piled up in a savage kind of order. Rocks, sand, white earth and cliffs are heaped together like a gigantic fortress. And climbing up the side of the *wadi* is the fortress-monastery. Its walls rise out of the rocks so naturally that you cannot see where they really begin, its terraces are hewn out of the cliff and its towers mount buttressed in tiers up into the sky. Its balconies are bridged over frightful chasms and its walls lie in winding curves up and down the ground like monstrous snakes. The whole makes the most incredibly picturesque group of buildings that one could conceive, all carved and fretted in dazzling white and shining gold as the heart of a superb and awful scene. Two notes of green alone relieve the barren splendour, the miraculous palm-tree planted by St Sabas, whose dates have no stones, and the bright green copper dome of the church. It is now a place of punishment for refractory monks of the Orthodox Church. They feed doves and tame jackals in their courtyard and throw bread from the strong ramparts to the Bedawin who ride up and demand it with awful threats. All night the wolves howl and the jackals bark outside; and the wailing chant of the *kalogeroi*, the "good old men," comes from the beautiful church, where they stand

---

[1] The sky is generally the most wonderful part of any Syrian landscape. In summer it is often almost indigo, deeper in tone than the shadows, so that everything stands out against a dark background; and yet those dark skies give one an impression of glowing heat that is even greater than that of the dazzling whites and yellows of the earth.

under stern Byzantine frescoes and sing their
hours. And when they do the honours of their
laura they take you to make the great salam
before the now empty tomb of our Father among
the Saints, John Mansur, called Chrysorroas.

It was soon after the year 730 that John and
Cosmas[1] came to this monastery. As monks they
went on writing pious books, and especially hymns.
But the community, true to the ideas that still rule
every eastern monastery, did not approve of
this at all. These newcomers, instead of fleeing the
world and accepting the proper ideal of the angelic
life, namely, to fast, pray, and do nothing else at all,
were introducing disturbing elements into the
monastery. To write books was bad, to sing hymns
or compose verses was very much worse. Monks—
it is the unchanging idea in the east—must not do
anything at all. So there was great discontent.
Things came to a climax when St John wrote a
poem about death, though one would think that,
at any rate, this subject would not seem too
worldly. One of the monks died and his brother,
very much distressed at his loss, came to John,
who was already a famous poet, and asked him to
compose a Canon that could be sung by the mourner
to comfort his soul. John said he would do so and
wrote the verses that are still famous:

> All human things are foolish,
> For death destroys them all.
> We keep no wealth nor glory
> That death shall not recall.
> So we in Christ confiding,
> Our one immortal King,
> Pray that he grant us mercy,
> Who takes from death its sting.

[1] Cosmas the Singer, John's fosterbrother. The Roman
breviary confuses him with Cosmas, the old Sicilian monk, who
had been John's master (S. Joh. Dam. 27 martii, lect. iv).

And when the hour determined
Shall bring us to the grave,
May he in heaven receive us,
Who died our souls to save.[1]

The Latin reader will not consider the composition of this hymn scandalous for a monk. He does not know the good old men. It is scandalous to do anything at all in a Byzantine laura. John, having written his hymn, proceeded to compose a tune for it, and he sang it "with a sweet sound"[2] in his cell. An old monk who was passing heard him and was perfectly furious. "Is this the way you forget your vows," he said, "and instead of mourning and weeping you sit in joy and give yourself delight by singing?"[3] This old monk was John's "master," that is, the person whose cell he shared and from whose teaching and example he was to learn the angelic life.[4] The master then, having reproached him, turned him out of the cell and refused to allow him back. After some days he relented and said he would forgive all, on condition that John went round the whole laura and cleared up all the filth with his own hands. Of course John did so at once, "and he did not hesitate to stain that very right hand that Christ had healed."[5] The end of the story is that the all-holy Lady appears to this old monk and tells him to let his disciple write books and poetry as much as he likes. So from this time

[1] This is the hymn: Πάντα ματαιότης τὰ ἀνθρώπινα, composed by St John on this occasion. It does not, I believe, occur in any part of the Byzantine liturgical offce, but it is still a well-known hymn among Greeks. The Greek text is printed by Le Quien in a note to the *Vita*, xxvii, p. 16.

[2] *Vita*, xxviii, p. 17.   [3] *Ib.*

[4] This was the regular system. Each new arriver put himself under obedience to an old and experienced monk who became what we should call his novice master.

[5] *Vita*, xxx, p.17.

the saint spends time in study and writing—an
almost unique case in the long history of eastern
monasticism. We hear of him being sent to
Damascus to sell baskets, too; his biographer is
duly impressed by the fact that he was not ashamed
to do so in the very city in which he had once held
so great a place.[1] His chief works, the logic, the
"fount of knowledge," etc., and most of his poems
were written at this time. St Cosmas, too, was
writing his odes. And then a great change came for
both of them.

6. St John ordained priest (c. 734)

The Patriarch of Jerusalem, John V († 735) had
heard of the fame of these two friends, and he
thought he would like to have them among his
clergy instead of at Mar Saba. First he took
Cosmas and ordained him bishop of Maiumas, the
port of Gaza in Southern Palestine, on the road to
Egypt. We are told that Cosmas gave way and was
ordained, "not freely but by force."[2] However,
once he was ordained, he became a very good
bishop, "ruled his flock admirably, as is pleasing
to God, and in a good old age went to rest with his
fathers, or rather went to God."[3] St Cosmas the
Singer apparently outlived his friend. The date of
his death is not known.

The same patriarch ordained John priest, and
brought him to Jerusalem, that he might fill some
place in that church. But the saint did not stay long
in the world; he went back almost at once to his

[1] *Ib.* xxvi, p. 15.
[2] *Vita*, xxxiv, p. 20. This fear of ordination is the com-
monest feature among holy men in the eastern Church at all
times (*see* above, pp. 94, 97, etc.). It seems to be part of the
normal programme that they should resist and be compelled
to be ordained. [3] *Ib.*

monastery, "this eagle flying away sought his old nest."[1] The only difference in his position now was that he had become a *Hieromonachos*, a Priest-monk. The old idea that a monk could not be a priest[2] had quite died out by now and there were, as a matter of course, a certain number of priest-monks in each laura who celebrated the holy Liturgy and administered sacraments to the others. On the other hand, our western principle that every choir-monk should be a priest is unknown to this day in the east.[3] St John as a hieromonachos thought that "priests must practise double humility and must do all their religious duties with double zeal."[4] He revised all his writings carefully, "and wherever they flourished with blossoms of rhetoric or seemed superfluous in style he prudently reduced them to a sterner gravity, lest they should have any vice of display or levity or want of dignity."[5] By this time his works in defence of the eikons were known and read everywhere; the faithful Catholics in the empire found in them comfort and arguments against the image-breakers. So naturally the persecuting emperors hated John Mansur. Leo III's attempt to have him killed by the khalifah had failed, he never put himself in the power of the Roman government by crossing the frontier of the empire, so they could not really hurt him. However, they showed their hatred by cursing him copiously. It was an age of playful nicknames. Constantine V (741–775) was called *Kopronymos* because of an accident at his bap-

[1] *Ib.* xxxv, p. 21. [2] *See* p. 57.
[3] When a *Kalogeros* tells you he is a monk, he is not a priest; if he were he would describe himself as a Hieromonachos. You should say πάτερ μου to a monk, αἰδεσιμώτατε πάτερ to a priest-monk and σεβασμιώτατε πάτερ to the Hegumenos. In Arabic (they speak both at Mar Saba) *Abūna* will do for anyone.
[4] *Ib.* xxxv, p. 21. [5] *Ib.* xxxvi, p. 22.

tism,[1] and he shared the general taste. So he changed John's name from Mansur and called him *Manzeros*, which is a very bad attempt at the Hebrew for bastard.[2] It was a little far-fetched, perhaps, but (when explained) agreeably offensive.

7. St John's philosophy and theology

Our saint, the last of the Greek fathers, had the mission of collecting and classifying what had been said by the others. He is the most systematic of all. His only original contribution to theology was his defence of holy images, and that defence is, perhaps, his chief title to fame. But it is not his only one. He was a poet of very rare merit, an ardent Aristotelian philosopher and a theologian who wrote of every question of theology that had been raised before his time. Since his works contain very complete courses of philosophy and dogmatic it is easy to understand his view on each point. In philosophy he is entirely a disciple of Aristotle († B.C. 322). He wrote a treatise of logic (p. 243), which in his time included a great deal of metaphysic and psychology. He has an unbounded respect for science and no sympathy with people who despise it in the name of faith and Christian simplicity. "Science is the light of the reasonable soul as ignorance is its darkness." "Nothing is better than knowledge."[3] "Philosophy is the science of beings, inasmuch as they are beings, that is, of their nature."[4] But since we live not only in our

[1]Κοπρόνυμος, *Dirt-named*. When he was baptized as a baby he had dirtied the font.
[2]*Mamzer*. One wonders how many Greeks would have even seen the joke.
[3]*Dialectic* (the first part of his *fount of knowledge*), i (M. P. G. XCIV, 529).
[4]*Ib.* LXIX (*ib.* 669).

soul, but also in a body, we have no philosophy from ourselves, so we need a master. The master is infallible Truth, Christ himself, who is subsistent wisdom and truth, in whom are hidden all treasures of knowledge.[1]

Although John is peripatetic, he proposes to take what is good from all Greek philosophers,[2] and he "will say nothing of his own but only gather up what has already been said by approved teachers."[3] That is an exact account of his method in general. He distinguishes four kinds of logic—*division* (διαιρετική), *definition* (ὁριστική), *analysis* (ἀναλυτική) and *demonstration* (ἀποδεικτική).[4] In metaphysic the root of his system is Aristotle's distinction of *actus* (ἐνέργεια) and *potentia* (δύναμις), with which St Thomas Aquinas has made us familiar. *Essence* (οὐσία) does not exist in itself but in a hypostasis (our *subiectum*).[5] *Nature* (φύσις) is the principle of movement and rest.[6] *Form* (μορφή, forma substantialis) gives to each being its specific nature, the being then is an *informed essence* (οὐσία μεμορφωμένη).[7] Essence, nature and ultimate actual species are the same thing.[8] Evil is nothing but the privation of Good.[9] Real being is either *substance* (σύστασις) or *accident* (συμβεβηκός).[10] He distinguishes these two exactly according to Aristotle.[11] *Hypostasis, person* (πρόσωπον) and *individual* (ἄτομον) are the same thing.[12]

In psychology he distinguishes four internal faculties—*Imagination* (φανταστικόν), *memory* (μνημονευτικόν), *reason* (διανοητικόν) and *will* (θέλημα). The reason generates a *word* (λόγος, our verbum

[1] *Ib.* i (*ib.* 529). [2] Introd. to the *fount* (524). [3] *Ib.* (525).
[4] *Dial.* lxviii (672). [5] *De fide orth.* iii, 6 (xciv, 1004).
[6] *Dial.* xl (605). [7] *Dial.* xli (608). [8] *Ib.*
[9] *Ctra manich.* xiii (M. P. G. xciv, 1517).
[10] *Dial.* xxxix (xciv, 605). [11] *Ib.* xlvii (621).
[12] *Ib.* xliii (613).

mentale).[1] Like all Greeks, John Damascene insists very much on *free will;* man is free because he is reasonable, all actions that depend on us are free.[2] It is also characteristic of his nation that John is little concerned about the mysteries of God's co-operation (in philosophy) and predestination (in theology). In all his philosophy, then, we see a faithful reflection of Aristotle, who has become through him the "master of them that know,"[3] to Greeks and the Orthodox Church as much as he has to Latins and Catholics through St Thomas.

In St John's theology we find that he produces three of the five scholastic arguments for the existence of God, namely, those from motion, from the conservation of the world and from the order of nature.[4] The attributes of God, his unity, simplicity, perfection, immensity, etc., are demonstrated as in our schools.[5] God can be known, but not comprehended by us.[6]

The Arian and Pneumatomachian controversies had left a very clear consciousness of their faith in the holy Trinity to Greeks as to Latins: "I believe in the Father, the Son and the Holy Ghost, one consubstantial Trinity and Unity in three Persons, one principle, having no principle, one will, one action, one power, one royalty, three hypostases (persons) having no difference except that one is unborn ($\dot{a}\gamma\acute{\epsilon}\nu\nu\eta\tau o\varsigma$), one born and one proceeding."[7] The Incarnation was the redemption of man from sin, especially from original sin.[8] Here, too, one sees that St John knew about the Pelagian heresy and definitely defends the faith against it. It is because

---

[1]*De fide orth.* ii, 17–20 (933–940).   [2]*Ib.* 26–27 (957–960).
[3]Dante, *Inferno*, iv, 131.   [4]*De fide orth.* i, 3 (796–797).
[5]*Ib.* i, 1–5 (789–801).   [6]*Ib.* i, 1 (789).
[7]*Libellus de recta sent.* i (XCIV, 1421).
[8]*De fide orth.* iv, 13 (*Ib.* 1137).

his date is so late and because all the great controversies had already taken place that he is able to
write so clearly and systematically on each point. He
argues at length against the Christological heresies.
He defends the word *Theotokos* against Nestorians,
the blessed Virgin is "truly mother of God,
because she gave birth to the true God made
flesh from her;"[1] he wrote a whole treatise against
that heresy.[2] He also wrote a book against the
Monophysites[3] and another against the Monotheletes.[4] It is, therefore, hardly necessary to
insist on his orthodoxy on these points.

He has very little, hardly anything, to say about
the Church, an omission that can only be an accident
in the eighth century, but he writes at length on
baptism,[5] speaks in passing of confirmation with
chrism,[6] and has much to say about the holy
Eucharist:[7] "the bread and the wine are not
figures of the Body and Blood of Christ, God forbid,
but the divine Body of the Lord, for he said: This
is—not the figure of my Body but—my Body, and
—not the figure of my Blood, but—my Blood."[8]
And he teaches Transubstantiation: "We may say
that just as bread and wine are changed by diges-
tion into the body and blood of him who eats and
drinks them and they become, not a different body
but his very body, so the bread, the wine and the
water of the oblation by the invocation and power
of the Holy Ghost are changed supernaturally into
the Body and Blood of Christ; and they are not a
different thing, but one and the same thing."[9]

[1] *De fide orth.* iii, 12 (1028–1032).
[2] *Against the heresy of the Nestorians (see* p. 245).
[3] *To the Jacobite Bishop of Daraias* (p. 246).
[4] *Of the two wills in Christ* (*ib.*).
[5] *De fide orth.* iv, 9 (1117–1121).
[6] *Ib.* iv, 9 (1125).   [7] *Ib.* iv, 13 (1137–1149).
[8] *Ib.* (1148).   [9] *Ib.* (1144).

The honour we pay to saints is part of the theology of the holy eikons of which St John was the
chief defender, so naturally he explains and
proves the rightness of this at great length,[1] as also
the use of relics.[2]

He is always very uncompromising in his resistance to the interference of the secular government
in affairs of the Church. One of the worst features
of the Iconoclast persecution was that it was a
shameless attempt of the emperors to dictate to the
Church. "The emperors have no power to make
laws for the Church. Listen to what the Apostle
says: God placed in the Church, first apostles, then
prophets, thirdly shepherds and teachers to make
the Church perfect. He does not say emperors. . . .
We will obey you, O emperor, in the things of
this world, in paying taxes and duty-money, in
accepting your office and in those things in which
our affairs are committed to you; but for the things
of the Church we have shepherds who speak the
word and give us ecclesiastical laws."[3]

Two points, lastly, that will interest Catholics
are his attitude towards the Roman Primacy and
about the Procession of the Holy Ghost. Concerning the *Primacy*, he says practically nothing. The
omission is less to be regretted since he lived in an
age when no one disputes that it was acknowledged
by all the Orthodox in the east, and since he was a
leader of those image-worshippers who looked up
to the Pope with special reverence as their head
and champion against the Iconoclasts.[4] There is,

[1] *De fide orth.* iv, 15 (XCIV, 1164–1165). *De Imaginibus*, Orat.
iii, 33 (*Ib.* 1352–1353).
[2] *De fide orth.* iv, 15 (1165).
[3] *See* the whole passage, *de S. Imag.* ii, 12 (XCIV, 1295–1298).
[4] On the other hand his fellow defender of the eikons, St
Theodore of Studion, has the plainest things to say about the
Pope's authority and primacy (cfr. *Orth. Eastern Church*, pp.

however, one place in which he speaks plainly of the Primacy of St Peter.[1] About the *Procession of the Holy Ghost* he repeats what he has learned from St Basil and other Greek fathers, and so sums up that attitude that was characteristic of the Byzantine Church before the schism, that the Council of Florence (1439) accepted as correct and Catholic.[2] Namely, God the Father is the *cause* (αἰτία) of the other Persons and the Holy Ghost proceeds *from* the Father, *through* the Son.[3] St John Damascene explains many other points of philosophy and theology at length, giving for each the arguments he has learned from Aristotle and the fathers. There is not space to quote more here, but a glance at his works, especially the *Fount of Knowledge* and quite especially its third part, *Of the Orthodox Faith*, will show that his people have done well in taking them as the standard work of theology, and that it is by a very right comparison that he is called the Aquinas or the Peter Lombard of the eastern Church.

8. St John's poetry

Our saint has a further title to fame as a poet. Both he and his friend St Cosmas wrote a great quantity of poetry, and that of John is certainly the better. He uses sometimes the old measure of quantity, as in his poems for Christmas, the Epiphany and Whitsunday,[4] and sometimes the

65–66) and the Council of Nicæa in 787 that was the triumph of St John's side and declared his orthodoxy (*see* below p. 240) also declared its belief that "The see of Peter shines as holding the primacy over the whole world and stands as head of all the Churches of God" (*op. cit.* p. 81).

[1] *Sacra parall.* (but *see* below p.   , about this work), iii (150).
[2] *Orth. Eastern Church*, pp. 379–380.
[3] Ἐκ πατρὸς μὲν δι' υἱοῦ ἐκπορεύεται. *De fide orth.* i, 12 (XCIV,849).
[4] They are in Iambic Trimetres.

new rhythm of stress-accent. Nearly all his poems
are hymns in honour of feasts of the Church or
about points of the Christian faith. He wrote,
besides poems strictly so called, a great number
of canons, that is, pieces in rhythmical prose to be
sung in the Byzantine office. The Orthodox
ascribe the whole of the canons in their Oktoechos[1]
to him.

Dr J. M. Neale, in his *Hymns of the Eastern
Church*,[2] has translated twelve Odes, a Sticheron,
and an Idiomelon of St John. Dr Neale is less happy
as a translator of Greek than of Latin poems. The
task in the case of Greek chants is also very con-
siderably more difficult. In order to make them
acceptable and fit for singing in English, he turned
their prose into English metres with rhymes. His
metres when compared with the originals seem, as a
rule, undignified; and his versions are so free that in
many cases he has practically written a new poem on
the same subject. For people who wish to see his
translations the book is easily accessible. I will give
a more exact idea of one or two of St John's most
famous odes by translating them into the same
sort of rhythmical prose as the originals.

The most famous of all are those of his *Golden*

[1] The *Oktoechos* is the book that contains the offices for the
Sundays from All Saints' Sunday (first after Pentecost) to the
tenth before Easter, arranged according to the eight modes
(ὀκτὼ ἤχοι).

[2] First edition, 1862, and often reprinted. I have the fourth
edition with music by S. G. Hatherly (London: J. T. Hayes,
1882).

[3] A *Canon* is divided into nine *Odes* (of which the second is
left out except on Tuesdays in Lent), the Odes into *Troparia*.
A Troparion (τροπάριον) is a short verse. The first is called
Heirmos (εἱρμός) because it fixes the mode and drags the others
after it. A *Sticheron* (στιχηρόν) is a longer poem modelled on a
verse (στίχος) of a Psalm. An *Idiomelon* (ἰδιόμελον) does not
follow a Heirmos, but has its own melody. All are composed in
rhythmic prose.

Canon (for Easter day). During the holy night, between Easter eve and Easter day, the clergy of the Byzantine Church assemble with their people and wait with unlit candles for midnight. As soon as midnight strikes the metropolitan or chief priest lifts up a cross and cries out: *Christ has risen* (Χριστὸς ἀνέστι), the cry is taken up by every one, the candles are lit and a sea of fire spreads over the crowd. Then St John Damascene's Paschal ode is sung, announcing the feast of feasts, as the three Alleluias on Holy Saturday do to us. It is the dramatic moment of the year in the Byzantine Church, the sudden glare of the candles, the shout of *Christos anesti*, and then the rolling chant of this glorious canon[1] make an impression as great as that of our Gloria and bells and organ at the first Easter Mass. The first ode is:

The day of Resurrection,
Let us make glorious the Pasch, the Pasch of the Lord.
From death to life, from earth to heaven Christ our
    God has led us,
As we sing his victory.

Let us cleanse our senses,
And wo shall see Christ radiant in the glorious light of
    his Resurrection,
And we shall hear him greet us clearly,
As we sing his victory.

The heavens rejoice and the earth is glad,
All the world both seen and unseen keeps this feast,

[1] The first Easter hymn at midnight is, however, not this canon (which is sung rather later) but the short verse, repeated continually throughout the feast:

> "Christ has risen from the dead;
> By death he trampled on death
> And to those who are in the tomb
> He gives back life."

For Christ who is our everlasting joy
Has come back to life.[1]

There follow then the other odes, from III to IX
(No. II being left out). It would be too long to
quote all. The ninth is:

Be enlightened, new Jerusalem, be enlightened, for the
 glory of the Lord has risen in thee.
Sion, leap and rejoice,
And do thou exult, all holy Theotókos,
For thy Child has risen again.

Oh blessed, holy and most sweet promise,
That thou wilt be with us all days to the end,
These are thy words, Christ, who canst not deceive,
And we, trusting to them, with firm hope rejoice.

Oh, great and most sacred Pasch of Christ,
Do thou, Wisdom, Power and Word of God,
Grant that we may see thy presence in thy kingdom,
In that day that has no evening.[2]

There is a beautiful canon for Lady-day, of which
the first troparia end with the first line of the
Benedicite, and the last with St Gabriel's greeting:

Listen, maiden, purest Virgin, Gabriel tells of God's
 high counsel,
And thou art ready to receive thy Lord,
Through thee the Almighty comes down to mortal
 men,
Wherefore I sing: Bless the Lord, all ye his works!

and further down (Trop. VII):

[1]These irregular lines give, I think, very nearly the effect
of the original. For instance, the first troparion is:

Ἀναστάσεως ἡμέρα,
λαμπρυνθῶμεν λαοὶ πασχα κυρίου, πάσχα,
ἐκ γὰρ θανάτου πρὸς ζωὴν καὶ ἐκ γῆς πρὸς οὐρανὸν Χριστὸς ὁ θεὸς ἡμᾶς
 διεβίβασεν,
ἐπινίκιον ᾄδοντας

[2]The whole *Golden Canon* will be found among St John's
works. In Lequien's edition (Venice, 1748) it comes in vol. 1,
pp. 685–686.

Living Ark that shelters God,
No impure hand shall dare to touch thee,[1]
But the lips of the servants of the Theotókos always
    sing the Angel's words,
Hail, full of grace, the Lord is with thee.

A number of these canons and poems are ana-
grams, so arranged that the initial letters of each
line, if read downwards, make a verse. Thus the
poem for Christmas mentioned above (p. 234)
begins:

> The Lord has saved his people; God's own Son,
> Who dried for them long years ago the sea.
> Born of a Virgin greater things has done
> Who coming down to earth has set us free.

And the first letters of the lines make this verse:

> With joyful sound this canon tells the birth
> Of Christ the Son of God, who came to bring
> Salvation to his people here on earth;
> And may he bless us while we gladly sing.

As a last specimen of St John's poetry, this is a long
rhyme in short Anacreontic verse, expressing contrition, shame for sin and hope of forgiveness:

> Christ, from a wicked tongue,
> From a heart that yet may dare
> With shame and sorrow wrung
> To turn to thee in prayer,
> Receive my humble cry,
> Nor turn away thy face,
> And when I mourn and sigh
> Refuse me not thy grace.
> My soul with sin is black,
> I have no right to plead,
> Yet, Saviour, take me back
> And pity my great need.

[1] A reference, of course, to Oza, who touched the Ark of the
Covenant and was struck dead (2 Kings, vi, 6–7). Their canons
are full of such allusions to the Old Testament, as types, many
of them being very far-fetched.

For lowly, poor and meek,
I come to thee in fear;
Teach me then how to speak
So that thou mayest hear.
Let me thy mercy feel
When I come to entreat
Before thy throne to kneel
And kiss thy sacred feet.[1]

9. St John's death (*c.* 754)

There is nothing more to say of our saint's life.
He spent the rest of it in his monastery, writing
theology and poetry. Here at Mar Saba he died,
sometime not long before the year 754, and here
he was buried. His relics were taken to Constantinople in the fourteenth century; but the tomb,
though now empty, that once held them is still the
chief treasure of the laura. He had been the great
defender of the holy eikons, so it was natural that
the eikon-breakers should hate and revile his
memory. The Iconoclast Synod of Constantinople
in 754 (p. 218) curses him at great length. It
remembers three defenders of the images specially,
the Patriarch Germanos of Constantinople (p. 217),
a certain George of Cyprus, and John Mansur of
Damascus; and it declares that "the Trinity
destroyed these three."[2] Our Saint receives a special
series of curses: "To Mansur of evil name, Saracen
at heart,[3] Anathema. To Mansur, the image-worshipper and writer of falsehoods, Anathema. To Mansur, who denied Christ and betrayed his sovereign,
Anathema. To Mansur, the teacher of impious doc-

[1] There are over 100 lines altogether. In Lequien's edition,
i, 691–693.

[2] ἡ Τριὰς τοὺς τρεῖς καθεῖλεν (quoted by the second Synod
of Nicæa, Act. 6, Mansi xiii, 356.

[3] This is preposterous. It was the Iconoclasts who got their
ideas from the Saracens.

trine and the perverter of holy Scripture, Anathema."[1] It is equally natural that all image-worshippers should look upon John of Damascus as their great hero. The seventh general Council,[2] that restored the honour of the eikons, was also concerned to restore his honour. The fathers expressly repudiate the anathemas of the Iconoclast synod, declare in opposition that "the Trinity made these three glorious,"[3] and proclaim that "John, who has been called Mansur in scorn,[4] imitating Matthew the Evangelist, left all and followed Christ, counting the reproach of Christ as better than all the treasures of Arabia, choosing rather to suffer with the people of God than to enjoy worldly pleasure."[5]

And since the image-breakers disappeared, together with the triumph of his cause, the honour of his name has spread throughout Christendom. Theophanes[6] says that John is rightly surnamed *Chrysorroas*, after the chief river of his city, "because in his life and in his teaching gold-gleaming spiritual graces shine."[7] This name, however, has not become the common one. It is rather as John Damascene (δαμασκηνός, damascenus) that he is known and honoured in east and west. We have seen how important his writings are in eastern theology. His own people keep his feast on Dec. 4;[8] on that day they sing: "Let us,

---

[1]Mansi, *Ib.*   [2]Nicæa, II, in 787; *see* p.

[3]ἡ Τριὰς τοὺς τρεῖς ἐδόξασεν (Mansi, *loc. cit.* p. 400).

[4]This is a mistake; it was an honourable name inherited from his father. Possibly the council has Constantine V's nickname in mind (above, p. 229).

[5]Mansi, *ib.*

[6]Theophanes, surnamed *the confessor*, was a chronicler who died about 817 (Krumbacher: *Byz. Litt.* 1891, pp. 120–124).

[7]*Chronogr.* ad ann. 734.

[8]With St Barbara, the Megalomartyr.

oh faithful people, praise the venerable John, the hymn-writer, teacher and light of the Church, our defender against enemies; for lifting up the cross of Christ with this weapon he defeated all wiles of heresy, and now as a true intercessor with God he obtains forgiveness for all our sins."[1] St John is remembered in the Roman martyrology on May 6[2]: "At Damascus the birth of blessed John Damascene, famous for his piety and learning, who valiantly strove against Leo the Isaurian by word and writing for the worship (cultus) of holy images, who, when his right hand had been cut off by this man's order, praying for himself before the image of the blessed Virgin Mary which he had defended, straightway received it back cured and whole."[3]

Pope Leo XIII declared St John Damascene a Doctor of the Church and appointed March 27 as his feast. The gospel (in allusion to the story of the saint's right hand) is Luke vi, 6–11, about the healing of the man whose hand was withered; and the collect is: "Almighty and eternal God, who didst give to blessed John heavenly knowledge and admirable strength of mind to defend the worship of holy images; grant by his prayers and example that we may copy the virtues and enjoy the protection of those whose pictures we honour."

10. Table of dates

661. The Ommeyade khalifahs set up their throne at Damascus.

[1] In the *Horologion* for Dec. 4, Kontakion to the fourth authentic tone.

[2] It is the feast of St John (the Evangelist) before the Latin Gate.

[3] *Martyr. Rom.* ad 6 maii.

16

680–690(?). St John Damascene born. Cosmas the Monk from Sicily his teacher. Cosmas the Singer his foster-brother. *John revenue-officer at Damascus.*

717–741. Leo III the Isaurian.

726. *Leo III's first edict against eikons.* St John's first treatise against the Iconoclasts.

730. Leo's second edict. The story of John's right hand. *He and Cosmas the Singer go to Mar Saba.*

732. Leo III excommunicated by Pope Gregory III. St John ordained priest.

741–775. Constantine V, Kopronymos.
Death of St John.

754. Iconoclast synod at Constantinople.

769. Roman synod against Iconoclasm under Stephen III.

775–780. Leo IV emperor.

780–797. Constantine VI, Porphyrogennetos. Irene regent.

787. SEVENTH GENERAL COUNCIL (NICÆA II).

813–820. Leo V, the Armenian. Second Iconoclast persecution.

842–867. Michael III, the Drunkard. Theodora regent.

842 (Feb. 19). First Sunday of Lent, *Feast of Orthodoxy.*

11. Works

The first complete edition of St John Damascene was made by the learned Dominican, Michael le Quien[1] (Paris, 1712, two folio volumes), with a parallel Latin version (reprinted at Venice, 1748). Migne reprints this in his *Patrol. Græca*, XCIV–XCVI

---

[1] Le Quien is the author of the great *Oriens Christianus* (Paris, 1740).

(Paris, 1864), with a supplement containing additions since discovered, most of which are spurious or at least doubtful. Hurter has published the *De fide orthodoxa* in his *SS. Patrum opuscula selecta*, vol. XLI (Innsbruck, 1880) and seven sermons about the blessed Virgin in the same series, vol. XXXIV (pp. 4–156).

DOGMATIC WORKS. The great compendium of St John Damascene (the summa theologica, and philosophica too, of the Byzantine Church) is his *Fount of Knowledge* (πηγὴ γνώσεως, fons scientice, XCIV, 517–1228), dedicated to his friend, Cosmas the Singer, Bishop of Maiumas. It has three parts. The first is entitled *Chapters of Philosophy* (κεφάλαια φιλοσοφικά, capita philosophica), but is generally known as the *Logic* (διαλεκτική, dialectica). This part contains, not only what we call logic, but a complete course of Aristotelian ontology as well. The second part is *A Compendium about heresies* (περὶ αἱρέσεων ἐν συντονίᾳ, de hæresibus compendium), arranged under their names, giving in each case an account of their teaching. Most of this part is only a new edition of the *Panarion* (πανάριον, "Hæreses") of Epiphanios (†403); but at the end St John adds paragraphs about Mohammedans, Iconoclasts and other later heretics. The third part is the most important; it is his great work *On the Orthodox Faith* (ἔκδοσις ἀκριβὴς τῆς ὀρθοδόξου πίστεως, Expositio accurata fidei orthodoxœ, quoted always as *de fide orthodoxa*). This is the classical compendium of theology in Greek. The Latins have divided it into four books, in imitation of Peter Lombard's four books of sentences.[1]

---

[1]Peter Lombard († 1164) knew the *de fide orth.* in a Latin version made by Burgundio of Pisa († 1194); he used it as his model for the *Sententiœ*.

The first book (nineteen chapters) treats of God, the second (thirty chapters) of creation, angels and demons, nature, man and Providence, the third (twenty-nine chapters) of the Incarnation and its consequences (against Nestorians, Monophysites, etc.), and the fourth (twenty-seven chapters) of various other questions in no very definite order, namely, of the glory of God the Son, of sacraments, saints, relics, and images, of the canon of holy Scripture, of the problem of evil, of the last things. The Fount of Knowledge was written towards the end of St John's life. It is, as he declares (Prolog.), a gathering up of tradition on these subjects. Earlier and shorter dogmatic works are: *A treatise about right opinion* (λίβελλος περὶ ὀρθοῦ φρονήματος, Libellus de recta sententia, XCIV, 1421–1432), which is a short profession of faith, an *Elementary Introduction to dogmas* (εἰισαγωγὴ δογμάτων στοιχειώδης, Institutio elementaris ad dogmata (XCV, 99–112) addressed to John, Bishop of Laodicea in Syria. It is another work on logic and metaphysic, covering the same ground as Part I of the Fount of Knowledge. Three more dogmatic works should be mentioned: *Of the Holy Trinity* (περὶ τῆς ἀγίας Τριάδος, de S. Trinitate, XCV, 9–18) in the form of a dialogue, a *Treatise on the Trisagion* (Περὶ τοῦ τρισαγίου ὕμνου, de hymno Trisagio, XCV, 21–62), in the form of a letter to an Archimandrite Jordanes, in which he declares that the Trisagion is sung of the Holy Trinity and not of the second Person only; wherefore the Jacobite addition about the Crucifixion should not be made.[1] Lastly, there is a

---

[1] The *Trisagion* is the verse: "Holy God, Holy Strong One, Holy Immortal One, have mercy on us." We sing it in Latin and Greek on Good Friday; it occurs often in the Byzantine rite. Peter the Dyer of Antioch, a Monophysite (470–488), had added to the form the words, "who wast crucified for us."

short treatise *On Confession* (περὶ ἐξομολογήσεως
de confessione, XCV, 283–304), of doubtful authenticity, written to defend the practice (that occurred
intermittently in both east and west for a long
time) of confessing one's sins to a holy man (generally a monk),[1] who is not a priest and therefore
cannot absolve.

POLEMICAL WORKS. The most important of these
are the three *Treatises against those who destroy
holy Images* (λόγοι ἀπολογητικοὶ πρὸς τοὺς διαβάλ-
λοντας τὰς ἁγίας εἰκόνας, orationes apologeticæ adv.
eos qui sacras imagines abiiciunt, XCIV, 1231–
1420, generally quoted as: *Pro sacris Imaginibus*).
The first was written in 726 before St John became a monk, the second about 730, the third a
few years later. They are the classical apology
for the use of images and for reverence paid
to them, with a clear distinction between the
adoration due only to God (λατρεία) and worship
in the sense of *cultus* (προσκύνησις). Other polemical works are a *Dialogue against the Mani-
chæans* (κατὰ μανιχαίων διάλογος, ctra manichæos
dialogus, XCIV, 1505–1584), the *Argument of John
the Orthodox against a Manichæan* (διάλεξις Ἰωάννου
ὀρθοδόξου πρὸς Μανιχαῖον, disquisitio Joh. orthod.
adv. Manichæum, XCVI, 1319–1336), a *Disputation*

This addition was considered unsound, if not heretical, as
implying that the Divinity itself was crucified. It was very
much discussed during the Monophysite controversy, and is
still a speciality of the Jacobite rite.

[1] In the west confession to a deacon was a not uncommon
practice at one time, especially in England. It is referred to in
synods at York in 1195, London 1200, Rouen 1231, and Canterbury 1236. There does not seem to be any mistake as to the
power of absolving. It was merely an act of humility and
protest of contrition. The deacon then prayed for the peni-
tent's forgiveness without any idea of conferring a sacrament
(cfr. J. N. Seidel: *Der Diakonat*, §32, *Bei der Bussdisciplin*,
Regensburg, 1884, pp. 141–144).

between a Saracen and a Christian (διάλεξις σαρακηνοῦ
καὶ χριστιανοῦ, disceptatio Saraceni et Christiani,
XCIV, 1585–1598, another text in XCVI, 1335–1348),
two treatises *Against the Nestorians* (κατὰ τῆς αἱρέ-
σεως τῶν νεστοριανῶν, adv. hær. Nest. XCV, 187-224,
and περὶ συνθέτου φύσεως, de natura composita,
XCV, 111–126), a *Letter to a Jacobite Bishop* (πρὸς
τὸν ἐπίσκοπον δῆθεν Τουδαρίας τὸν Ἰακωβίτην,
ad episcopum Tudariœ jacobitam, XCIV, 1435–
1502), *Of the two wills in Christ* (περὶ τῶν ἐν τῷ
Χριστῷ δύο θελημάτων, de II voluntatibus Christi,
XCV, 127–186), and a curious fragment *On dragons
and witches* (περὶ δρακόντων καὶ στρυγγῶν, de dra-
conibus et strygibus, XCIV, 1599–1604) that contains a great deal of information as to the habits
of these little understood creatures.[1]

EXEGETICAL WORKS. St John wrote a *Commentary
on St Paul's Epistles,* that is a compilation from
Theodoret of Cyrus, St Cyril of Alexandria, and
especially St John Chrysostom (XCV, 441–1034).

ASCETIC WORKS. The *Sacred Parallels* (τὰ ἱερὰ
παράλληλα, sacra parallela, XCV, 1039; XCVI,
442) is a long collection of texts and quotations
from the Bible, the fathers, and even heathen
philosophers, arranged to illustrate various points
of faith and morals. The collection was made
before the time of our saint; there are many
editions of it, of which he made the one included
among his works. He wrote treatises *On Fasting*
(περὶ τῶν ἁγίων νηστειῶν, de s. jeiuniis, XCV, 63–78),
On the eight evil spirits (περὶ τῶν ὀκτὼ τῆς πονηρίας
πνευμάτων, de VIII spiritibus nequitiæ, XCV, 79–86),

---

[1] He says that dragons never turn into men, they have no
poison and are not liable to be killed by lightning. Witches
cannot go through closed doors nor fly about in the air, nor do
they eat babies. On the whole, both dragons and witches turn
out to be much less harmful than one had thought.

and *On Virtues and Vices* (περὶ ἀρετῶν καὶ κακιῶν, de virtutibus et vitiis, xcv, 85–98).

HOMILIES. Thirteen sermons of John Damascene are preserved, of which three are about the *Falling asleep of the holy Theotokos* (εἰς τὴν κοίμησιν τῆς ἁγίας θεοτόκου, de dormitione S. Dei genitricis, xcvi, 699–762), all preached on one day. There are others on her *Birth* (xcvi, 661–698) and *Annunciation* (xcvi, 643–662).

HYMNS AND CANONS. We have already seen specimens of these; they are collected in M. P. Gr. xcvi, 817–856, 1363–1408. Some of them are of doubtful authenticity.

The *Life of Barlaam and Joasaph*, in which J. Robinson discovered the lost Apology of Aristides (in the second century), is included (in one version) among St John Damascene's works (xcvi, 859–1240). It was not composed by him, but by another monk of Mar Saba, also named John. It is a novel about the conversion of an Indian prince, named Joasaph, through the discourses of a hermit, Barlaam, that had a very great vogue in the middle ages, and it is a most curious and valuable example of a legend that has travelled all over the world. The original story was an Indian legend about Buddha; it was altered and re-edited to form a Christian one.

12. Literature

The source for our saint's life is the *Life of our holy Father John Damascene* by John, Patriarch of Jerusalem (in Migne, P. Gr. xciv, 429–490), written apparently in the tenth century. This is the work I have quoted throughout. It contains, however, much that is legendary, and many of its stories must not be taken seriously. J. Langen:

Johannes von Damaskus (Gotha, 1879). V. Ermoni: *S. Jean Damascène* (Paris, Bloud, *La Pensée chrétienne*, 1904). J. H. Lupton: *St John of Damascus* (London, S.P.C.K. *The Fathers for English Readers*, 1882). Mary H. Allies: *St John Damascene's Treatise on Holy Images*, Burns & Oates, 1898. Le Quien adds a series of dissertations on various points concerning St John (Dissertationes damascenicæ) to his edition of the works (Venice, 1748, pp. 1–127). *See* also Krumbacher: *Gesch. der Byzantinischen Litteratur* (Munich, second edition, 1897), pp. 68 *seq.* and 674 *seq.*

This brings us to the end of the great Greek fathers. The line that began in Greek Egypt with the mighty Athanasius and the thunder of the Arian storm led us for two centuries through Asia Minor, Constantinople and Palestine through the chain of heresies that rent the eastern Church. Now, after a break, we leave it at the close of the last of those heresies in Moslem Syria.

The age of the fathers is over. The khalifah sits at Damascus, a new line of emperors will begin at once in the west, Photius is a promising cavalry officer with a grudge against Ignatius, the long ships of the Northmen have begun to be a terror to all the coasts of Europe, people are just discovering that what they talk is no longer Latin—we have reached the great turning-point. The old world is dead and the middle ages have begun.

INDEX

ACHILLAS, Pt of Alexandria before Alexander, 4

Adrian I, Pope († 795), 218

Aetios, leader of Arians, 20

Akakios, (340) Metropolitan of Cæsarea, 20, 155, 156, 158, 159

Alexander, Patriarch of Alexandria († 328), 3, 7, 10, 11, 12, 13, 14, 16

Alexander, Bishop of Constantinople, 24

Alexander III, Pope († 1181), ix

Alexandria, 13, 37, 52, 57, 90, 102, 110, 110n, 114, 182, 183, 184, 218

Ambrose, St († 397), 72, 73, 119n

Ammonios, 174

Amphilochios, Bp of Ikonion, 70, 80

Anastasios, Nestorian leader, 180, 181

Anastasios Sinaitikos, 213

Andrew of Samosata, 186

Ankyra, 20n; Synod of, 33

Annesos, Basil's monastery, 58, 59, 74, 77, 93, 94

Anomoios, 19

Anthimos, 68, 69, 96, 97

Antioch, 65, 66, 102n, 110, 113, 115, 119, 120, 122, 129, 134n, 152n, 184n, 206, 218

Antony, St, the hermit, 11, 33, 42, 56

Anthusa, St John Chrysostom's mother, 111, 112, 114–116

Apollinaris of Laodicea, heretic († c. 392), ix, 36, 82, 84n, 85n, 101; Apollinarists, 176

Arcadius, Emperor (395–408), 130, 132, 140, 141

Arcadius, Papal legate at Ephesus, 188

Arianism, gradual development, 4; extreme subordinationism, 6; condemned by Nicæa I, 15; favoured by Constantine and Constantius, 18, 26; Arian sects, 18–21; downfall, 35, 36

Arians, the antagonists of St Athanasius, 1, 2; depose and banish Athanasius, 22–24, 27, 29, 31, 35; evaded synod of Rome, 27, 29; synods of, 22, 27, 29, 30, 31, 33; persecution by, 32

Arius (293–336), early history of, 3, 4, 6; excommunicated, 7, 11; makes converts in Asia Minor, 12; defies Alexander, 13; Constantine tries to pacify, 13; excommunication confirmed by Nicæa I, 15; banished, 15; triumphant return, and death, 24, 25

Armenia, 65, 66; Armenians, 91, 92n

Arsakios, anti-Patriarch of Constantinople (404–405), 139, 140, 174

Arsenios, of Hypsele, 22, 23

Athanasius, St (293–373), birth and education, 8–10; ordained reader, then deacon, 10, 11; at synod of Alexandria, 7, 11; Patriarch of Alexandria, 16; trial at Tyre, 22; deposed and banished, 22–24, 27, 29, 31, 35, last years and death, 35, 36, 37; defends Divinity of Christ, 1, 16, 65, 125; dates, 38–40; works, 40–44; literature, 44, 45

Athens, 50–54, 90

Attikos, anti-Patriarch of Constantinople (406–425), 139, 140, 173n, 174

Augustine, St, Bp of Hippo, (354–430), 125, 128

Auxentius of Milan, semi-Arian leader, 20

BASIL, St (330–379), his family, birth and early years, 46–49; description of, 46, 77; at Athens, 50–54; and St Gregory of Nazianzos, 51, 70, 82, 90, 91, 96–99; teaches rhetoric at Cæsarea, 54; his baptism, 55; studies monasticism, 55–57; founds monastery at Annesos, 58, 59; fixes the monastic rule, 60; ordained by Eusebeios, 62; defends Cæsarea against Arian influence, 63–65; reforms the liturgy, 63, 82; consecrated Metropolitan of Cæsarea, 64; represses the Arians, 63, 65, 66, 68; his struggle with Anthimos, 69, 96, 97; his friends, 70–73; 90, 96–99; letters, 70–73; his death and burial, 76, 77; dates, 78, 79; works, 79–85; literature, 86

Basil, St Basil's father, 47, 49, 50

Basil, friend of St John Chrysostom, 113, 116

Basil of Ankyra, 20

Basiliskos, St, 141

Barsumas, Bp of Nisibis (453–489), 193

Baukalis Church at Alexandria, 4, 6

Berenice, St, 127n, 128n

Bernard, St († 1153), x

Byzantine Church, 46, 60, 63, 77, 83, 104, 142, 142n, 165, 195, 219, 234, 236

CÆSAREA, in Cappadocia, 49, 65, 158

Cæcilian, Bp of Carthage, 14

Candidian, Theodosius' emissary at Ephesus, 187–191

Cappadocia, 65

Celestin, St (422–432), Pope, 183, 184, 185, 188, 189

Celibacy of clergy, 88, 89, 124

Chalcedon, Council of (451), 130n, 158, 182, 192, 206n

Chiliasm, 134n

Christmas, date of, 94n

Chrysostom, St John (344–407), birth, 110; family, 111; studies, 113; Meletian schism, 114; baptized and ordained reader, 115; Doctor Eucharisticus, 125, 126, 128n; Patriarch of Constantinople, 109, 129–131; and Eutropios, 131, 132; Oak-Tree Synod, 133–136; exiles, 137–139; appeals to Rome, 139–140; death, 141; honour after death, 141–143; his liturgy, 94; sermons, 117–127; dates, 143; works, 144–148; literature, 148, 149

Constans, Emperor in Illyricum and Italy, 26, 29

Constantia, Constantine's sister († 328), 18

Constantine, Emperor (306–337), edict of Milan, 23; writes to Alexander and Arius, 13, 14; summons council of Nicæa, 14; banishes Arius, 15; favours Arianism, 18, 23, 24; builds Constantinople, 49n, 117; baptism and death, 25, 153n; honoured as saint by Orthodox Church, 25; division of empire after his death, 26; cross of, 213n

Constantine II, Emperor in Gaul, 26

Constantine V, Emperor (741–775), 217, 218

Constantine VI (780–797), 218

Constantinople, 49, 65, 69n, 101n, 110, 130n, 133, 183, 184n, 217

Constantinople I, Council of, 65n, 75, 100–103, 157, 164,

Constantius, Emperor (353–361), 26, 27, 29, 31, 33, 34, 35, 61, 153n, 161, 161n

Cosmas, St John Damascene's master, 209, 210, 225n

Cosmas the Singer, St John Damascene's foster-brother, 223, 225, 227, 234

Councils, General, Nicæa I (325), 11–19, 24, 150n, 158; Constantinople I (381), 75, 100–103, 157, 164, 182; Ephesus (431), 169, 186–192; Chalcedon (451), 130n, 158, 182, 192, 206n; Constantinople II (553), 134n; Nicæa II (787), 218, 219, 234n, 240, 243

Cyprian, St, 94n

Cyril of Alexandria, St († 444), and Nestorians, 169, 179–192; influenced by Isidore of Pelusium, 170; and Orestes, the governor, 171–174; Paschal letter (429), 182; accused of Arianism, 184; Legate at Ephesus, 188–192; returns to Alexandria, 192; pacifies Syrians, 194, 195; death, 195; dates, 197; works, 197–201; literature, 201

Cyril of Jerusalem, St (c. 315–386), early years, 150; ordained deacon, 151; teaches

catechism, 151; anti-Arian, 156, 157; on Holy Eucharist, 157; Bishop of Jerusalem, 158; friction with Akakios, 158, 159, 166; deposed and banished twice by Arians, 160, 164; at second general Council, 164; death, 165; dates, 166; works, 166–168; literature, 168

DAMASCUS, 203–207

Damasus, St, Pope († 384), 36, 71, 72

Demophilos, Arian Bishop of Constantinople (369–379), 99

Demosthenes, Governor of Cæsarea (375), 75

Dianeios, Bp of Cæsarea, 55, 61

Didymos the Blind (310–395), 101

Diodore, Bp of Tarsus (378–394), 115, 116, 193, 194

Dioskoros, Monophysite Patriarch of Alexandria, 183, 184n, 195

Domitius Modestus, Valens' prefect, 66

Dorotheos of Markianopolis, 180, 181

EASTER, date settled by Nicæa I (325), 15

Edena, centre of Nestorianism, 193

Emmelia, St Basil's mother, 47, 48, 58, 59, 78

Ephesus, 65, 169, 186; council of (431), 169, 187–191, 194

Ephrem, St, 70, 71, 94

Eudokia, Theodosius II's wife, 183

Eudoxia, Arcadius' wife, 131–139, 143

Eudoxios, Arian bishop († 360) of Antioch, 20, 114

Eulalios, Bp of Nazianzos, 104

Eunomios of Kyzikos, Arian leader, 20

Eusebeios of Cæsarea, St Basil's Metropolitan (†370), 61–64

Eusebeios, Metropolitan of Cæsarea, the father of Church history († 340), 13

Eusebeios, Bishop of Nicomedia, 12, 16, 23, 25

Eutropios, Eunuch, fall of (399), 130–133

Eustathios, Pt of Antioch (banished 330), 14, 22, 114

Eustathios, Bp of Sebaste, 71

FATHER of the Church, title of, ix

Flavian, Pt of Antioch († 386), 103, 115n, 117, 119–122

GALATOS, son of Valens, 67

Gelasios, Metropolitan of Cæsarea, 165

Germanos I, Patriarch of Constantinople (715–730), 217, 239

George, Arian usurper at Alexandria, 32, 34

George of Laodicea, semi-Arian leader, 20

Glykeros, deacon at Cæsarea, 69

Gratian, Emperor (375–383), 75, 164

Gregory the Great, St, Pope (590–604), 63, 64n

Gregory II, Pope (715–731), 217

Gregory III, Pope (731–741), 217

Gregory of Nazianzos, St (330–390), birth and family, 88, 89, 112; studied at Athens, 51–54, 90, 91; Kaisarios, his brother, 92; baptized, 93; at Nazian-

zos, 95, 96; monk at Annesos, 58, 59, 93, 95; urges St Basil to go to Cæsarea, 62, 63; struggle with Anthimos, 69; bishop of Sasima, 69, 87, 97; and St Basil, 46, 51, 70, 76, 77, 82, 87, 90, 91, 97, 99; and St Athanasius, 37; and St Gregory of Nyssa, 74, 75; and Origenism, 134n; at Constantinople, 100, 109n; Second general Council, 100–103; returns to Nazianzos, 103; retirement and death, 104; his feast, 78; dates, 104; works, 105–107; literature, 107

Gregory, Bp of Nazianzos († 374), father of the Saint, 66, 88, 90, 93–98

Gregory of Nyssa, St (c. 331–c. 395), birth and family, 48, 78; education, 51–53, 73; an orator, 54, 74; married, 74; ordained by St Basil, 69, 74, 97; buries St Basil, 76, 77; visits Annesos, 77; his feast in Eastern Church, 78; and Origenism, 134n; dates, 78; works, 83–85, literature, 86

Gregory, Arian usurper at Alexandria, 27, 29, 30, 34

Gregory Thaumaturgos, St († 270), 48, 49, 85, 134n

Gregory of Tours, St (c. 593), 213

Goths, 75

HELLADIOS, Metropolitan of Cæsarea after Basil, 75, 102

Himerios, professor at Athens 53

Honorius, Emperor, in the West (395–423), 130, 140

Hosius of Cordova, 13, 14, 15

Hussain, 208

Hypatia, 169, 170–173

IBAS, Bp of Edessa (435–457), 193
Iconoclasts (726–842), 15, 212, 218, 233
Ignatius of Constantinople (†877), 109, 140
Innocent I (401–417), 140
Irenæus, St (†202), 153, 178
Irene, Empress, 218
Ischyras, 22, 23
Isidore of Pelusium († c. 440), 125, 170, 171, 183
Isidore, Origenist, 135

JEROME, St, (†410), 34, 36, 100, 101n, 134n
Jerusalem, 17, 65, 94n, 152
John of Damascus, St († c. 754, last of the Greek Fathers, x, 169n; his father, 208, 211; early years, 209; and the Iconoclasts, 212–220, 240; monk at Mar Saba, 223–227; ordained and sent to Jerusalem, 227; returns to desert, 227; philosophy, 229–234; poetry, 234–239; death, 239; dates, 241–242; works, 242–247; literature, 247,248
John the Evangelist, St, 1st Bp of Ephesus, 186n, 187
John, father of St John Damscene, 208, 209
John V, Patriarch of Jerusalem (†735), 227
John, Patriarch of Antioch, Nestorius' friend, 183, 185–186, 188–192
John of Monagria, martyred by Iconoclasts, 218
Jovian, Emperor (363–364), 35, 164
Julian, Emperor (361–363), 34, 35, 50, 53, 54, 61, 62, 92, 113, 161–164, 214n
Julius I, (337–352), 27–29
Justin, St (†166), 153n
Justinian I (527–565), 130n, 193n, 206

KAISARIOS of Nazianzos, St Gregory's brother, 16, 90, 92

LEO I, St, Pope (†461), 185
Leo III, the Isaurian (717–741), 216, 217, 221, 228, 241
Leo IV, Emperor (775–780), 218
Leo V, Emperor (813–820), 219
Libanios, philosopher, Julian's friend, 112
Liberius, Pope, 31, 33
Lucian of Antioch (†311), 6, 12
Lucifer, Bishop of Calaris, 31, 114

MAGNENTIUS, 26
Makarios, Bishop of Jerusalem, 14, 150, 151
Makedonios, semi-Arian Bishop of Constantinople (†360), 100
Makrine, St, St Basil's sister, 47, 54, 55, 58, 77, 85
Makrine, St Basil's grandmother, 47, 49, 54, 77
Manicheism, 127
Marathonios, a Pneumatomachian monk, 100
Marcionism, 127
Markellos of Ankyra, 23, 24
Mar Saba, 223, 239
Maximian, Bp of Constantinople (†434), 192
Maximos, bishop at Constantinople, 100, 102, 151, 157
Maximinus, Bishop of Trier, 26
Meletios of Antioch, 4, 102, 103, 114, 115, 117
Meletios of Lykopolis, 4, 111; Meletians, 12, 15
Melkites, 15, 38n, 60n, 11n, 219, 220
Memnon of Ephesus, 187, 190

Michael II, the Stammerer (†829), 219
Milan, edict of, 2, 3
Mithraism, 161n
Modalism, 5
Monophysites, 38n, 44, 85n, 206

NAUSIKRATES, or Naukratios, 48, 54
Nazianzos, 88; see Gregory, St, of
Nektarios of Constantinople (†397), 75, 103, 129, 130
Nestorius, Patriarch of Constantinople, 175–192; Nestorianism, 6n, 44, 127, 169
Nicæa, Council of (325), summoned by Constantine, 14; declares Christ equal to the Father, 15; excommunicates Arius, 15; St Athanasius the Catholic leader, 11, 16; refuses Jerusalem rank of a metropolitan see, 17, 158; settles the time of keeping Easter, 15; the validity of doubtful baptism, 15
Nicæa, 2nd Council of, 18, 219, 234n, 240
Nonna, St, mother of St Gregory of Nazianzos, 88–90, 98, 112
Novatian, 172n; Novatians, 175
Nyssa, 74; see St Gregory of

OMMEYADES, 206, 208
Orestes, Governor, 171–174
Origenes (†254), x, 6, 83, 133, 134n, 151
Orthodox Church, 15, 63, 111, 195, 202n, 203, 219n

PARABOLANI, 172
Paphnutios of the Thebais, 14
Patripassianism, 5

Paul, St, 88, 110, 125, 187, 205
Paul of Samosata, 6, 12
Paulinos, 72, 102n, 114
Paulinus of Trier, St, 31
Pelagius, 185n; Pelagianism, 128, 231
Peter, St, Bp of Sebaste, St Basil's brother, 48, 54, 58, 71, 73, 78
Philip, Legate at Ephesus, 188, 189
Photius, Patriarch of Constantinople (857), 109, 140, 141n, 212, 248
Pistos, Arian anti-bishop at Alexandria, 27
Pneumatomachians, 100–102, 231
Politianos of Alexandria, 218
Potamon of Herakleia, 14
Prohairesios, 53
Proklos of Kyzikos, 181
Projectus, Papal Legate, 188
Prosdoce, St, 127, 128
Pulcheria, Theodosius' sister-in-law, 183

QUARTODECIMANS, 175

ROME, 110, 114, 184n, 218; synods at, 28, 184, 218

SABAS, St (†531), 223
Sabellius, 5, 6
Sacraments, intention in, 10, 94, 94n
Sanctuary, right of, 132
Secundus, St John Chrysostom's father, 111
Secundus of Ptolemais, 7
Seleucia, port of Antioch, 110, 159
Seleukos I, founder of Antioch, 110
Semi-Arianism, compromise between Catholicism and Arianism, 13, 20

Stephen III, Pope (768–772), 218

Stephen, Abbot, martyr, 218

Subordinationism, 4, 6, 12

Sylvester I, St Pope (314-335), 24

Synods—Alexandria (321), 74; Antioch (330), 22; Tyre (335), 22; Constantinople (335), 24; Antioch II (340), 27; Rome (341), 28; Antioch III, " in encæniis " (341), 29, 137n, 159, 160; Sardica (343), 29; Philippopolis (343), 29; Laodicea (345), 30; Antioch IV (344), 30; Milan (345), 30; Sirmium I (351), 30; Arles (353), 30, 31; Milan (355), 31; Sirmium II (357), 33; Ankyra (357), 33; Sirmium III (358), 33; Cæsarea (358), 159; Sirmium IV (359), 33; Seleucia in Isauria (359), 159, 160; Ariminium (359), 33, 61, 95, 159n; Constantinople (360) 160; Alexandria (362), 101; Zele c. 363), 101; Antioch (379), 75; Constantinople, (394), 75; Constantinople (399), 135; of the Oak Tree (403), 135, 136; Rome (430), 184, 185; Alexandria (430), 185; Tarsus (c. 431), 192; Antioch (c. 431), 192; Constantinople (754), 218, 239; Lateran (769), 218

TALL BROTHERS, the, 134

Tarasios of Constantinople, 218

Tertullian, ix, 153, 172n

Theodora, Empress, Theophilos' wife, 219

Theodore of Herakleia, semi-Arian leader, 20

Theodore of Mopsuestia (†428), 127, 176n, 193, 194

Theodore of Studion, St. (†826), 202, 219, 220, 233n

Theodosius I, Emperor (379–395), 75, 76, 99, 101, 119, 122, 130, 164

Theodosius II, Emperor (408–450), 141, 172, 183, 186, 187, 190, 191, 192

Theon, Hypatia's father, 171n

Theonas of Marmarica, Arian leader, 7

Theophilos, Emperor (829–842), 219

Theophilos of Alexandria (†412), 115, 129, 130, 133, 134, 134n, 135, 136, 140, 169–171, 183, 184n

Theopompos, the Novatian bishop, 172

Theosebeia, St Gregory of Nyssa's wife, 74

Theotokos, 180–182; Theotokians, 184

Timothy, St Basil's chorepiscopus, 70

Trier, St Athanasius banished to, 24, 25, 26

Tyana, 68, 90, 97

URANIOS of Tyre, Homoian leader, 21

VALENS, Cæsar (364–378), 35, 63, 66–68, 75, 92, 99, 164

Valentinian I, Emperor (364–375), 35, 164

Venantius Fortunatus (†603), 213

XENAIAS, the Nestorian bishop of Hierapolis, 216

YARMUK, Battle of (634), 206

ZENO, Emperor (474–491), 193

THE ARDEN PRESS

W. H. SMITH AND SON
FETTER LANE LONDON EC
AND LETCHWORTH